Finite Elements and Optimization for MODERN MANAGEMENT

G. A. MOHR, PHD
WORLD HONS MULT

Finite Elements and Optimization for MODERN MANAGEMENT

G. A. MOHR, PHD
WORLD HONS MULT.

© G. A. Mohr, 2019

All rights reserved. No part of this publication may be reproduced, stored in a retrieval system, or transmitted in any form or by any means, electronic, mechanical, photocopying, recording, or otherwise, without the prior written permission of both the author and publisher.

G. A. Mohr
Finite Elements and Optimization for
MODERN MANAGEMENT

TRI
Transworld Research & Innovation
9 Hampstead Drive
Hoppers Crossing VIC 3029
AUSTRALIA

Also by G. A. Mohr

Finite Elements for Solids, Fluids, and Optimization

A Microcomputer Introduction to the Finite Element Method

The Pretentious Persuaders,
A Brief History & Science of Mass Persuasion

Curing Cancer & Heart Disease,
Proven Ways to Combat Aging, Atherosclerosis & Cancer

The Variant Virus: Introducing Secret Agent Simon Sinclair

The Doomsday Calculation: The End Of The Human Race

The War of the Sexes, Women Are Getting On Top

Heart Disease, Cancer, & Ageing:
Proven Neutraceutical & Lifestyle Solutions

2045: A Remote Town Survives Global Holocaust

The History & Psychology of Human Conflict

Elementary Thinking for Modern Management

The 8-Week+ Program to Reverse Cardiovascular Disease

The Scientific MBA;   Mohr's Law of Hierarchies

The DIY Cardiovascular Cure,
A Comprehensive Program to Reverse Atherosclerosis

Combating Cancer: Proven Neutraceutical & Lifestyle Remedies

The Psychology of Life;   The Psychology of Depression

The Bullying Epidemic;   New Ideas for the 21st Century

Economics: A Concise Introduction

With R.S. Mohr/Richard Sinclair & P.E. Mohr/Edwin Fear

The Evolving Universe: Relativity, Redshift and Life from Space

World Religions: The History, Psychology, Issues & Truth

The Population Explosion;   World War 3: When & How Will It End?

The Brainwashed: From Consumer Zombies to Islamic Jihad

Human Intelligence, Learning & Behaviour

New Theories of The Universe, Evolution, and Relativity

World Religions: From to Animism to Mohronism

Human Conflict: An Attitudinal Psychology Model

The Psychology of Hope;   The Psychology of Success

Human Psychology, Learning & Intelligence

Real Democracy;   DIY Psychology & Psychotherapy

Contents

Preface   1

1 Introduction   3
    1.1 New features of the book
    1.2 A brief history
    1.3 A brief history of the finite element method
    1.4 Applications of FEM in structural mechanics
    1.5 Applications of FEM and optimization in management science
    1.6 Conclusion
    1.7 References

2 Mathematics and Optimization   15
    2.1 Mathematical functions
    2.2 Standard mathematical curves and functions
    2.3 Basic calculus
    2.4 Differential equations
    2.5 Matrices
    2.6 Classical optimization problems
    2.7 Multivariate optimization problems
    2.8 References

3 Numerical Methods   43
    3.1 Iterative and search techniques
    3.2 Predictor-corrector methods
    3.3 Solution of matrix equations
    3.4 Direct solution of matrix equations
    3.5 Inversion routine with pivoting
    3.6 Finite differences
    3.7 Numerical integration
    3.8 Lagrangian interpolation.
    3.9 Hermitian interpolation
    3.10 Statistical correlation
    3.11 References

4 Finite Element Network Models   73
    4.1 Linear one dimensional elements
    4.2 FEM modeling of DC networks
    4.3 Program for DC networks
    4.4 The dual problem for DC networks
    4.5 References

5 Linear Programming — 85

5.1 Introduction
5.2 Linear Programming
5.3 The Simplex Method
5.4 Alternative pivoting rules for the Simplex Method
5.5 The dual LP problem
5.6 Equality constraints
5.7 Distribution problems
5.8 Program for sequential MIN + MAX
5.9 Direct LP method program for distribution problems
5.10 References

6 Nonlinear Programming — 107

6.1 Classical theory of optimization
6.2 Unconstrained nonlinear problems
6.3 Constrained nonlinear problems
6.4 Steepest descent exercise
6.5 Conjugate gradient method
6.6 References

7 Finite Element Distribution Models — 121

7.1 Finite Element Distribution Models
7.2 Optimizing FEM distribution models
7.3 Program for optimization of FEM distribution models
7.4 Inventory problems modeled as distribution problems
7.5 References

8 Finite Element Traffic Flow Models — 133

8.1 Finite element traffic flow models
8.2 Optimizing the network
8.3 Program for traffic flow network optimization
8.4 Alternative flow laws
8.5 References

9 Flow Ratio Design Method — 143

9.1 Optimality criterion methods
9.2 FRD for FEM distribution models
9.3 Distribution network with dummy routes
9.4 Application of FRD to traffic flow problems
9.5 Program for FRD of distribution problems
9.6 References

10 The Critical Path Method — 157
10.1 The Critical Path Method
10.2 Bar charts and resource scheduling
10.3 Crashing a project
10.4 PERT
10.5 Optimization of the critical path
10.6 Simple CPM program
10.7 CPM Program with quadratic elements
10.8 References

11 Production/operations Management — 175
11.1 Line of balance systems
11.2 The flow line method
11.3 Assembly lines
11.4 Group technology
11.5 Dynamic programming
11.6 Other network problems
11.7 Inventory models
11.8 Simulation
11.9 Queueing theory
11.10 Project control and assessment
11.11 References

12 Numerical Methods for Econometrics — 205
12.1 Input-output analysis
12.2 Optimizing IOA problems
12.3 Applying constraints to matrix problems
12.4 Time stepping macroeconomic models
12.5 Finite element IOA models
12.6 References

13 Two dimensional Finite Elements — 221
13.1 Two dimensional finite elements
13.2 Potential flow
13.3 The quadratic triangle element
13.4 FEM analysis of potential flow
13.5 Program for potential flow
13.6 Inclusion of line elements
13.7 Infinite boundary modeling
13.8 Conclusions
13.9 References

14 Conclusions — 241
14.1 Key applications of the present work
14.2 Future research of the present work
14.3 Conclusion

Appendices

A   Introduction to BASIC   **249**

    A.1 A brief history of BASIC
    A.2 Introduction to BASIC programming
    A.3 Sorting routines
    A.4 Visual BASIC (VB)
    A.5 Using programs listed in this book
    A.6 References

B   Block equation solution routine   **263**

KEY PROGRAMS IN THE TEXT

Section	Program
3.3	Gauss-Mohr reduction
3.6	Gauss-Jordan matrix inversion routine with pivoting
4.3	FEM for primal and dual DC networks
5.4	LP MIN using optimal pivots
5.8	Sequential LP MIN + MAX using dual pivoting rules
5.9	Direct sequential LP MIN + MAX for distribution problems
6.4	Steepest descent method
6.5	Conjugate gradient method
7.3	FEM analysis and optimization of distribution networks
8.3	FEM analysis and optimization of traffic flow networks
9.5	Flow Ratio design for distribution networks
10.6	Critical path method program
10.7	Program for optimization of CPM networks
11.5	Shortest route program
11.9	Queue simulation program
12.3	Routine for Lagrange multiplier, penalty factor and Basis constraints
12.4	Time stepping GNP models
12.5	Solution routine for banded (unsymmetric) matrices
13.5	2D potential fields using quadratic triangular elements
A.2	Several programming examples
A.3	Quicksort routine
A.4	Visual Basic programming and example VB programs
B	Block equation solution routine

Note: Most programs are in QBASIC but readable into Visual Basic 5+ as program 'modules', as discussed in Section A.4.

PREFACE

This book introduces many new developments in *Management Science*, including:

[1] The powerful *Finite Element Method (FEM)*, along with other *matrix methods* of modeling and analysis of management and business systems.

[2] *Optimization* of these models by both exact search and approximate iteration techniques,

from their source, in a concise, simple manner, including many short BASIC programs along the way.

Management Science and *Operations Research* are sometimes taken to be the same field, and in OR the major tool is *Linear Programming (LP)* and most OR books devote much attention to it. Here LP is dealt with far more concisely and simply than hitherto, for example only one type of supplementary variable *(slack variables)* is used, rather than the usual three. Then, rather than dwell on the mathematics of LP, three short BASIC programs which use optimum pivots, successively obtain both MIN and MAX solutions, and deal efficiently with distribution problems, are given.

The major intention of the present work is to expand Management Science to include: the Finite Element Method to model network problems, the Critical Path Method of scheduling with *element interpolations,* Input-Output Analysis between companies, sectors of the economy and nations, and time stepping macroeconomic models. Again short BASIC programs are given to demonstrate these developments.

A decade ago application of FEM in these areas was foreshadowed at the close of the author's book *Finite Elements for Solids, Fluids, and Optimization* (Oxford University Press, Oxford, 1992).

In 1995 the author began developing a course in management science as a modern alternative to the ubiquitous MBA. This included application of FEM techniques to scheduling networks and discussion of input-output analysis, concluding by suggesting the form of element matrix needed for FEM models of distribution problems.

In 1997 the first FEM distribution models were developed, and new techniques for optimizing them quickly followed.

In 2001 FEM models for traffic flow were developed and in 2002 the new optimization techniques were also applied to these.

Preface

These exciting new advances, along with several others, are discussed in the present book. It is hoped that it will prove of interest to a very wide range of people, including:

- Students in any business/management course.
- Students and practitioners of Operations Research (OR)
- Students & practitioners of Quantitative Management Techniques (QMT).
- Computing, Engineering, Maths and Science students.
- People in business and management practice.
- People in the distribution, logistics, roads and transport industries.
- Anyone interested in computer modeling and computing with BASIC.

The text should find its way into existing MBA etc. courses, to improve these with a modest dose of new material, rather than replace them with alternative more specialized courses with much more of this material.

So where does this new material fit into existing business courses?

Some possibilities, perhaps, are:

- Project and construction management subjects.
- Production and operations management subjects.
- Mathematical and computer modeling subjects.
- Systems analysis and optimization subjects.
- Financial modeling /quantitative economics/econometrics subjects.
- Logistics/transportation subjects.
- Distribution/marketing subjects.

Production, operations and optimization come through as major application areas, actually producing something concrete perhaps being the most important part of any ongoing business. As intended, however, the scope has widened to include other areas.

In choosing a title I felt that the terms OR and MS defined above were not quite appropriate. I am here not concerned with research or science, that is the acquisition of new knowledge, but the application of knowledge (some of it new) in *management.* And QMT might be taken to include accounting, which along with business law, are the only other major essential subjects of a 'real' business course not considered here.

Noting that our numerical computer models can then be linked to accounting, inventory and other management information systems, therefore, *Finite Elements and Optimization for Modern Management* can greatly influence almost any facet of almost any business or other organization and I am sure that it will.

Geoff Mohr, 2019

Chapter 1

INTRODUCTION

"I have no great intelligence, I have imagination",
"You are the hope of the future", John Argyris,
(said to the author by phone from Stuttgart circa 1998 & 1999).

1.1. New features of the book

This short book, though having, of course, to devote some time to introductory material, is a groundbreaking one, that is:

➤ It introduces the *Finite Element Method* (FEM) to *Management Scien*ce or *Operations Research* (OR).
➤ It is first to describe applications of FEM to the analysis of distribution networks,
➤ It is the first to describe application of FEM to the analysis of traffic flow networks.
➤ These new FEM network models are then optimized by using the *steepest descent* method to modify *element access* parameters and thence eliminate *redundant* (to the optimal solution) routes.
➤ It is the first to describe the *Flow Ratio Design* (FRD) method of iterative optimization of numerical models, and this concept has unlimited application.
➤ Linear programming is done with only *slack variables* added and thence without recourse to additional surplus variables or artificial variables.
➤ A simple *direct* linear programming method and *dual pivoting rules* are used to obtain comparison MIN and MAX solutions for distribution networks.
➤ *Elements* of scheduling networks are allowed interpolations in time, thence allowing optimization of the network.
➤ Simple 'single number' *infinity conditions* for modeling potential field problems with infinite domains are described.

There are several other notable features, for example:

➤ Many simple programs in BASIC are given throughout the text, with a useful introduction to BASIC in Appendix A
➤ Used as an introduction, both the *primal* and *dual* models of direct current (DC) networks are modeled using the same program.

1. Introduction

➢ A short routine for *time stepping* of Klein's structural equations for the US economy 1921 - 1941.
➢ Demonstration of application of optimization and constraints to *input-output* analysis problems.

It should be noted that *Management Science* is often taken to be a synonym for *Operations Research,* a branch of modern mathematics, but here a broader focus is intended, for example including *Quantitative Economics* or *Econometrics,*

Indeed *quantitative* is a key word here, as in most books on management most attention will be given to qualitative matters involving lists of do's and don'ts and the like. Matters such as leadership, personnel management and marketing are also largely qualitative and in areas such as advertising and attitudinal psychology quantitative theories are few.

More precisely, however, the focus of the present book is upon *matrix methods* of modeling business and management systems, including economic managements systems between companies, economic sectors and nations. This has particular emphasis on introducing the *Finite Element Method* and optimization of the resulting models.

It should be remembered, however, that our numerical computer models can then be linked to accounting and other management information systems.

1.2. A brief history

This book is in part based on the *Diploma of Business Science* at the *International Arts and Sciences College* (IASC), Melbourne, Australia. Some of the motivations for this course were well stated by F.W. Taylor, *"the father of management science",* in his *Principles of Scientific Management* (Harper, New York NY 1911) where he argued that:
1. The whole country loses daily by inefficiency in everything we do.
2. The remedy? Systematic management based on scientific principles, not some 'super manager(s).'
3. Business science rests on clear laws, rules and principles applicable to individual acts and to large corporations and will yield big results.

The course included the usual MBA material and then much more.

For example, a little on input-output analysis, a good deal on Critical Path Method and other project/operations management techniques and ending with a chapter on FEM, the last pages of which gave an example of dividing traffic flows between parallel routes according to their capacity parameters and noted that *it must be possible to model distribution problems as FEM networks using the simple matrices that apply to DC networks.*

1. INTRODUCTION

Earlier in the course I introduced Gauss-Jordan reduction to invert matrices, and thence solve simultaneous equations, using the neat 10 line routine given in Sec. 3.4. In the last chapter a short program used this to model DC networks as in Sec. 4.3, an exercise I had once given to all early Auckland University Engineering students in a three hour computing lab. Generally they had little or no prior knowledge of coding and none of FEM but, without exception, they coded in the program and got it running OK.

A few years later and working on FEM rectilinear flow models and a 'direct' LP method for distribution problems prior to that time, I added a boundary 'reaction' calculation to the DC network program and added the data for the optimum solution of the distribution problem of Figure 7.1, trying its route unit costs in place of electrical resistance R, or its reciprocal. Literally arbitrary potential values appeared, but the single boundary reaction, where I had specified the potential to be zero as a datum, was equal to the demand flow at that point. The program didn't even calculate element current flows, but adding this, the results were as required, irrespective of the route costs, and here was a promising beginning!

A *steepest descent* method of optimizing these FEM distribution models was soon found, quickly followed by an optimality criterion method, the *Flow Ratio Design* (FRD) method which has almost universal applications potential.

A few years later FEM traffic flow models were developed, first using the simple parallel route traffic flow example in the original Dip. Biz Sci. course, this simple example having been used in class notes and an exam question for a post graduate traffic engineering course at Monash University in 1978.

1.3. A brief history of the finite element method

The *Finite Element Method (FEM)* will be new to all but a few readers of this book. This method is based on *matrix structural analysis* of aircraft structures in the mid 1940s, in which the *elements* of the structure were modeled mathematically by small matrices. For simple spar or *line elements* this could be done exactly, but to model patches of the aircraft 'skin' approximate *lumping* techniques were used to represent them as, for example, three line elements to represent a triangular patch.

In 1954 Turner (Boeing), Clough (UC Berkeley), Martin (U Washington), and Topf (Boeing) produced the first paper on *continuum* finite elements at a meeting in New York and it was published in 1956.

Argyris (U Stuttgart & U London), the best known pioneer of matrix structural analysis, provided a bridge between the 1940s 'lumping' work and these continuum elements with his *natural strains* on the sides of simplex elements (i.e. triangles in 2D and tetrahedra in 3D).

1. INTRODUCTION

Since then FEM has gone on to be applied to a wide range of problems in engineering and science, the main field of application being in *Computational Mechanics*, particularly the mechanics of solid buildings and manufactured products, including cars and aircraft.

In that time much effort has been directed at developing better element 'recipes', for example for the analysis of curved shell structures and shock fronts in supersonic air flows. Much effort too has been directed at *optimizing* FEM models, and the author has devoted much of over three decades to both these areas.

1.4. Applications of FEM in structural mechanics

The aim of this book is to introduce FEM applications in management science as simply as possible. It is, however, perhaps worthwhile to sketch a couple of applications of the method in its original field of application, namely the mechanics of structures, hoping to give some indication of the power of the method and the almost unlimited prospects that exist for its application to management science.

Figure 1.1(a) shows a spar element with two *degrees of freedom*, horizontal and vertical displacement *u* and *v*, at a *node* at each end, thus having a total of *four freedoms*.

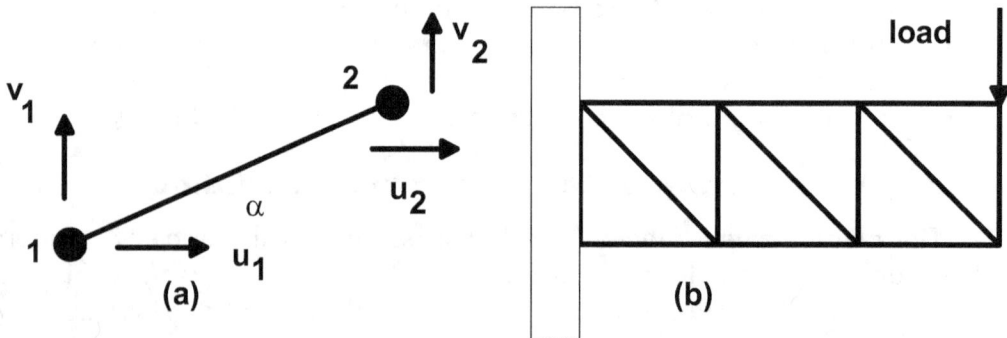

Figure 1.1. (a) Four freedom spar element. (b) Truss structure.

Figure 1.1(b) shows a truss modeled by a number of these elements, subjected to a load at its end. The nodal loads $\{q\}$ for each element are related to its nodal displacements $\{d\}$ by its *Element Stiffness Matrix (ESM)* k_e:

$$\{q\} = \begin{Bmatrix} q_{x1} \\ q_{y1} \\ q_{x2} \\ q_{y2} \end{Bmatrix} = (EA/L) \begin{bmatrix} k_n & -k_n \\ -k_n & k_n \end{bmatrix} \begin{Bmatrix} u_1 \\ v_1 \\ u_2 \\ v_2 \end{Bmatrix} = k_e\{d\} \quad (1.1)$$

1. INTRODUCTION

where $k_n = \begin{bmatrix} c^2 & -sc \\ -sc & s^2 \end{bmatrix}$ with $c = \cos\alpha$, $s = \sin\alpha$ \hfill (1.2)

and (EA/L) is the extensional stiffness of the element, α is its angle of inclination from the horizontal x axis, and $\{q\}$ and $\{d\}$ are its load and displacement *vectors*.

In FEM the ESMs for each element are assembled into a *System Stiffness Matrix (SSM)* K to model the behaviour of the whole structure, symbolically stated as

$$\boxed{\{Q\} = K\{D\} \text{ where } K = \Sigma k_e} \hfill (1.3)$$

Specifying the loads on the structure $\{Q\}$ and the *boundary conditions*, that is the supporting points at which $u = 0$ and/or $v = 0$, the problem is solved by solving the *simultaneous equations* of Equation 1.3 to determine the nodal displacements $\{D\}$, then calculating the forces in each element of the structure from these.

Generally the elements must have *flexural* or beam action, in addition to *extensional* behaviour. To model this rotational freedoms are added at each node and the ESMs are now 6 X 6.

In more advanced work the nonlinear effects of large displacements are included, when the ESMs must be calculated using *numerical integration* to include *large strains* and Mohr's *large curvature correction*, the latter correction being comparable to the small time changes resulting from the bending of light in the special theory of relativity.

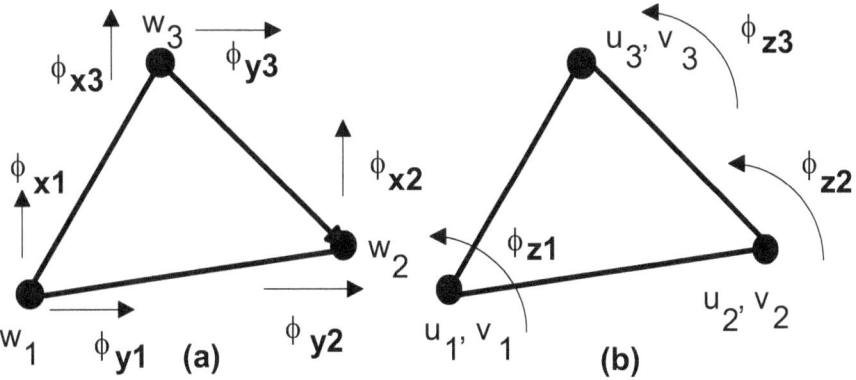

Figure 1.2. Components of facet shell element.

1. INTRODUCTION

Figure 1.2(a) shows a nine freedom thin plate bending element with nodal freedoms w, ϕ_x, ϕ_y, that is transverse displacement w and its derivatives in the x and y directions, corresponding to the rotations about those axes. Figure 1.2(b) shows a nine freedom plane stress element with nodal freedoms u, v, ϕ_z that is displacements parallel to the axes and the *drilling freedom* or rotation about the transverse z axis. Using Mohr's method of 'nested interpolations', both elements use the same quadratic interpolation used in Chapter 13 to formulate a six node element for modeling of potential field problems.

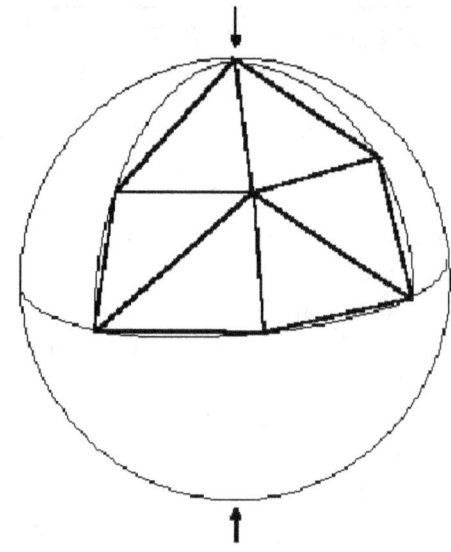

Figure 1.3.
Octant of a pinch loaded spherical shell modeled by facet shell elements.

These two elements are easily combined to form an 18 freedom facet shell element, conveniently with displacement and rotation freedoms for all three axes, and Figure 1.3 shows an example use of these elements to model a quite demanding problem. In fact only about 20 - 30 elements are needed to obtain a reasonable result for the deflection of the sphere at its crown, but many more elements are needed to approximate the stresses in this region.

There are, in fact, almost countless applications of FEM in both the mechanics of solids and fluids, as well as in many other areas of engineering and science.

1.5. Applications of FEM and optimization in management science

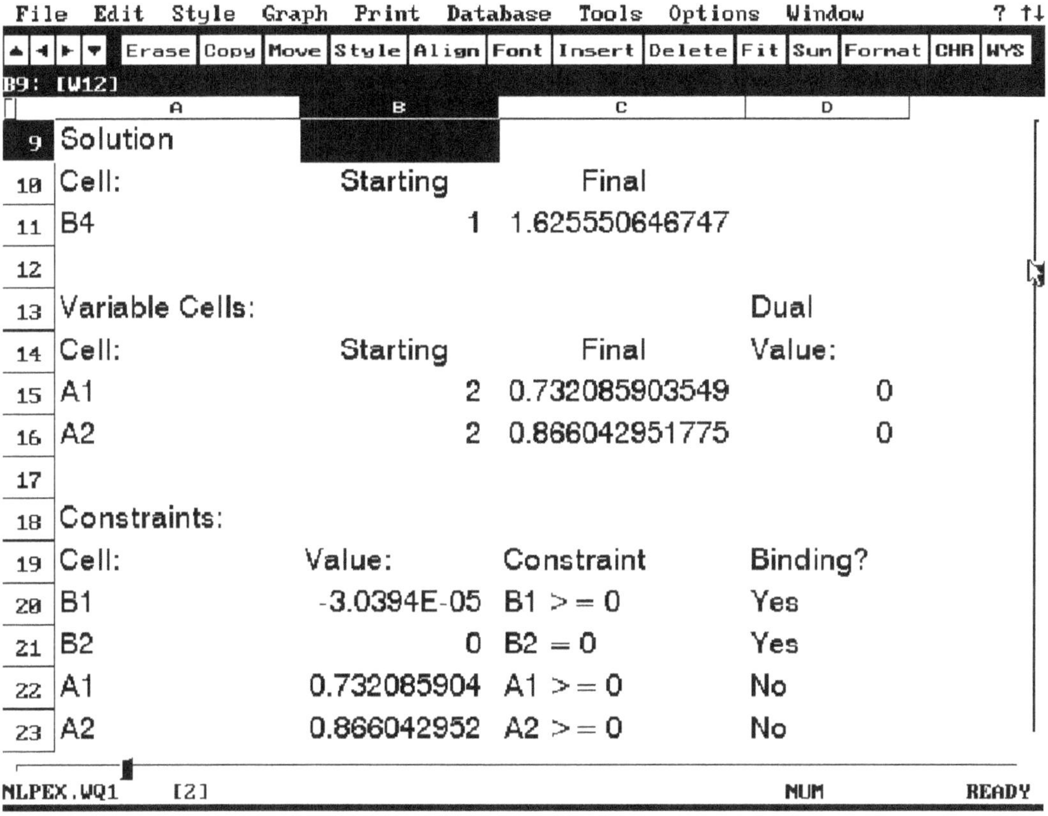

File Edit Style Graph Print Database Tools Options Window ? ↑↓

Erase Copy Move Style Align Font Insert Delete Fit Sum Format CHR WYS

B9: [W12]

	A	B	C	D
9	Solution			
10	Cell:	Starting	Final	
11	B4	1	1.625550646747	
12				
13	Variable Cells:			Dual
14	Cell:	Starting	Final	Value:
15	A1	2	0.732085903549	0
16	A2	2	0.866042951775	0
17				
18	Constraints:			
19	Cell:	Value:	Constraint	Binding?
20	B1	-3.0394E-05	B1 >= 0	Yes
21	B2	0	B2 = 0	Yes
22	A1	0.732085904	A1 >= 0	No
23	A2	0.866042952	A2 >= 0	No

NLPEX.WQ1 [2] NUM READY

Figure 1.4. Nonlinear optimization results,

Figure 1.4 shows the results for a small nonlinear optimization problem, also used as an example in Section 6.3. These results were obtained using the spreadsheet program Quattro Pro V4.

This illustrates the degree to which such techniques are now applied and in the present text much attention is given to both linear and nonlinear optimization methods and application of them to numerical computer models of physical and management systems.

1. INTRODUCTION

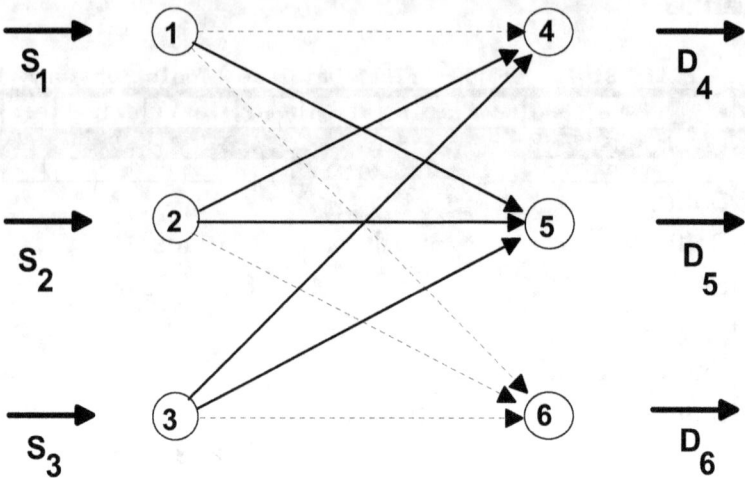

Figure 1.5. A distribution problem with 3 supply points and 3 demand points. In the optimum system the routes shown by dashed lines are omitted.

Figure 1.5 shows a distribution problem with supplies S_i and demands D_j at six points, connected by nine routes. Specifying a cost c_{ij} for transporting a single unit from supply point i to demand point j, six equations can be written equating the sum of the route flows at a point to its supply or demand value.

The problem can then be solved by *Linear Programming* (LP) to determine the route flow values that minimize the total transportation cost, in the process eliminating the four routes, such as those shown dashed in Fig. 1.5.

In this text we shall model the problem using very simple two freedom finite elements for which the constitutive parameter for each element is its unit transportation cost. Such models are useful in their own right to show the effects of changes in the system.

We shall also use the method of *steepest descent*, a powerful and very widely applicable technique, to optimize the distribution network, obtaining the same solutions as by LP. Then, indeed, with a little experimentation, it is possible to obtain 'better than optimal' solutions, for example by finding that a small increase in one supply flow can be accommodated without increasing the total transportation cost in the system.

Further, we shall introduce the *Flow Ratio Design* (FRD) method of iteratively modifying the distribution network until an improved, approximately optimal solution is obtained. The simple *optimality criterion* of this is very widely applicable in flow problems in both engineering mechanics and management science.

1. INTRODUCTION

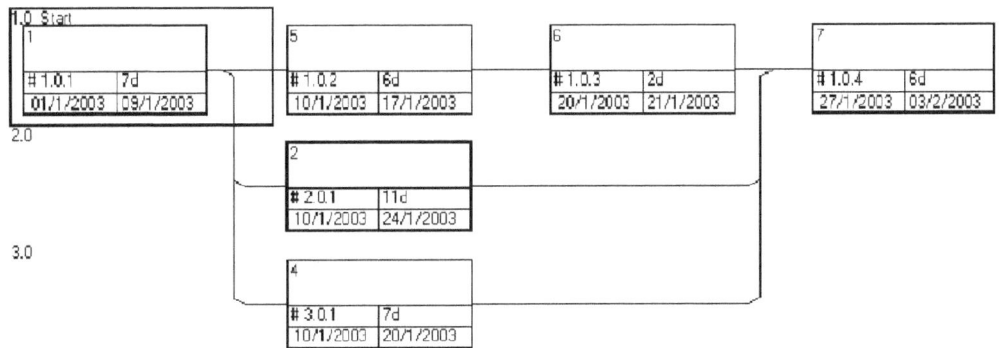

Figure 1.6. CPM project schedule.

Figure 1.6 shows a Critical Path Method (CPM) project schedule, the elements on the critical path having heavier borders. In the present text quadratic time/cost interpolations are allowed for each element and the critical path optimized using the steepest descent method.

Elsewhere in the text, *Finite Element* models and concepts and *optimization* are applied to several other problems. It is expected that many other such applications will follow in the years to come.

Finally, the text gives many QBASIC programs and Appendix A gives a brief introduction to BASIC programming. As an immediate introduction, the following coding plots a diagram of the *Reception-Yielding Model* of attitudinal psychology, giving the result shown in Figure 1.7.

```
SCREEN 1: COLOR 15, 4: a1 = 0: a2 = 0: A3 = 0
WINDOW (0, 0)-(300, 200)
VIEW (20, 10)-(180, 110)
FOR I = 0 TO 100 STEP 10: X = 3 * I: XL = X - 30
LINE (0, 0)-(0, 200): LINE (0, 1)-(300, 1)
y = 200 * 50 / (X + 50): LINE (XL, a1)-(X, y): a1 = y
y = 200 * X / (X + 100): LINE (XL, a2)-(X, y): a2 = y
y = a1 * a2 / 150: LINE (XL, A3)-(X, y): A3 = y
NEXT
LINE (71, 0)-(71, 85)
LOCATE 2, 2: PRINT "Probability": LOCATE 15, 21: PRINT "IQ"
LOCATE 4, 6: PRINT "Yielding": LOCATE 6, 15: PRINT "Reception"
LOCATE 13, 9: PRINT "Attitude change"
```

1. Introduction

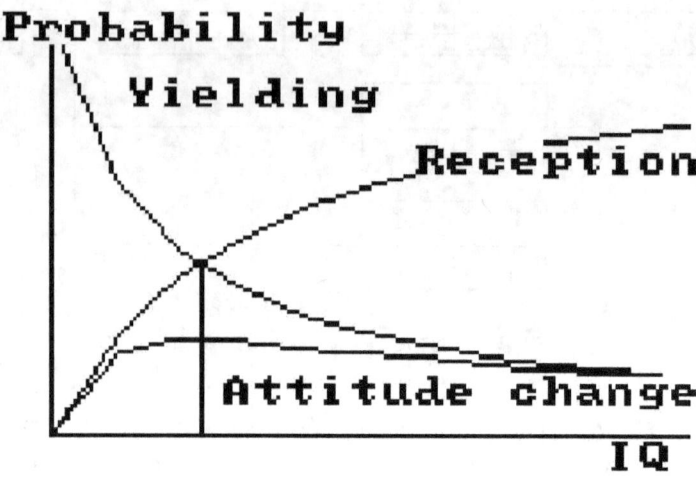

Figure 1.7. Reception-Yielding Theory plot.

In this theory the impact of advertising is the product of 'up' and 'down' functions, respectively for reception and yielding vs IQ, and the maximum impact is when the two curves intersect. A similar result appears frequently in quantitative management and economics, for example for supply (up) and demand (down, a useful mnemonic) curves when they intersect at the most efficient equilibrium point.

1.6. Conclusion

Some experts in FEM would insist that *finite elements* must be those of a 2D or 3D continuum, not naturally *discrete* 1D line elements. The late John Argyris, a pioneer of FEM, recently agreed with me that FEM might be defined by the process of *assembly of element matrices* to form a *system matrix* of Equation 1.3, and it is that process that we introduce here for distribution and traffic flow networks.

Indeed it is this 'sub matrix assembly' process that is the power of FEM, not its ability to model continua which methods like its predecessor the *Finite Difference Method* were originally used for. Then, as we shall see, many alternative types of distribution network to those traditionally analyzed using Linear Programming can be modeled.

That in the 'FEM' distribution models the constitutive parameter for each element is a *cost* emphasizes that we have a new area of application.

1. INTRODUCTION

It is hoped that such innovations as application of FEM or 'sub matrix assembly' to distribution and traffic network models will be just the beginning of application of FEM in Management Science.

Indeed the simple '1 -1' matrices used for networks here are irreducibly simple and, as foreshadowed in the final chapter, there is much scope for further work to be done, for example perhaps using 1D elements to model major routes and 2D elements to model 'background flow' in traffic flow network.

It is also hoped that such concepts as *Flow Ratio Design* will find very wide application. Here the idea is to favour routes with higher flows and thus reduce their cost or 'resistance'.

That FRD results in MIN models, in which the remaining elements all have the same minimum cost limit is reminiscent of Michell's celebrated 1904 'constant strain' criterion for optimum building truss structures, indicates an analogous 'constant cost' criterion for optimum business systems.

Such simple and obviously almost universally applicable concepts as these should, therefore, be of wide interest and be widely applied for a long time.

1.7. References

Argyris JH, *Energy Theorems and Structural Analysis*, Butterworth, London 1960. Reprinted from Aircraft Engineering 1954-1955.

Argyris JH, Mohr GA, The large curvature correction in finite element analysis - II, *Computer Methods in Applied Mechanics & Engineering*, paper CMA2085, 1999.

Argyris JH, Mohr GA, The large curvature correction in finite element analysis - I, *Int. J. Arts & Sciences* 1 (2001) 1-9.

Battersby, A, *Mathematics in Management*, Penguin, Harmondsworth, 1966.

Budnick FS, Mojena R, Vollmann TE, *Principles of Operations Research for Management*, Irwin, Homewood IL, 1977.

Enrick, NL, *Management Operations Research*, Holt, Rinehart & Winston, New York, 1965.

Eagly AH, Chaiken S, *The Psychology of Attitudes*, Harcourt Brace Jovanovich, Orlando FA, 1992.

Kempner, T (Ed.), *The Penguin Management Handbook*, 4th edn, Penguin Harmondsworth, 1987.

Koonz H, O'Donnell C, *Principles of Management*, 3rd edn, McGraw-Hill, New York, 1964.

1. Introduction

Livesley RK, Analysis of rigid frames by an electronic computer, *Engineering* 176 (1953) 230-238.

Michelle AGM, On the limits of economy in frame structures, *Phil. Mag.* series 6, 8 (1904) 589-595.

Mohr GA, Design of shell shape using finite elements, *Computers & Structures* 10 (1979) 745 - 749.

Mohr GA, Milner HR, Accurate finite element analysis of large displacements in skeletal frames, *Computers & Structures* 13 (1981) 533-536.

Mohr GA, Finite element formulation by nested interpolations: application to the drilling freedom problem, *Computers & Structures* 15 (1982) 183-190.

Mohr GA, *Finite Elements for Solids, Fluids, and Optimization*, Oxford University Press, Oxford, 1992.

Mohr GA, Improving an accurate thin plate element, *Computer Methods in Applied Mechanics & Engineering* 166 (1998) 341-348.

Mohr GA, Finite element modeling of distribution problems, *Applied Mathematics & Computation* 105 (1999) 69-76.

Mohr GA, Optimization of primal and dual network models of distribution, *Computer Methods in Applied Mechanics & Engng* 188 (2000) 135-144.

Mohr GA, Argyris JH, The large curvature correction in finite element analysis - II, *Int. J. Arts & Sciences* 1 (2001) 27-35.

Mohr GA, *The Pretentious Persuaders, A Brief History & Science of Mass Persuasion,* 2nd ed., Horizon Publishing Group, Sydney (2013).

Mohr GA, Fear E, *The Brainwashed: From Consumer Zombies to Islamism and Jihad,* Inspiring Publishers, Canberra (2016).

Mohr GA, Mohr PE, Mohr RS, *Brainwashed Zombies: Religious, Political & Consumer Persuasion,* Amazon-Kindle (2018).

Mohr WE, Bawden AW, *Network Analysis Reference Manual*, 6th edn, EPAC, Melbourne, 1974.

Mohr, WE, *Project Management and Control*, 3rd edn, University of Melbourne Dept of Architecture & Building, 1981.

Schmenner RW, *Production/Operations Management,* 4th edn, MacMillan, New York, 1990.

Turner MJ, Clough RW, Martin HC, Topp LJ, Stiffness and deflection analysis of complex structures, *Jour. Aero. Sciences* 23 (1956) 805-823.

Chapter 2

MATHEMATICS AND OPTIMIZATION

This chapter briefly reviews some basics of classical mathematics as a prelude to the introduction of *numerical methods* in the next chapter. Some knowledge of *polynomials, calculus* and *matrices*, for example, is needed in the Finite Element Method and the optimization techniques that are the core of this book.

The chapter then concludes with a few simple but useful optimization problems which draw upon the material of earlier sections.

2.1. Mathematical functions

<u>Explicit functions</u>. Explicit functions are expressed symbolically in the form $y = f(x)$ where x is the *independent variable* and y is the *dependent variable*. An example is

$$y = x^2 \qquad -3 < x < 3 \qquad (2.1)$$

where the function is defined in the range or interval -3 to 3 and is a parabola passing through the origin (as an exercise plot this on graph paper and on your computer if you have never done so).

<u>Implicit functions</u>. Implicit functions are expressed symbolically in the form $f(x,y) = 0$. An example is

$$x^2 + y^2 = 9 \qquad (2.2)$$

which is a circle of radius 3 centred at the origin (convert the equation to explicit form and plot it as an exercise).

<u>Single valued functions</u>. For these solutions of $f(x,y) = 0$ give one and only one value of y corresponding to each value of x. Examples are $f(x,y) = x - y + 2$ (straight line) and $f(x,y) = x^2 - y + 1$ (parabola). On the other hand relations such as $y^2 = |x|$ and $sin(y) = x$ define *two-valued* and *many-valued* functions of x respectively.

2. MATHEMATICS AND OPTIMIZATION

<u>Polynomials</u>. A polynomial of *degree n* is a function of the form

$$a_n x^2 + a_{n-1} x^{n-1} + - - - - + a_1 x + a_0 \qquad (2.3)$$

in which the coefficients (the *a's*) are constants and *n* is an integer. The quotient *p(x)/q(x)* of one polynomial by another is called a *rational* function of x (a rational number can be expressed in the form *r/s* where *r* and *s* are integers whereas an irrational number cannot be expressed in this way, for example π and $\sqrt{2}$).

<u>Transcendental functions</u>. These are infinite polynomials. Examples include the trigonometric functions and the exponential, hyperbolic and logarithm functions. Examples of these infinite polynomials are given in the next section.

<u>Periodic functions</u>. These repeat themselves at regular intervals. For example sin (x) and cos (x) are periodic with period 2π, tan (x) has period π and sin $(\pi x/a)$ has period π.

The *trigonometric* functions are so called because they are defined by the ratios of the sides of a right angled triangle:

sin(A) = BC/AC
cos(A) = AB/AC
tan(A) = BC/AB = *slope* of AC

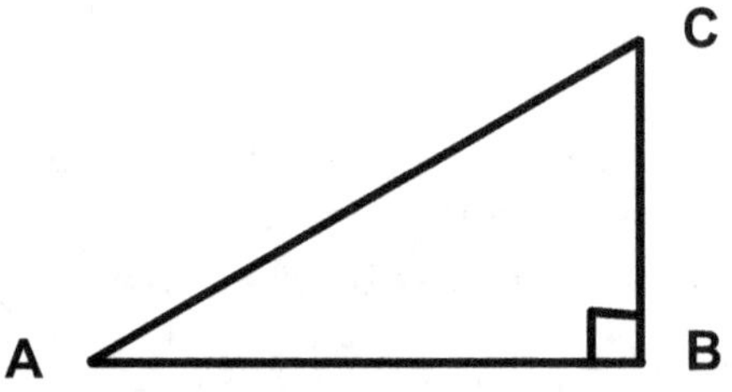

Figure 2.1. Trigonometric functions.

and their periodicity arises as the hypotenuse AC revolves through successive circles of rotation (anticlockwise so that angle A increases). Here recall that 360 degrees (a full revolution) equals 2π in *radians*.

Then it can easily be shown that, for example, sin (180 - A) = sin (A) and sin (180 + A) = - sin (A). The signs of these relationships are remembered by the CAST rule which is represented by the simple diagram shown in Figure 2.2.

2. MATHEMATICS AND OPTIMIZATION

Figure 2.2. The CAST rule.

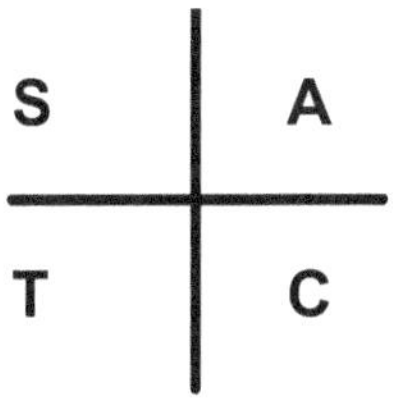

```
S | A
-----
T | C
```

It indicates that sin( ) is positive in the second quadrant, tan( ) in the third, cos( ) in the fourth and all are positive in the first. This is a very good example of a *mnemonic* (here taking the form of an *acronym*).

As an exercise verify the CAST rule for 90 ±, 180 ± and 270 ± using such simple cases as $A = 30°$ (given by $BC = 1$, $AC = 2$ and $AB = \sqrt{3}$, so that $\sin(30°) = ½ = \cos(60°)$) or $A = 45°$ (given by $AB = BC = 1$ and $AC = \sqrt{2}$, so that $\tan(45°) = 1$).

Even functions. $f(x)$ is an even function if $f(-x) = f(x)$ and is an *odd function* if $f(-x) = -f(x)$. For example, x^2, $\cos(x)$ and $x\sin(x)$ are even functions and x^3, $\sin(x)$ and $x\cos^2(x)$ are odd functions. Generally functions are neither even nor odd but any function can be expressed as a sum of even and odd functions using the identity:

$$f(x) = (1/2)\{f(x) + f(-x)\} + \{f(x) - f(-x)\}$$

Logarithms. If $y = b^x$ we say that x is the logarithm of y to the *base b* and write $x = \log_b(y)$. Historically logarithms were used to calculate the products of numbers using the rule

$$\log_b(yz) = \log_b(y) + \log_b(z) \quad (2.4)$$

and tables of logarithms, a task eliminated by the electronic calculator.

Generally the base 10 is used so that, for example, $\log_{10}(10) = 1$ and $\log_{10}(100) = 2$ etc. *Natural logarithms*, however, where the base is the *exponential number e* are perhaps more important theoretically.

The exponential function $y = e^x$ or exp (x) is the solution of the *differential equation* $dy/dx = y$ when $y = 1$ at $x = 0$. This solution is discussed in Section 2.4 and the infinite series expression for exp (x) is given in Section 2.2.

2. MATHEMATICS AND OPTIMIZATION

Finally the following rules for logarithms are worth note:

(i) $y = e^{\ln(y)}$

(ii) $x = \ln(e^x)$

(iii) $a^x = e^{x \ln(a)}$, where $\ln(\ ) = \log_e(\ )$.

2.2. Standard mathematical curves and functions

Some standard functions which should be familiar in graphical form include:

Straight line: $y = ax + b$ is a straight line with *intercepts* $x = -b/a$ and $y = b$ on the x and y axes respectively and *slope a*.

Circle: $(x - a)^2 + (y - b)^2 = R^2$ is a circle of area $A = \pi R^2$ centred at $x = a$ and $y = b$, that is at the point (a,b).

Ellipse: $(x/a)^2 + (y/b)^2 = 1$ is an ellipse of area $A = \pi ab$ centred at the *origin* $(x = y = 0)$.

Hyperbola: $(x/a)^2 - (y/b)^2 = 1$ is a pair of rectangular hyperbolae with asymptotes $y = \pm bx/a$.

$y = ax/(b + x)$ is a pair of hyperbolae with asymptotes $y = a$ and $x = -b$. This particular case is used as an example Sec. 3.2.

Polynomial: $y = a + bx + cx^2 + dx^3 + ex^4 + fx^5 - - - (const.)^n$ and the special cases $n = 2$ (parabola or *quadratic*), $n = 3$ (*cubic*), $n = 4$ (*quartic*) and $n = 5$ (*quintic*) are much used in practice (for example in the Finite Element Method).

Note that a parabola has one *turning point*, a cubic curve two (because the equation for the *slope dy/dx* is quadratic and therefore has two *roots*, that is, solutions to $dy/dx = 0$), a quartic curve has three 'TPs' and so on.

Exponential: $y = ak^x$ or $y = e^{kx}$ in the special case of the exponential function and the infinite series expression for this is given below.

Periodic: $y = \sin(kx)$, $\cos(kx)$ and $\tan(kx)$. The $\sin(\ )$ and $\cos(\ )$ functions are much used in the study of alternating electrical currents and the vibration of machinery.

2. MATHEMATICS AND OPTIMIZATION

<u>Curve sketching</u>. In drawing such functions attention should be given to:
i. Symmetry (?), intercepts (with the axes) and asymptotes.
ii. Turning points, curvature at TPs (> 0 for a minimum, < 0 for a maximum, and = 0 for a point of inflexion).
iii. Range restrictions and discontinuities (e.g., $y = \tan(x)$).

<u>Translation of axes</u>. To shift the origin of a function to $x = a$, $y = b$ simply replace x by $(x - a)$ and y by $(y - b)$ throughout the function.

<u>Rotation of axes</u>. If the axes are rotated anticlockwise by an angle ϕ then the coordinates x', y' relative to these new axes are given by

$$\begin{Bmatrix} x' \\ y' \end{Bmatrix} = \begin{bmatrix} c & s \\ -s & c \end{bmatrix} \begin{Bmatrix} x \\ y \end{Bmatrix} \qquad (2.5)$$

where the result is written in matrix form and $c = \cos(\phi)$, $s = \sin(\phi)$.
 [As a useful exercise see if you can prove this with a simple diagram].
 It can easily be shown that the inverse of the 2 x 2 matrix is the *transpose* of the original matrix (see Section 2.5), so that $x = cx' - sy'$ and $y = sx' + cy'$.
 As an exercise substitute these results into the equation $x^2 - y^2 = 1$ to obtain the equation for hyperbolae with the axes as asymptotes (note: use $c = s = 1/\sqrt{2}$ for angle = 45 degrees).

<u>The transcendental functions</u>. These are represented by infinite series or polynomials. These are obtained using *McLaurin's formula*. To develop this from first principles we write an infinite polynomial for some function $g(x)$:

$$g(x) = c_1 + c_2 x + c_3 x^2 + c_4 x^3 + - - -$$

Differentiating $g(x)$ several times [differentiation is discussed in the next section]

$$g'(x) = c_2 + 2c_3 x + 3c_4 x^2 + - - -, \text{ that is, } c_2 = g'(0)$$
$$g''(x) = 2c_3 + 6c_4 + - - -, \text{ that is, } c_3 = g''(0)/2$$
$$g'''(x) = 6c_4 + - - -, \text{ that is, } c_4 = g'''(0)/6$$

and so on.

2. MATHEMATICS AND OPTIMIZATION

Thus, the coefficients of the polynomial can be expressed in terms of the various derivatives at the origin. Then substituting these results into the original polynomial for $g(x)$ we obtain by induction

$$g(x) = g(0) + xg'(0) + x^2 g''(0)/2 + x^3 g'''(0)/6 + --- + x^2 g^n(0)/n!$$
(2.6)

which is McClaurin's formula.

From this the infinite series for the transcendental functions can be obtained, for example

$$e^x = 1 + x + x^2/2 + x^3/!3 + x^4/4! + --- \qquad |x| < \infty$$
$$\ln(1+x) = x - x^2/2 + x^3/3 - x^4/4 + --- \qquad -1 < x \le 1$$
$$\sin(x) = x - x^3/3! + x^5/5! - x^6/6! + --- \qquad |x| < \infty$$
$$\cos(x) = 1 - x^2/2! + x^4/4! - x^6/6! + --- \qquad |x| < \infty$$

In each of these cases the ratio of successive coefficients is less than unity and approaches zero so that the series converges.

Note also that e^x repeats itself upon differentiation and this is the unique property of the exponential function for which it was created.

<u>Taylor's theorem</u>. This is for the value of a function at a distance (usually small) h from the point $x = a$. This is obtained simply by replacing zero by 'a' and x by h in Equation 2.6.

Conclusion. In following chapters some familiarity with the equations for such simple functions as straight lines, parabolas and hyperbolae will be needed, for example in attempting to fit curves to graphs of share or currency variations.

To have some understanding of the mathematical forms involved in the oscillations in functions, therefore, it is also important to have familiarity with the exponential function and its series expression.

2. MATHEMATICS AND OPTIMIZATION

2.3. Basic calculus

Differentiation. The *first derivative f'(x)* of a function *f(x)* with respect to *x* is defined as

$$f'(x) = d(f(x))/d(x) = \lim_{\delta x \to 0} [f(x + \delta x) - f(x)] / \delta x \quad (2.7)$$

where δx is an infinitesimal increment in *x*. Then to take second and higher order derivatives the process is repeated successively.

Using this definition the first derivative of x^2, for example, is

$$f'(x) = d(f(x))/d(x) = \lim_{\delta x \to 0} [(x + \delta x)^2 - x^2]/\delta x = \lim_{\delta x \to 0}[2x + \delta x] = 2x$$

from which it can be inferred that $d(x^n)/dx = nx^{n-1}$.

Three rules which are especially useful for calculating derivatives are:

Product rule (PR): $d(uv)/dx = u(dv/dx) + v(du/dx)$ \quad (2.8)

Quotient rule (QR): $d(u/v) = [v(du/dx) - u(dv/dx)]/v^2$ \quad (2.9)

Chain rule (CR): $dy/dx = (dy/du)/(du/dx)$, $y = f(u)$ \quad (2.10)

where *u* and *v* are functions of *x*.

As simple exercises the reader may verify the following examples:
(i) PR: $y = e^x \tan(x)$ gives $y' = e^x \sec^2(x) + \tan(xe^x)$
(ii) QR: $y = \ln(x)/x$ gives $y' = (1 - \ln(x))/x^2$
(iii) CR: $y = (2x^2 + 3)^3 + 2$ gives $y' = 12x(2x^2 + 3)^2$

Applications of differentiation. Elementary examples include:

(a) Calculation of velocities (dx/dt) and accelerations (d^2x/dt^2).

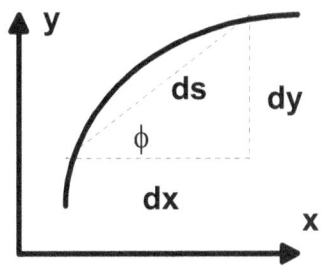

Figure 2.3.
Arc length and slope for a curve.

(b) Properties of curves:

Slope = $\phi = \tan^{-1}(dy/dx)$
Arc length $ds^2 = dx^2 + dy^2$
giving $s = \int \sqrt{(1 + (dy/dx)^2)}\, dx$

2. Mathematics and Optimization

Curvature:
$$\kappa = 1/R = d(slope)/d(arc)$$
$$= d\phi/ds = (d\phi/d\tan\phi)(d\tan\phi/dx)(dx/ds)$$
$$= (1/\sec^2\phi)(dy'/dx)(1 + (y')^2)^{-1/2} = y''/[1 + (y')^2]^{3/2}$$

Centre of curvature: $x_c = x - R\sin(\phi)$, $y = y + R\cos(\phi)$

Turning points: $y'' > 0$ for a minimum
  $y'' < 0$ for a maximum [before the TP $y' > 0$, after it $y' < 0$ so that y' is Decreasing, hence y'' (the rate of change in y') is < 0.
  $y'' = 0$ indicates a point of inflexion.

Finally, a list of some standard derivatives is given in the following table.
As shown this also can be used to obtain indefinite integrals (i.e. without *numerical* limits) by reverse differentiation (i.e., reading the table backwards)

Integral ←←←	→ → → Derivative	Derivative deduced using
x^n	nx^{n-1}	PR
e^x	e^x	Take as definition
e^{ax}	ae^{ax}	PR
log (x)	$1/x$	log definition and CR
log (f(x))	$f'(x)/f(x)$	CR
a^x	log (a) a^x	from $a^x = e^{x\log a}$
sin (x)	cos(x)	from $\sin x = (e^{ix} - e^{-ix})/2$
cos(x)	- sin(x)	from $\cos x = (e^{ix} + e^{ix})/2$
tan(x)	$\sec^2(x)$	QR
cosec(x)	- cosec (x) cot (x)	CR
sec(x)	sec (x) tan (x)	CR
cot(x)	$-\csc^2(x)$	CR
sinh(x)	cosh(x)	from $\sinh x = (e^x - e^{-x})/2$
cosh(x)	sinh(x)	from $\cosh x = (e^x + e^{-x})/2$
tanh(x)	$\mathrm{sech}^2(x)$	QR
$\sin^{-1}(x)$	$1/\sqrt{(1-x^2)}$	These usually appear as integration exercises by substitution but may also be deduced directly by substitutions (e.g. $y = \sin^{-1}(x)$ and invert and differentiate etc.) or the 'e' definitions.
$\cos^{-1}(x)$	$-1/\sqrt{(1-x^2)}$	
$\tan^{-1}(x)$	$1/(1+x^2)$	
$\sinh^{-1}(x)$	$1/\sqrt{(x^2+1)}$	
$\cosh^{-1}(x)$	$1/\sqrt{(x^2+1)}$	

2. MATHEMATICS AND OPTIMIZATION

Integration. The two basic types of integral are:

Definite integral: $\int_a^b f(x)\, dx$, $\int_c^d y(t)\, dt$ where a, b are boundary conditions and c is an initial condition.

Indefinite integral: $\int f(x)\, dx = F(x) + C$ where $F(x)$ is the antiderivative and C is a constant.

Analytical integration. Useful examples include:
(a) *Back or reverse differentiation:*
$de^{kx}/dx = ke^{kx}$ gives $\int e^{kx}\, dx = e^{kx}/k + C$

(b) *Substitution:* for the integral $\int (1 + x^2)^{-3/2}\, dx$ put $x = \tan(u)$, giving

$$I = \int (\sec^2(u)\, du)/(\sec^2(u))^{3/2} = \int \cos(u)\, du = \sin(u) + C = x/\sqrt{\{1 + x^2\}} + C$$

(c) *Integration by parts:* based on the product rule the formula for this is

$$\int u\, (dv/dx)\, dx = uv \mid - \int (du/dx)\, v\, dx$$

where $\mid$ denotes term evaluated at the boundary.
 A useful example of the latter 'IBP' process is:

$$\int x^2 e^x\, dx = x^2 e^x - 2\int x e^x\, dx = x^2 e^x - 2[xe^x - \int e^x dx]$$
$$= x^2 e^x - 2xe^x + 2e^x + C$$

from which the *reduction formula* for integration of $x^n e^{ax}$ is obtained by inference.

2. MATHEMATICS AND OPTIMIZATION

Applications of integration.

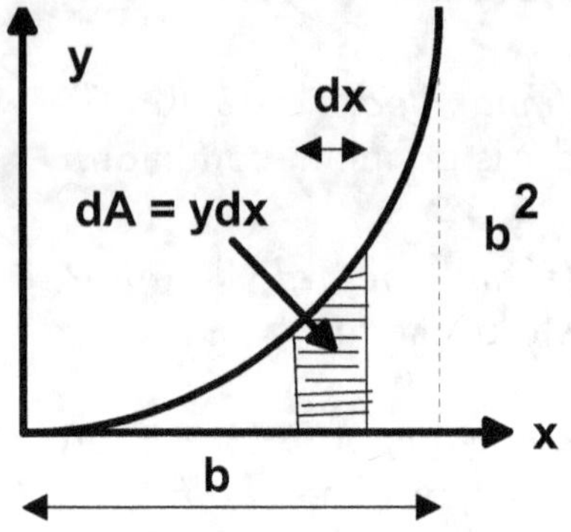

Figure 2.4.
Infinitesimal strip
of the area under a curve.

(a) Areas under curves are calculated as
$$\int_a^b y\, dx$$

(b) Centroids of areas are given by

$$x_c = \int x\, dA / \int dA, \quad y_c = \int y\, dA / \int dA$$

(c) Volumes, for example for a solid of revolution (about the x axis)
$$V = \int \pi y^2\, dx$$

(d) First and second moments of area are calculated as $\int y\, dA$ and $\int y^2\, dA$, first moments of area being used in (b).

As a very simple example we calculate the area under the parabola $y = x^2$ between $x = 0$ & $x = b$.

$$A = \int dA = \int y\, dx = \int_0^b x^2\, dx = [x^3/3]_0^b = b^3/3$$

or one third of the rectangle bounded by $x = b$, $y = b^2$ and the axes.
As an exercise the reader should verify that $x_c = 3b/4$ and $y_c = 3b^2/5$

Conclusion

At least a little calculus is useful, for example to find turning points in cost functions in economics and in the theory of optimization. Indeed, optimization is of crucial importance in business science and one of the major objectives of this text.

2. MATHEMATICS AND OPTIMIZATION

2.4. Differential equations

Ordinary differential equations. ODEs are those involving only one independent variable and of these useful examples are:

(1) $dy/dx - x = 0$

is a *first order* ODE (involving only first derivatives) the solution of which is given by integration as

$$y \mid = x^2/2 \mid$$

where $\mid$ denotes that boundary values must be given for the interval over which the DE applies.

(2) $dx/dt = kx$ \hfill (2.11)

is the growth law for populations and is *separable* which means that it can be written in the form

$$\int dx / x = \int k \, dt$$

giving, with the inclusion of the initial values, the exponential growth law

$$\ln x - \ln x_0 = k(t - t_0), \text{ or } x - x_0 = \exp[k(t - t_0)]$$
(2.12)

where k is the *growth factor*.

As an example, suppose that every 25 years 0.5[children - deaths] result per person, giving $k = 0.02$. This will give a 22% increase in population in 10 years, 2.7 times in 50 years (not very different from what happened from 1935 to 1985) and 2.7 times in the next 50 years (i.e. 7.3 times for 100 years). Now the growth factor is closer to 0.014, doubling us in 50 years, but the disturbing message should be clear.

Mohr's law of money, perhaps the fundamental principle of capitalism is another example:

$$d\$/dt = const. \times a \, (= activity) \text{ where } a = const. \times \$$$

that is, the rate at which money is made is proportional to the rate of business activity, this in turn proportional to the amount money so that again we have an exponential growth law.

2. MATHEMATICS AND OPTIMIZATION

(3) $\quad x = A\cos(\omega t + a)$

describes vibration and writing

$x' = -A\sin(\omega t + a)$ and $x'' = -\omega^2 A\cos(\omega t + a)$

it is clear that

$$x'' + \omega^2 x = 0 \qquad (2.13)$$

which is the form of differential equation that governs vibrations.

Analytical solution of ODEs

(1) ODEs take the general form $F(y'', y', x$ etc.$) = f(x)$ and analytical solutions seek a *complementary function* for the case when $f(x) = 0$ and a *particular solution* to augments this for the right side function.

(2) Such solutions can be obtained by techniques such as:
a. *Integration factors* $\lambda = \exp(\int P(x)dx)$ for the equation $y' + Py = Q$.
b. *Auxiliary equations* formed by substituting $y = \exp(mt)$.
c. The *Laplace transform*, multiplying $F()$ by an exponential term.
d. *Power series*, giving a polynomial solution.

Compared to numerical methods, such techniques have limited application, though the Laplace transform is worth note when discontinuities are involved.

For the purposes of this very limited introduction, therefore, simple cases that can be directly integrated or are separable must suffice.

Partial differential equations

PDEs are those involving two or more independent variables. For example, in *potential flow* problems the distribution of the *potential function* $\phi = \phi(x,y)$ in two dimensions possesses *partial derivatives* $\partial\phi/\partial x$ and $\partial\phi/\partial y$ which are calculated by respectively holding y and x constant and then obtaining an expression for the partial derivatives in the normal way. For example if

$$\phi = ax^2 + 2hxy + by^2 + 2gx + 2fy + c$$

then $\phi_x = \partial\phi/\partial x = 2ax + 2hy + 2g$

$\phi_y = \partial\phi/\partial y = 2hx + 2by + 2f$

2. Mathematics and Optimization

The PDE governing potential flow problems is *Laplace's equation* which is

$$\nabla^2 \phi = \partial^2 \phi / \partial x^2 + \partial^2 \phi / \partial y^2 = 0 \quad (2.14)$$

where $\nabla^2 \phi$ is the *Laplacian* operator.

Then the particular case $\nabla^2 \phi = const.$ is *Poisson's equation* and this governs *plane torsion* problems.

Including the time dimension two other well known PDEs are the *wave equation*

$$\partial^2 u / \partial t^2 = c^2 \nabla^2 u \quad (2.15)$$

and $\partial^2 T / \partial t = c \nabla^2 T \quad (2.16)$

which is the *diffusion equation*, respectively having application to vibration and transient heat flow problems.

Analytical solution of PDEs

PDEs for steady state two dimensional problems can be solved analytically using *Fourier series*. This involves 'fitting' solutions which are the sum of sin( ) or cos( ) terms to each direction to satisfy the boundary conditions and then the product of these solves the 2D problem.

When the problem is time dependent also then the Laplace transform and fast Fourier transform techniques prove useful. Such techniques have limited application, however, and numerical techniques are now more popular.

Numerical solution of PDEs

When numerical methods are used four basic types of physical problem can be written in matrix form:

(i) *Equilibrium problems.*
These are steady state distributions of stress, temperature, electrical or magnetic potential, fluid pressure or potential etc. For these only the *K* and *Q* terms of Equation 2.17 are needed.

(ii) *Diffusion problems.*
These involve transient fluxes of matter or energy governed by a *velocity law*. These require the *C, K, Q* and *Q(t)* terms of Equation 2.17.

(iii) *Inertial problems.* These involve vibrations governed by an *acceleration law*. These are expressed as a matrix equation of the form

$$M\{D''\} + C\{D'\} + K\{D\} = \{Q\} + \{Q(t)\} \qquad (2.17)$$

where M, C and K are *mass*, *damping* and *stiffness* matrices, D' and D'' are the derivatives of the field variables and Q and $Q(t)$ are constant and time dependent forcing loads.

(iv) *Eigenvalue problems.*
Omitting the load and C terms in Equation 2.17 and writing each element of the vector $\{D\}$ as $e_i \sin(\omega t + a_i)$ so that each element of the acceleration vector $\{D''\}$ is $-\omega^2 e_i \sin(\omega t + a_i)$ we obtain the eigenvalue problem

$$(K - \lambda M)\{e\} = \{0\} \qquad (2.18)$$

in which various *eigenvalues* of $\omega^2 = \lambda$ correspond to *eigenvectors* $\{e\}$ which are in vibration problems, for example, the modes of *free vibration*.

Conclusion

PDEs are largely beyond the scope of the present text at present but the potential flow problem of Equation 2.14 is solved in Chapter 12, providing a useful example of application of the *Finite Element Method (FEM)* to a two dimensional equilibrium problem. Such solutions can be used to approximately analyze traffic flow and other problems of relevance in business science.

2.5. Matrices

We have already encountered matrices in passing and here some of the basic manipulations with matrices are discussed. First, however, we observe that matrices are used as a way of writing simultaneous equations such as

$$2x + 2y + 2z = 12$$
$$2x + 3y + 4z = 20$$
$$2x + 4y + 3z = 19$$

which can be written

2. MATHEMATICS AND OPTIMIZATION

$$A\{x\} = \begin{bmatrix} 2 & 2 & 2 \\ 2 & 3 & 4 \\ 2 & 4 & 3 \end{bmatrix} \begin{Bmatrix} x \\ y \\ x \end{Bmatrix} = \begin{Bmatrix} 12 \\ 20 \\ 19 \end{Bmatrix} = \{b\}$$

(2.19)

using a 3 (rows) x 3 (columns) coefficient matrix A.

Special matrices
Special types of matrix include:
(i) *Diagonal matrix:* the entries are elsewhere zero.
(ii) *Unit matrix:* a diagonal matrix with all non-zero entries = 1.
Denoted *I* and the *leading diagonal* (starting top left) entries all = 1.
(iii) *Null matrix:* all entries zero. Denoted O.
(iv) *Symmetric matrix:* entry ij = entry ji (row j & column i), that is symmetric across the *leading diagonal* which runs from top left to bottom right.
(v) *Triangular matrix:* entries above or below leading diagonal zero.

Addition and subtraction of matrices: add or subtract corresponding entries (the matrices must be the same size).

Scalar multiplication of matrices: multiply all entries by the number.

Differentiation and integration of matrices: operate in the same way on each entry.

Transpose of a matrix: interchange rows and columns. For example:

$$A = \begin{bmatrix} 1 & 2 & 3 \\ 0 & -1 & 4 \end{bmatrix} \qquad A^t = \begin{bmatrix} 1 & 0 \\ 2 & -1 \\ 3 & 4 \end{bmatrix} \quad (tranpose)$$

Matrix multiplication. As an example we multiply a 3 x 3 matrix *A* with a 3 x 2 matrix *B*, yielding a 3 x 2 matrix *C* = *AB* which is given by the *algorithm*

$$c_{ij} = \Sigma_{k=1}^{3} a_{ij}b_{kj} = \{\text{row i of } A\} \text{ multiplied into } \{\text{column j of } B\}$$

(2.20)

and we say that row *i* of *A* is multiplied with column *j* of *B*, but only multiplying corresponding entries together and summing the result (this corresponds to a vector dot product).

2. MATHEMATICS AND OPTIMIZATION

Note that to permit such multiplication A and B must be *compatible*, that is the number of columns in A must equal the number of rows in B, as in the following

$$AB = \begin{bmatrix} 1 & -1 & 2 \\ 0 & 3 & 4 \\ -2 & 5 & -1 \end{bmatrix} \begin{bmatrix} 2 & 0 \\ -1 & 3 \\ 1 & 1 \end{bmatrix} = \begin{bmatrix} 5 & -1 \\ 1 & 13 \\ -10 & 14 \end{bmatrix} = C$$

The following rules pertaining to matrix multiplication are also noteworthy:
a. $AI = A$ (I = unit or identity matrix)
b. $A(B + C) = AB + AC$
c. $(AB)^t = B^t A^t$
d. AA^t yields a symmetric matrix.

Determinant of a matrix. The determinant of a (square) matrix

$$A = \begin{bmatrix} x & y & z \\ a & b & c \\ d & e & f \end{bmatrix}$$

is
$$\det(A) = |A| = \Sigma(\text{entries of any row or column} \times \text{their 'cofactors'})$$

where the cofactor of an entry is the *signed minor*, that is the determinant of the matrix given by omitting the row and column of that entry and given the sign corresponding to the pattern of alternating signs through rows and columns begun with a + sign at the top left.

Hence we obtain the *Laplace expansion*

$$|A| = x \begin{vmatrix} b & c \\ e & f \end{vmatrix} - y \begin{vmatrix} a & c \\ d & f \end{vmatrix} + z \begin{vmatrix} a & b \\ d & e \end{vmatrix} \quad (2.21)$$

where the first 2 x 2 determinant = $bf - ce$ (*cross product*), likewise the others.

Determinants have important application in some techniques of solving eigenvalue problems. They also provide a formal (but not practical) means of inverting matrices and solving matrix equations.

2. MATHEMATICS AND OPTIMIZATION

Another application of determinants is given by

$$\begin{vmatrix} 1 & 1 & 1 \\ x_1 & x_2 & x_3 \\ y_1 & y_2 & y_3 \end{vmatrix} = 0 \qquad (2.22)$$

which gives the equation for the line joining the points (x_1, y_1) and (x_2, y_2).

Replacing x and y by x_3 and y_3 above one also obtains three times the area of a triangle with vertices at (x_1, y_1) etc.

Matrix inverse

The inverse of a matrix A is defined as

$$A^{-1} = adj(A)/|A| = [cof(A)]^t/|A| \qquad (2.23)$$

where adj(A) denotes the *adjoint* of A which is the transpose of the matrix of cofactors.

Note that an inverse does not exist if $|A| = 0$ when A is said to be *singular*. This occurs if any two or more rows of columns of A are not independent (and $|A| = 0$ can be used as a test for this).

Using Equation 2.23 the inverse of the matrix of Equation 2.19 is obtained and used as shown below to obtain the solution for $\{x\}$ in this equation.

$$\begin{Bmatrix} x \\ y \\ x \end{Bmatrix} = (-1/6) \begin{bmatrix} -7 & 2 & 2 \\ 2 & 2 & -4 \\ 2 & -4 & 2 \end{bmatrix} \begin{Bmatrix} 12 \\ 20 \\ 19 \end{Bmatrix} = \begin{Bmatrix} 1 \\ 2 \\ 3 \end{Bmatrix} \qquad (2.24)$$

and the reader should check the cofactor calculations etc. leading to this result as an exercise.

Finally, the following identities involving matrix inverses are worth note:

(a) $A^{-1}A = I$, (b) $(A^{-1})^t = (A^t)^{-1}$, (c) $(AB)^{-1} = B^{-1}A^{-1}$

Conclusion

Matrices are much used in the remainder of the text, for example in linear programming and in input-output analysis. For these and other applications efficient methods of inverting matrices and thus solving matrix equations will be discussed.

2. MATHEMATICS AND OPTIMIZATION

2.6. Classical optimization problems

In the following section we discuss problems which can be solved by simple classical calculus. In these a simple objective function is formed and differentiation used to establish turning points. Though they are very simple and often neglected in favour of larger scale 'number crunching' techniques, the examples given here are, in fact, amongst the most useful optimization exercises, often giving a 'one-off' one line answer that can be used in the long term.

(1) Determination of cost functions

To determine the data for a function $y = f(x)$ of a production process cost y where x is the number of units produced the following guidelines are useful:

1. x and y must be related (by such a function).

2. Production should be observed when production is 'constant' or steady.

3. Sufficient observations must be made to give a reasonable spread of data (in fact the range of production is often underestimated).

4. Observations of variation in y as a result only of those in x are required (and not as a result of other contributing factors).

Then a suspected form for the function must be established. Usually a polynomial function with unknown coefficients is used and the values of the coefficients can be determined by linear regression.

(1) Short and long run supply curves

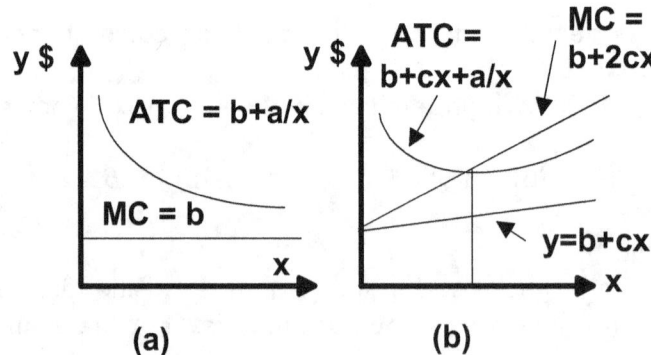

Figure 2.5. Linear and quadratic cost functions.
(a) $y = a + bx$
(b) $y = a + bx + cx^2$

2. MATHEMATICS AND OPTIMIZATION

Suppose the long run supply curve for a production process has been found to be of the form:

$$y = a + bx - cx^2 + dx^3 \qquad (2.25)$$

where a minus sign for c is often the suspected form for such curves.

Then the average total cost (ATC) and marginal cost (MC) are immediately given as:

$$y/x = ATC = a/x + b - cx + dx^2 \qquad (2.26)$$

$$dy/dx = MC = b - 2cx + 3dx^2 \qquad (2.27)$$

In practice, in fact, linear and quadratic cost functions are generally satisfactory and examples of these are shown in Figure 2.5.

Finally, for the minimum in ATC shown in Figure 2.5(b), we have the *marginal average cost* given by the quotient rule of differentiation:

$$d(y/x)/dx = (xy' - y)/x^2 \qquad (2.28)$$

$$= 0 \quad \text{when} \quad y' = y/x \qquad (2.29)$$

so that the minimum in the ATC curve occurs when marginal cost (MC) equals average cost (ATC), that is the MC curve intersects the average (total) cost curve at its minimum point and this is the break-even point for production.

(2) Demand functions

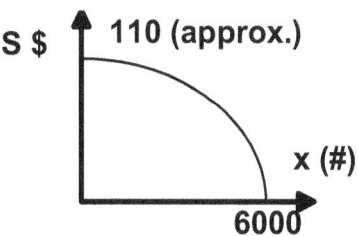

Figure 2.6.
Quadratic demand function

As an example assume that demand x and price S are related by

$$2x + S^2 - 12000 = 0 \qquad (2.30)$$

giving $\quad p(x) = \sqrt{(12000 - 2x)} \qquad (2.31)$

as the demand function and this is shown in Figure 2.6.

Then it follows immediately that

marginal demand function = $p'(x)$ (2.32)

(total) revenue function = $R(x) = xp(x)$ (2.33)

marginal revenue function = $R'(x) = (12000 - 3x)/\sqrt{(12000 - 2x)}$ (2.34)

and setting the latter to zero gives $x = 4000$ as the number of units produced for maximum revenue, each at price $p(x) = \$63.25$, so that this maximum revenue is $R(x = 4000) = 4000(63.25) = \$235,000$.

(3) Profit functions

Profit functions are given by subtracting the production cost function $y = C(x)$ from the revenue function $R(x)$:

$$P(x) = R(x) - C(x) \qquad (2.35)$$

and the marginal profit function is given by

$$P'(x) = R'(x) - C'(x) \qquad (2.36)$$

so that profit is maximum when

$$R'(x) = C'(x) \qquad (2.37)$$

so that maximum profit occurs when marginal revenue and marginal cost are equal and, it then follows from Equation 2.29, these are both then equal to the average cost y/x.

As an example let $C(x) = x^3 - 3x^2 - 80x + 500$ and $S = 2800$ so that $R(x) = 2800x$. Then equating $C'(x)$ and $R'(x)$ we obtain

$3x^2 - 6x - 80 = 2800$; $x^2 - 2x - 960 = 0$; $(x - 32)(x + 30) = 0$ (2.38)

giving the roots $x = 32$ and $x = -30$.

Then with the 'sensible' solution $x = 32$ we test the nature of the turning point:

$$p''(x) = R''(x) - C''(x) = 0 - (6x - 6) = -6(32) + 6 < 0 \qquad (2.39)$$

so that the turning point is a maximum and the value of the profit at this maximum is given by

$$P(32) = 2800(32) - [32^3 - 3(32)^2) - 80(32) + 500] = \$61,964$$

2. MATHEMATICS AND OPTIMIZATION

(4) Replacement models

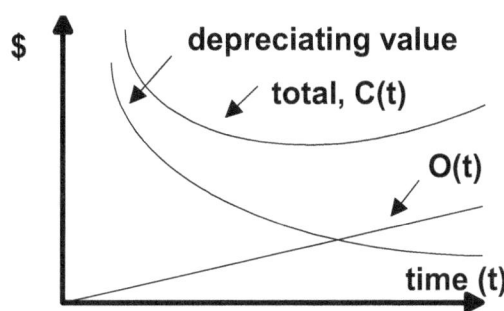

Figure 2.7.
Total cost for a machine or plant.

Figure 2.7 shows the depreciation in capital value of a machine or plant with time as well as the increasing operating cost as the machine gets older, resulting in a total cost function with a distinct minimum, as shown.

Writing this total cost as

$$C(t) = K(t)/t + O(t) \quad (2.40)$$

where $K(t) = P - S$ is the capital value expressed as the difference of the principal P and the salvage value S.

Then if the operating cost function $O(t) = a + bt$ we have

$$C(t) = (P - S)/t + (a + bt) \quad (2.41)$$

and taking the first derivative we have for the optimum replacement time t^*,

$$C(t) = -(P - S)/t^2 + b = 0, \text{ giving } t^* = \sqrt{\{(P - S)/b\}} \quad (2.42)$$

If, for example, $P = \$k\ 100$, $S = \$k\ 20$, $a = \$k\ 5/\text{year}$ and $b = \$k\ 1/\text{year}$ then we obtain the time for replacement as $t^* = 8.94$ years and the associated total cost $= C(t^*)t^* = \$k\ 204.63$.

Once again a potentially very useful result is obtained relatively easily and, not for the first time, a combination of a 'down curve' and a linear cost function appears in Figure 2.7 to provide a problem with an optimum point.

2. MATHEMATICS AND OPTIMIZATION

(5) Advertising periods

Suppose that the *response function* for an advertisement is

$$r = 1 - \exp(-0.02t) \tag{2.43}$$

and this is the proportion of a target population which buys a product at time t after an advertisement.

Suppose the market size of the target population reached is 100,000 people and the unit profit for the product is \$2 then the revenue function is

$$R = 200{,}000\{1 - \exp(-0.02t)\} \tag{2.44}$$

Then if the advertising costs are given by the function

$$C = 2000t + 2500 \tag{2.45}$$

the profit function can be written (in \$1,000s) as

$$P = R - C = 197.5 - 200\exp(-0.02t) - 2t \tag{2.46}$$

and calculating the first derivative we obtain

$$dP/dt = 4\exp(-0.02t) - 2 = 0 \tag{2.47}$$

from which $\exp(-0.02t) = 2/4 = 1/2$, giving $-0.02t = \ln(1/2) = -0.6931$

giving $t = 34.66 = 35$ days for which the maximum profit is given as

$$P_{max} = 197.5 - 200(1/2) - 70 = 27.5 \text{ (k\$)} \tag{2.48}$$

In this case the profit function is an 'exponential parabola' which intersects the time axis at $t = 1.28$ and $t = 77.54$ (this is most easily verified numerically using search, such methods being discussed in the following chapter).

Indeed the exponential model for the response function proposed here is of considerable usefulness though, of course, the problem requires more detailed study in practice as advertising campaigns will have to be repeated periodically, response function parameters may vary owing to seasonal factors or for different media and so on.

Conclusion

Deterministic problems involving a single variable can model many management science problems readily. With the use of classical calculus simple optimum solutions to such problems can be obtained.

Finally, the last example given provides a useful application of one of the techniques (Newton's method) discussed in Section 3.1, reminding us that numerical methods are complementary to classical techniques.

2. MATHEMATICS AND OPTIMIZATION

2.7. Multivariate optimization problems

In the last section we dealt only with problems with a single variable and these are, of course, immediately amenable to basic calculus. In the present section we consider two variable problems and then generalize the discussion to problems with more than two variables.

Two variable problems

For these we presume an objective function

$$z = f(x,y) \tag{2.49}$$

and this is a turning point with respect to both variables if

$$\partial f / \partial x = 0 \tag{2.50a}$$
$$\partial f / \partial y = 0 \tag{2.50b}$$

and the simultaneous Equations 2.50 are solved to find (x,y) at the turning point.

Then to determine the nature of the turning point we calculate the determinant

$$D(x^*, y^*) = f_{xx} f_{yy} - (f_{xy})^2 \tag{2.51}$$

where $f_{xx} = \partial^2 f / \partial x^2$, $f_{yy} = \partial^2 f / \partial y^2$, $f_{xy} = \partial f / \partial x \partial y$ are second partial derivatives.

Then
(a) if $D > 0$ we have a maximum if $f_{xx}, f_{yy} < 0$
    or we have a minimum if $f_{xx}, f_{yy} > 0$

(b) if $D < 0$ we have *a saddle point* (for example a maximum with respect to x and a minimum with respect to y)

(c) if $D = 0$ the test is indeterminate (in this unlikely event more investigation is needed to determine the nature of the stationary point.

2. MATHEMATICS AND OPTIMIZATION

Examples

As a simple introduction suppose we wish to maximize the revenue function

$$R = -3x_1^2 - 2x_2^2 + 20x_1x_2 \qquad (2.52)$$

subject to the constraint

$$x_1 + x_2 = 100 \qquad (2.53)$$

Using the latter to eliminate x_1 from the objective function R we have

$$R = -25x_2^2 + 2600x_2 - 30{,}000 \qquad (2.54)$$

Calculating the first derivative gives

$$R'(x) = -50x_2 + 2600 = 0, \text{ giving } x_2 = 52 \qquad (2.55)$$

and since $R''(X) = -50 < 0$ the turning point is a maximum with $x_1 = 48$, $x_2 = 52$ and $R = 37{,}600$.

Here, however, the constraint allowed us to reduce the problem to a single variable again (but well worthwhile when possible). Now consider the problem of two products with related demand functions (of their prices):

$$q_1 = 100 - 4p_1 - p_2, \quad q_2 = 90 - 2p_1 - 3p_2 \qquad (2.56)$$

where q_1, q_2 are their demands and p_1, p_2 their prices. The total revenue from the two products is then

$$R = p_1q_1 + p_2q_2 = p_1(110 - 4p_1 - p_2) + p_2(90 - 2p_1 - 3p_2) \qquad (2.57)$$

$$= 110p_1 - 4p_1^2 - 3p_1p_2 + 90p_2 - 3p_2^2$$

Taking the first partial derivatives we obtain

$$\partial R/\partial p_1 = 110 - 8p_1 - 3p_2 = 0 \qquad (2.58a)$$

$$\partial R/\partial p_2 = -3p_1 + 90 - 6p_2 = 0 \qquad (2.58b)$$

which are easily solved (for example by subtracting the second from twice the first) to give $p_1 = p_2 = 10$.

2. MATHEMATICS AND OPTIMIZATION

Now taking the second partial derivatives we obtain

$$\partial^2 R/\partial p_1^2 = -8, \quad \partial^2 R/\partial p_2^2 = -6, \quad \partial^2 R/\partial p_1 \partial p_2 = -3$$

so that Equation 2.51 yields $D() = (-8)(-6) - (-3)^2 = 39 > 0$ so that the point is a maximum as required and the demands and revenue are $q_1 = 60$, $q_2 = 40$ and $r = \$1000$ (for a given period).

Problems with *n* variables

For a function of *n* variables

$$z = f(x_1, x_2, x_3 - - -) \tag{2.59}$$

we have a turning point if

$$\partial f/\partial x_1 = 0, \quad \partial f/\partial x_2 = 0, \quad \partial f/\partial x_3 = 0 \text{ etc.} \tag{2.60}$$

and these simultaneous equations are solved to determine the coordinates of the turning point $(x_1^*, x_2^*, x_3^* - - -)$.

Calculating the second partial derivatives we can form a *Hessian matrix*

$$H = \begin{bmatrix} f_{x_1 x_1} & f_{x_1 x_2} & - - & f_{x_1 x_n} \\ f_{x_2 x_1} & f_{x_2 x_2} & - - & \\ - & - & - - & \end{bmatrix} \tag{2.61}$$

and the determinants of the 1 x 1, 2 x 2 etc. matrices H_1, H_2 - - formed beginning at the top left corner are called the *principal minors* of this matrix.

Then if

a. All principal minors are > 0 then H is positive definite and the turning point is a minimum

b. The principal minors alternate in sign (starting with a minus) then H is negative definite and the turning point is a maximum.

In general, however, turning points will be maxima with respect to some variables and minima with respect to others and investigation of the values of their individual second derivatives will reveal which situation applies. This allows the variables to be divided into two groups for further study of the problem.

2. Mathematics and Optimization

The Lagrangian function

For problems with constraints the Lagrangian function can be used to augment the objective function with the constraints, each multiplied by a *Lagrange multiplier*.

In the example of Equations 2.52 and 2.53 this gives

$$L(x_1,x_2,\lambda) = -3x_1^2 - 2x_2^2 + 20x_1x_2 - \lambda\{x_1 + x_2 - 100\} = f(x,y) - \lambda g(x,y) \qquad (2.62)$$

Calculating the first partial derivatives

$$\partial L/\partial x_1 = -6x_1 + 20x_2 - \lambda = 0 \qquad (2.63a)$$
$$\partial L/\partial x_2 = -4x_2 + 20x_1 - \lambda = 0 \qquad (2.63b)$$
$$\partial L/\partial x_3 = -x_1 - x_2 + 100 = 0 \qquad (2.63c)$$

which are solved simultaneously to give $x_1 = 48$, $x_2 = 52$ and $\lambda = 752$.

Calculating the determinant of the *bordered Hessian matrix* we obtain

$$|H| = \begin{vmatrix} 0 & g_x & g_y \\ g_x & L_{xx} & L_{xy} \\ g_y & L_{yx} & L_{yy} \end{vmatrix} = \begin{vmatrix} 0 & 1 & 1 \\ 1 & -6 & 20 \\ 1 & 20 & -4 \end{vmatrix} = 50 > 0 \qquad (2.64)$$

so that the turning point is a maximum (and had $|H|$ been less than zero the turning point would have been a minimum).

We can proceed in the same way in the case of inequality constraints and the signs of the Lagrange multipliers will indicate whether the constraints are *binding* or not.

When there are more than two variables, however, numerical solution is generally necessary using such techniques as the SUMT method for which an example program is given in Chapter 6.

Conclusion

In the case of only two variables nonlinear optimization problems present no great difficulty and constraints can easily be included. Here an equality constraint effectively reduced the problem to a single variable, such reduction being important in larger problems too. Such simple exercises, however, provide useful models in their own right as well as an understanding of the behaviour of multivariate systems.

2. MATHEMATICS AND OPTIMIZATION

2.8. References

Bajpai AC, Mustoe IR, Walker D, *Engineering Mathematics*, Wiley, Chichester. 1974.

Battersby A, *Mathematics in Management*. Pelican, Harmondsworth, 1966.

Chirgwin BH, Plumpton C, *A Course of Mathematics for Engineers and Scientists,* vol 1, Pergamon, London, 1961.

Coulson AE, *An Introduction to Matrices*, Longman, London, 1965.

Fairbank RE, Shultheis R, Piper EB. *Applied Business Mathematics,* 10th edn, South-Western, Cincinnati OH, 1975.

Hillier FS, Lieberman, GJ, *Introduction to Operations Research*, 3rd edn, Holden-Day, Oakland CA, 1980.

Kempner, T (Ed.), *The Penguin Management Handbook*, 4th edn, Penguin Harmondsworth, 1987.

Massey, HSW and Kestelman, H. *Ancillary Mathematics*, Pitman, London, 1958.

Mohr GA, *Finite Elements for Solids, Fluids, and Optimization*, OUP, Oxford, 1992.

Mohr GA, *Elementary Thinking for the 21st Century,* Xlibris, Sydney (2014).

Paul, RS, Haeussler, K. *Introductory Mathematical Analysis for Students of Business and Economics.* Reston Publ. Reston VA, 1985.

Steinberg, DI, *Computational Matrix Algebra*, McGraw-Hill Kogusaka, Tokyo, 1974.

Swokowski, EW, *Calculus with Analytic Geometry*, 3rd edn, Prindle, Weber & Schmidt, Boston MA, 1984.

2. Mathematics and Optimization

Chapter 3

NUMERICAL METHODS

With the PC so ubiquitous it is important to remember that computers were originally developed to perform numerical calculations, the use of *Graphical User Interfaces* (GUIs) and thence digital imaging being later developments.

Here numerical methods much used in computer applications are introduced and these are needed in following chapters. An example is numerical solution of matrix equations. Techniques for this are needed in *Linear Programming* and the *Finite Element Method,* and application of such methods to Management Science problems is a principal focus of this book.

In the present and following chapters simple QBASIC programs for key numerical methods are given, QBASIC being a version of BASIC that was included with DOS5 and still being used as an introduction to computer programming in recent books. QBASIC reads directly into VB as a *project module* and runs with only one or two changes, principally reading data from a file (rather than DATA statements) and writing output to a *form*.

3.1. Iterative and search techniques

In the following section a number of simple techniques for solving problems in a *stepwise* fashion are discussed. These are often used in conjunction with matrix methods of analysis, for example to provide powerful general techniques of tackling complex mathematical modelling problems.

Recurrence formulas

A simple example of a recurrence formula is *Newton's formula* for determining the square root of a number:

$$Lim_{n \to \infty}(x_n + A/x_n)/2 = \sqrt{A} \tag{3.1}$$

for which the *recurrence relation* is

$$x_{n+1} = (x_n + A/x_n) \tag{3.2}$$

where A is the number for which the square root is sought, x_n, is the last estimate of the root and x_{n+1} is an improved estimate.

3. NUMERICAL METHODS

For example, to obtain $\sqrt{4}$ we put $A = 4$ and begin with $x_0 = 1$, giving

$$x_1 = (1 + 4/1)/2 = 2.5$$
$$x_2 = 2.5 + 4/2.5) = 2.05 \text{ etc.}$$

so that clearly *convergence* is very rapid.

The reader is encouraged to write a short computer program of a few lines for this formula, including a tolerance number to test whether the root has been found with sufficient accuracy, if so terminating iteration.

Basic iteration

Basic iteration is a simple means of determining the solution of a problem by rearranging its equation and iterating the result in an attempt to obtain a solution. As an example suppose we wish to find the roots of the equation

$$x^2 - 5x + 4 = 0 \tag{3.3}$$

By factorization it is obvious that the roots are $x = 1$ and $x = 4$, but a more general method of solution is obtained by writing

$$x_{n+1} = (x_n + 4)/5 = F(x) \tag{3.4a}$$
$$x_{n+1} = \sqrt{(5x_n - 4)} \tag{3.4b}$$

Then (a) with $x_0 = 1$ gives the root $x = 1$, whilst with $x_0 = 5$ the solution *diverges*. The recurrence relation (b), on the other hand, gives the root $x = 4$ with $x_0 = 2, 3,$ or 5 but gives an imaginary solution when $x_0 = 0$ (which a computer program should not allow).

Here we notice the first of three important properties of basic iteration, these being:

[1] Only one root can be obtained from any particular arrangement.

[2] Convergence is guaranteed if $|F'(x)| < 1$ near the root.

[3] The method has *first order convergence*, that is dx is proportional to $(x - x^*)$ where x^* is the exact solution. In other words the rate of convergence is proportional to the distance from the solution.

Basic iteration can be used to solve nonlinear matrix equations, for example, by placing the nonlinear terms on the right hand side and retaining a left side of the form $A\{x\}$ where A is a matrix of constant entries and $\{x\}$ is a vector of variables x, y etc., for which a solution is sought.

3. NUMERICAL METHODS

Search methods

Search methods involve using successive *trial values* to 'locate' the solution to a problem. For example suppose we seek the solution of

$$f(x) = x^3 - x - 1 = 0 \qquad (3.5)$$

then we assume trial values of x and calculate the resulting value of $f(x)$. Beginning with $x = 0$ we obtain

$$f(0) = -1, \quad f(1) = -1, \quad f(2) = 5$$

and with $x = 2$ we observe a change in sign, indicating that $f(\ ) = 0$ has been passed. Then we can use *bisection* of the interval $x = 1 \to 2$, that is use $x = 1.5$ to give $f(1.5) = 0.875$.

Then, the sign having changed, we bisect the interval $x = 1.25 \to 1.5$ using $x = 1.375$ to give $f(1.375) = -0.225$.

Continuing in this fashion the solution is more closely bracketed but the solution can be obtained more quickly by using *linear interpolation* rather than bisection in the intervals in x. This can be written as

$$x' = x + \delta x/\delta f \qquad (3.6)$$

so that in place of the first bisection (with $x = 1.5$) we use

$$x' = 1 + 1/6 = 1.167$$

giving $f(x') = -0.579$. Interpolating again

$$x' = 1.167 + (2 - 1.167)/(5 - (-0.579)) = 1.3163$$

giving $f(x') = -0.0356$ which after two interpolations is much closer to the solution than we were after three bisections.

Note that Equation 3.5 has two other roots, however, and to obtain these other trial values of x some distance from the first root must be used. Sometimes this is achieved by *shifting* the origin of the problem using the substitution $(x - x^*)$ where x^* is the first root (estimate) for x in Equation 3.5. Then the search is for the distance of the next root from the first.

3. NUMERICAL METHODS

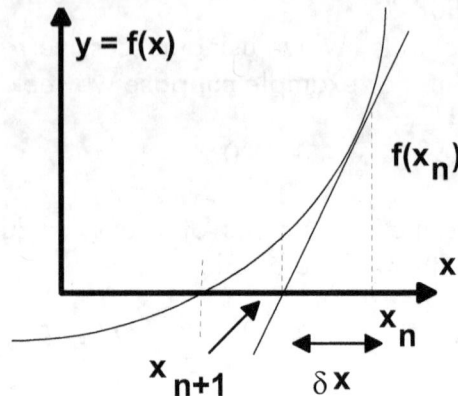

Figure 3.1
Newton's 'tangent' method of finding the roots of equations.

Figure 3.1 illustrates Newton's method of finding the roots of an equation. Here in seeking the root of $f(x) = 0$ we *extrapolate* along the tangent to the curve $y = f(x)$ at the current point x_n to obtain an improved solution x_{n+1}, so that the change in x is given by

$$\delta x = -(\text{residual error})/(\text{slope})$$

where the *residual* or residual error is the distance of $f(x_n)$ from the required value of zero and the *slope* is the derivative of the function $f(x)$ with respect to x evaluated at $x = x_n$.

Then the recurrence relation for Newton's method is written as

$$x_{n+1} = x_n - f(x_n)/f'(x_n) \tag{3.7}$$

and this might be described as the *tangent slope method*.

If, for example, we seek the roots of Equation 3.3, then we have

$$f(x) = x^2 - 5x + 4 \quad \text{and} \quad f'(x) = 2x - 5$$

so that the recurrence relation is

$$x_{n+1} = x_n - (x_n^2 - 5x_n + 4)/(2x_n - 5) = (x_n^2 - 4)/(2x_n - 5)$$

which with $x_0 = 5$ gives the successive results $x = 4.2, 4.012, 4.000$ so that convergence is a good deal faster than with basic iteration in Equations 3.4. Then $x_0 = 2$ quickly leads to the other root ($x = 1$) whilst $x_0 = 3$ will yield the first root again (i.e. $x = 4$).

3. NUMERICAL METHODS

Here we notice the first of three characteristics of Newton's method (sometimes referred to as the Newton-Raphson method), these being:

1. The root obtained depends upon the starting point.
2. The method has *second order convergence*, that is dx is proportional to $(x - x^*)^2$ (whereas basic iteration has only first order convergence).
3. No simple criterion for convergence exists (as it does for basic iteration).

Often search techniques are used to approximately locate a root (which may be of $f'(x) = 0$ when we are seeking turning points) and then Newton's method is applied to efficiently find an accurate solution.

Example application of Newton's Method

Suppose we have an asset whose present value is given by

$$P = R(t)\exp(-rt) \tag{3.8}$$

where $R(t)$ is a monotonically increasing function for which the rate of increase decreases. If the capital investment on the asset was C then the net present value is given by

$$N = R(t)\exp(-rt) - C \tag{3.9}$$

Taking the first derivative we obtain

$$dN/dt = R'(t)\exp(-rt) + R(t)(-r)\exp(-rt)$$
$$= \{R'(t) - rR(t)\}\exp(-rt) = 0, \text{ giving } R'(t) = rR(t) \tag{3.10}$$

as the condition for the maximum NPV.

Taking the second derivative gives

$$d^2N/dt^2 = \{R'(t) - rR(t)\}(-r)\exp(-rt) + \{R''(t) - rR'(t)\}\exp(-rt)$$
$$= \{R''(t) - rR'(t)\}\exp(-rt) < 0 \tag{3.11}$$

because $R'(t) = rR(t)$ from Equation 3.10 and $R''(t) < 0$, $r > 0$ and $R'(t) > 0$ are assumed at the outset, so that we have a maximum as required.

As an example consider the *return function* to be of the form

$$R(t) = 500(1 + t^{0.6}), \quad r = 0.08 \tag{3.12}$$

and substituting this into the result of Equation 3.10 gives $500(0.6)t^{-0.4} = 0.08\{500(1 + t^{0.6})\}$ and multiplying through by $t^{0.4}$ and dividing by 40 we obtain:

$$t + t^{0.4} - 7.5 = 0 \tag{3.13}$$

3. NUMERICAL METHODS

Solving this result using Newton's method we have

$$t_{n+1} = t_n - f(t)/f'(t) = t_n - (t + t^{0.4} - 7.5)/(1 + 0.4t^{-0.6}) \quad (3.14)$$

and beginning with $t = 1$ this recurrence relation yields the results

$$t_0 = 1 \text{ gives } t_1 = 1 - (1 + 1 - 7.5)/(1 + 0.4) = 4.9286$$

and then $t_2 = 5.5169$, $t_3 = 5.5196$ for which the return function value is $R(t) = 1{,}894$ so that the net present value is

$$N = 1{,}894\exp(-0.08(5.52)) - 700 = 1218 - 700 = 518 \quad (3.15)$$

if the capital outlay was $700, yielding a profit of $518.

Once again a very simple mathematical model yields a useful result but, of course, the parameters need adjustment for real applications. In addition, a useful example of the use of Newton's method results.

The initial slope method

In some types of problem calculation of the new value of $f'(x)$ required by Newton's method is laborious. In such cases we can use only the first or *initial value* of this slope, that, is $f'(x_0)$ in Equation 3.7 giving

$$x_{n+1} = x_n - f(x_n)/f'(x_0) \quad (3.16)$$

and this method must work as iteration will continue as long as there is a residual (value of $f(x)$).

Convergence is a good deal slower than with Newton's method (first order convergence, in fact) but numerous *acceleration* techniques have been proposed to remedy this in part. The simplest of these multiply the increment in x suggested by Equation 3.16 by a *convergence factor* which typically ranges from 0.8 to 1.5.

Conclusion

In econometrics, for example, the search and other techniques described here have obvious application, as they do in many areas of modern computer analysis of physical systems, including, of course, those in business.

3. Numerical Methods

3.2. Predictor-corrector methods

From their name predictor-corrrector methods sound like something we might be grateful to see used in the governance of our national economy and, indeed, such methods do have wide potential application. In such methods a prediction is made by such techniques as Newton's method and then we correct our 'aim' on the basis of the result of this prediction.

Euler's Method

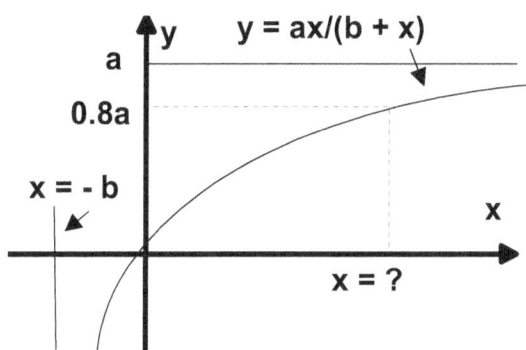

Figure 3.2
Rectangular hyperbola with asymptotes $y = a$ and $x = -b$.

Euler's method involves taking steps in some variable x, say δx, to calculated the value of a function $y = f(x)$ at some value of x several steps δx away. To explain this procedure we write a *linear interpolation* in terms of a *dimensionless coordinate* $s = dx/\delta x$ which varies from zero to one in the interval δx, that is, the interpolation for x is written as

$$x = (1 - s)x_i + (s)x_{i-1} \tag{3.17}$$

and the functions in brackets are called *interpolation functions*.

Then for a function $y = f(x)$ like that shown in Figure 3.2 we can write

$$\delta y x' = \delta y (dx/dy) = \delta y (dx/ds)(ds/dy) = dx/ds = x_i + x_{i+1} \tag{3.18}$$

using the chain rule of differentiation and noting that $dy/ds = \delta y$.

Rearranging this result we have

$$x_{i+1} = x_i + \delta y (dx/dy) \tag{3.19}$$

which is Euler's method.

3. NUMERICAL METHODS

Applying this to the rectangular hyperbola shown in Figure 3.2 we obtain the recurrence relation

$$x_{i+1} = x_i + \delta y(b + x_i)^2/ab \tag{3.20}$$

or $\quad x_{i+1}/b = x_i/b + (\delta y/a)(1 + x_i/b)^2$

in dimensionless form, yielding the results shown in Table 3.1 when eight equal steps in y are taken up to $0.8a$.

Table 3.1. Solutions to the problem of Figure 3.2

y/a	x/b Euler	x/b Runge-Kutta	x/b Exact
0.1	0.1000	-	0.1111
0.2	0.2210	0.2400	0.2500
0.3	0.3701	-	0.4286
0.4	0.5578	0.6607	0.6667
0.5	0.8005	-	1.0000
0.6	1.1247	1.4874	1.5000
0.7	1.5761	-	2.3333
0.8	2.2397	3.8164	4.0000

The results for the Euler method (sometimes called the *continuation method*) are poor, illustrating the need for an improved method such as the following one.

Predictor-corrector method

An improved method is obtained by replacing the linear interpolation of Equation 3.17 by the *quadratic interpolation*

$$x = (1/2)(s^2 - s)x_{i-1} + (1 - s^2)x_i + (1/2)(s^2 + s)x_{i+1}$$

in which the dimensionless coordinate s ranges from minus one to one (this interpolation is derived later in this chapter). Then the result of Eqn 3.18 is:

$$\delta y x' = (1/2)(2s - 1)x_{i-1} - 2s x_i + (1/2)(s^2 + 1)x_{i+1} \tag{3.21}$$

from which

$$\delta y x'_i = (x_{i+1} - x_{i-1})/2 \tag{3.22}$$

using $s = 0$ in Equation 3.21.

3. Numerical Methods

Eliminating x_{i-1} from these two results gives

$$x_{i+1} = x_i + \delta y(1 - 1/2s)x'_i + \delta y(1/2s)x'_{i+1} \qquad (3.23)$$

which is the second order Runge-Kutta predictor-corrector formula. Using this we obtain the following solution strategy:

$$x_1 = x_0 + \delta y(dx/dy)_0 \quad \text{- first predictor} \qquad (3.24)$$

$$x_{i+1} = x_{i-1} + 2\delta y(dx/dy)_i \quad \text{- subsequent predictors} \qquad (3.25)$$

$$x_{i+1} = x_i + (1/2)\delta y[(dx/dy)_i + (dx/dy)_{i+1}] \quad \text{- corrector} \qquad (3.26)$$

where Equation 3.24 results from Equation 3.23 when $s = \infty$ (this is also the Euler formula), Equation 3.25 is a rearrangement of Equation 3.22 and Equation 3.26 results from Equation 3.23 when the dimensionless coordinate $s = 1$.

This gives much better results than the Euler method using only half as many steps, as shown in Table 3.1 (where to make the comparison fair half as many steps are used but two gradient calculations are required for each step, namely the predictor and corrector).

This approach can also be used to modify Newton's method (see Figure 3.1) but in this case convergence is already sufficiently rapid for most purposes.

Conclusion

The Euler or continuation method is rather inaccurate in highly nonlinear problems and the predictor-corrector method described gives considerably better results. It is, perhaps, best understood in words than from Equations 3.24 - 3.26:

a. Use the last tangent at the present point to extrapolate from the last point to the next point (equivalent to using a chord approximation).

b. Calculate the slope at this *estimate* of the next point and use the average of this and that used to obtain the estimate to extrapolate to the next point.

Then this 'correct the aim' approach is much more accurate and much more logical than the Euler method.

3. Numerical Methods

3.3. Solution of matrix equations

In the following section two important methods of solving matrix equations of the form $A\{x\} = \{b\}$ are described. A concise program for one of these is then given in Section 3.4.

Gauss-Seidel Iteration

Gauss-Seidel iteration can be described by the *algorithm*

$$a_{ii}x_i^* = b - \sum_{j=1(j\neq i)}^n a_{ij}x_j \qquad (3.27)$$

and such algorithms can be coded almost literally. This method, however, is best understood from a simple example such as solution of the two simultaneous equations:

$$2x_1 + x_2 = 7, \quad x_1 + 2x_2 = 8$$

which are rewritten as $\quad x_1 = (7-x_2)/2, \quad x_2 = (8-x_1)/2$

$$(3.28)$$

Then beginning with $x_1 = x_2 = 1$ and iteratively using the rearranged Equations 3.28 we obtain:

Iteration	x_1	x_2
1	3	2.5
2	2.25	2.875
3	2.063	2.969
Exact	2	3

and the results are converging fairly well.

Note, however, that if the equations are first written in the form

$$x_1 + 2x_2 = 7, \quad 2x_1 + x_2 = 8 \qquad (3.29)$$

then the results diverge (try this as an exercise).

Then for convergence we require the magnitude of the *pivot* (the diagonal coefficient in the matrix expression of the equations) to be equal to or greater than the magnitude of the other coefficients for each row or equation.

A slight variation in the Gauss-Seidel method is *Jacobi* or *simultaneous iteration* where all the x_i are evaluated at each iteration or 'pass' through the values before being used for the next evaluation or iteration. Generally convergence will be slightly slower and this method is rarely used.

3. NUMERICAL METHODS

Boolean matrices

$$\begin{bmatrix} 1 & 0 & 0 \\ 0 & 0 & 1 \\ 0 & 1 & 0 \end{bmatrix} \begin{bmatrix} 1 & 2 & 3 \\ 4 & 5 & 6 \\ 7 & 8 & 9 \end{bmatrix} = \begin{bmatrix} 1 & 2 & 3 \\ 7 & 8 & 9 \\ 4 & 5 & 6 \end{bmatrix} \qquad (3.30)$$

The first matrix of Equation 3.30 *pre multiplies* the second, causing rows two and three to be swapped. Such matrices are called Boolean matrices and only have zero or 'one' entries.

If this same matrix had been used to *post multiply* the second matrix then its second and third columns would have been swapped.

Such matrices are rarely used in practice but the concept of a matrix which operates on another matrix, swapping or subtracting rows and/or columns is helpful in understanding the Gauss-Jordan reduction technique discussed below.

Gauss-Jordan reduction

Gauss-Jordan reduction is a practical numerical method of finding the inverse A^{-1} of a matrix A. Then the solution of the matrix equation $A\{x\} = \{b\}$ is given as $\{x\} = A^{-1}\{b\}$, where here $\{x\}$ = a one column matrix or *vector* of the unknowns or *variables* x_i and $\{b\}$ is a vector containing the right hand side values of the set of simultaneous equations whose coefficients are stored in matrix A.

This method involves performing such operations on matrix A so as to reduce it to an identity matrix (i.e. with entries = 1 on the *leading diagonal* running from top left, and = 0 elsewhere), expressing these operations as a matrix B (a complicated extension of the idea of a Boolean matrix). Then if matrix A is first *augmented* by an identity or unit matrix we can write:

$$B[A, I] = [I, C] \qquad (3.31)$$

then A has been reduced to a unit matrix and we have

$$BA = I \quad \text{so that} \quad B = A^{-1}$$

and $\quad C = BI = A^{-1}$

so that the pre multiplying matrix B was the required inverse (though we did not know it) and all the operations performed on matrix A to reduce it to a unit matrix (various row subtractions to produce the zero off-diagonal entries required) are recorded as matrix C.

3. NUMERICAL METHODS

Then it turns out that the operations required to reduce A to a unit matrix are straightforward so that, using these at the same time on a unit matrix, the inverse A^{-1} is obtained and this is done on an example in Table 3.2.

Table 3.2. Gauss-Jordan reduction tableau.

	2	2	2	1	0	0
	2	3	4	0	1	0
	2	4	3	0	0	1
row1/pivot → r1*	1	1	1	1/2	0	0
r2 - 2r1*	0	1	2	1	1	0
r3 - 2r1*	0	2	1	-1	0	1
r1(last) - 1 x 2r2	1	0	-1	3/2	-1	0
r2(last)/pivot →r2*	0	1	2	-1	1	0
r3(last) - 2 x r2*	0	0	-3	1	-2	1
r1(last) - (-1) x r3*	1	0	0	7/6	-1/3	-1/3
r2(last) - 2 x r3*	0	1	0	-1/3	-1/3	2/3
r3/pivot → r3*	0	0	1	-1/3	2/3	1/3

Here r2 denotes row 2 and so on, and r2* denotes the row after it has been divided by the pivot (the first operation of each reduction).

Here three reductions (of successive columns from left to right) have been performed, the first operation of each being division by the pivot (entry on the diagonal) of matrix A. This is followed by the operation

new row = old row - pivot row* x *row multiplier* (3.32)

where * denotes having been divided by its pivot and the *row multiplier* is the entry in each row directly above or below the pivot.

This method can easily be written as an *algorithm* and this will directly correspond to the key lines of the program given in Section 3.4. In this program the matrix is not actually augmented by a unit matrix but overwritten by the forming inverse.

Note that problems will occur when a pivot is zero is close to it and routines which use *pivotal condensation* or *pivoting* are used to overcome such difficulties. In these columns are swapped to obtain the largest possible pivot (from the columns remaining unreduced). These column swaps are recorded in a one dimensional array and corresponding rows are swapped at the conclusion of Gauss-Jordan reduction (reversing the swaps). This is necessary because swapping any two columns of a matrix results in a corresponding swap in the rows of the inverse.

A program which includes pivoting is given in Section 3.5 whilst a simpler program which does not is given as an introduction in Section 3.4.

3. NUMERICAL METHODS

3.4. Direct solution of matrix equations

Gauss reduction

Gauss reduction is a method of *direct solution* of matrix equations, that is, a solution is obtained without calculating the inverse of the connecting matrix A. This method is also called *triangular elimination* because it reduces the matrix A to an 'upper triangular' matrix *(U)*. The operations required to achieve this are exactly the same as in Gauss-Jordan reduction except that the 'row subtraction' operations are only carried out below the pivotal position. Thus, returning to the example of Table 3.2 we obtain:

Table 3.3. Example of Gauss reduction

(a) forward reduction

	Matrix A			{b}
	2	2	2	12
	2	3	4	20
	2	4	3	119
r1/pivot r1*	1	1	1	6
r2 - 2 x r1*	0	1	2	8
r3 - 2 x r1*	0	2	1	7
OK	1	1	1	6
r2(last)/pivot r2*	0	1	2	8
r3(last) - 2 x r2*	0	0	-3	-9
OK	1	1	1	6
OK	0	1	2	8
r3(last)/pivot	0	0	1	3

(b) back substitution
$b_3 = x_3 = 3$
$b_2 - 2x_3 = x_2 = 8 - 2(3) = 2$
$b_1 - x_2 - x_3 = x_1 = 6 - 2 - 3 = 1$

Here in the forward reduction or pass to reduce matrix A to upper triangular form the same operations are carried out on the RHS vector *{b}* (that is, *{b}* replaces *I* on the LHS of Equation 3.31). Then back substitution yields the solutions of A{x} = {b} in reverse order as

$$x_i = b_i - \sum_{j=i+1}^{n} a_{ij}(last) \times x_j \qquad (3.33)$$

and Equation 3.33 is, in fact, equivalent to inverting the upper triangular matrix to which A was reduced and pre multiplying the RHS vector by it (it must be as it yields the solution!). Inversion of triangular matrices, therefore, is a very simple exercise numerically.

3. NUMERICAL METHODS

Gauss reduction requires roughly n^3 operations (+, -, x, /) to obtain the solution whereas Gauss-Jordan reduction takes about twice as many operations when the inverse of A is calculated (but not the same number if A^{-1} is not formed as can be seen in the program given in this section). The classical Laplace expansion (Chapter 1), on the other hand takes $n!$ operations and hence is only practical for $n \leq 4$.

Coding of matrix operations

Computer coding of most matrix operations is relatively straightforward and, for example, multiplication of two matrices *A (M x L)* and *B (L x N)* to obtain a matrix *C* (which will be *M x N*) can be coded as

```
10 FOR I = 1 TO M: FOR J = 1 TO N
20 C(I,J) = 0 : FOR K = 1 TO L
30 C(I,J) = C(I,J) + A(I,K)*B(K,J)
40 NEXT : NEXT : NEXT
```

and here it is clear why for the matrices to be *compatible* (for the purposes of multiplication) the number of columns of the first must be equal to the number of rows of the second (so that rows and columns can be multiplied together in the required fashion).

Gauss-Mohr reduction subroutine

The following BASIC subroutine uses Gauss-Jordan reduction to form the inverse of a matrix *S*, overwriting it by its forming inverse. Underlining and [ ] are to indicate modifications discussed later but are not actual code. This incredibly short ten line routine was the basis of Mohr's *PC Finite Element Solution System (PC FESS)*, first developed for teaching on a 8 terminal 'midi computer' in 1983 and used on a Spectravideo PC in 1984. Version 2 was a far longer and more complex affair developed using MegaBasic and an XT PC in 1987.

```
10 FOR I = 1 TO N
20 X = S(I,I) : Q(I) = Q(I)/X [: S(I,I) = 1]
30 FOR J = 1 TO N
40 S(I,J) = S(I,J)/X : NEXT
50 FOR K = 1 TO N
60 IF K = I THEN 100
70 X = S(K,I) : [S(K,I) = 0 : ] Q(K) = Q(K) - X*Q(I)
80 FOR J = 1 TO N
90 S(K,J) = S(K,J) - X*S(I,J) : NEXT J
100 NEXT K : NEXT I
```

3. NUMERICAL METHODS

Then if the two underlined statements are added the reduction operations are also applied to a RHS vector $\{Q\}$ so that, at the completion of 'GJR' this vector contains the solution of the equation $S\{x\} = \{Q\}$.

In Gauss-Mohr Reduction (GMR) the bracketed statements are removed and the lower limits in lines 30 and 80 are changed from 1 (one) to I+1 so that reduction operations are carried out only to the right side of the pivot and the inverse of A is not formed but the solution of $S\{x\} = \{Q\}$ is still obtained with the amount of computation almost halved.

Note that before this program segment is entered matrix S and vector $\{Q\}$ (if used) must be appropriately dimensioned and filled, for example using

```
2 INPUT "INPUT N",N
4 DIM S(N,N), Q(N)
6 FOR I = 1 TO N
8 READ S(I,J) : NEXT : NEXT
9 FOR I = 1 TO N : READ Q(I) : NEXT
110 END
120 DATA 5/8, -1/2, 1/8
130 DATA -1/2, 1, -1/2
140 DATA 1/8, -1/2, 5/8
150 DATA 1,2,3
```

Here the data is for a 3 x 3 matrix of the form shown in Equation 3.34 so that the inverse should take the simple form shown (PRINT lines need to be added to print the results). Then the RHS vector is given by line 150, so that the solution of $S\{x\} = \{Q\}$, which will be contained in array Q( ), will be (10, 14, 14).

$$\begin{bmatrix} \frac{n+2}{2n+2} & -1/2 & 0 & - & - & \frac{1}{2n+2} \\ -1/2 & 1 & -1/2 & - & - & 0 \\ 0 & -1/2 & 1 & - & - & 0 \\ - & - & - & - & - & - \\ 0 & 0 & - & -1/2 & 1 & -1/2 \\ \frac{1}{2n+2} & 0 & - & 0 & -1/2 & \frac{n+2}{2N+2} \end{bmatrix}^{-1} \begin{bmatrix} n & n-1 & n-2 & - & 2 & 1 \\ n-1 & n & n-1 & - & 3 & 2 \\ n-2 & n-1 & n & - & 4 & 3 \\ - & - & - & - & - & - \\ 2 & 3 & 4 & - & n & n-1 \\ 1 & 2 & 3 & - & n-1 & n \end{bmatrix}$$

(3.34)

The form of matrix used here (that is a *tridiagonal matrix* with unit diagonal, -1/2 for all the off-diagonal entries on either side of the diagonal and exceptional corner values as shown in Equation 3.34) is very useful for testing matrix inversion or solution routines.

3. NUMERICAL METHODS

Conclusion

Gauss reduction is the fundamental means of solving matrix equations though there are a few minor and major variations on the theme. Gauss-Jordan reduction, however, can also be used for direct solution of matrix equations (when the inverse of the connecting matrix is not formed) as the short program given shows.

3.5. Inversion routine with pivoting

The numerical methods of inverting matrices and solving matrix equations we have just described all involve division of each row by its *pivot*. Where this is zero or very small the solution will be aborted. The following program solves the IOA problem example of Section 12.1 using an inversion routine which includes pivoting, using a *flag vector* M( ) to record column/row swaps and another vector (i.e. column matrix) is used to store columns during swapping.

```
DECLARE SUB inverta (A!(), n!)
  n = 3: DIM M(n, n), X(n), B(n)
  B(1) = 120: B(2) = 260: B(3) = 50
  FOR I = 1 TO n: FOR J = 1 TO n
  READ M(I, J): NEXT: NEXT
  inverta M(), n
  FOR I = 1 TO 3: FOR J = 1 TO 3
  X(I) = X(I) + M(I, J) * B(J): NEXT: NEXT
  PRINT "Solution"
   FOR I = 1 TO 3: PRINT I, " = ", X(I): NEXT: END
   DATA 1,-0.15,-0.2
   DATA -0.2,1,-0.5
   DATA -0.25,-0.25,1

SUB inverta (A(), n)
REM Inversion routine with pivoting
   DIM M(n), COL(n): AMIN = 1E-20
   FOR I = 1 TO n: M(I) = -I: NEXT
   FOR II = 1 TO n: D = 0
   FOR J = 1 TO n: IF M(J) > 0 THEN 100
   FOR I = 1 TO n: IF M(I) > 0 THEN 90
   IF ABS(D) >= ABS(A(I, J)) THEN 90
   L = J: K = I: D = A(I, J)
90 NEXT I
100 NEXT J
```

3. Numerical Methods

```
   TEMP = -M(L): M(L) = M(K): M(K) = TEMP
   FOR I = 1 TO n: COL(I) = A(I, L): A(I, L) = A(I, K)
   A(I, K) = COL(I): NEXT I
   IF ABS(D) <= AMIN THEN PRINT "SINGULAR"
   FOR J = 1 TO n: A(K, J) = -A(K, J) / D: NEXT
   FOR I = 1 TO n: IF I = K THEN 180
   FOR J = 1 TO n: A(I, J) = A(I, J) + COL(I) * A(K, J): NEXT J
180 NEXT I
   COL(K) = 1
   FOR I = 1 TO n: A(I, K) = COL(I) / D: NEXT
   NEXT II
   FOR I = 1 TO n: IF M(I) = I THEN 270
   FOR L = 1 TO n: IF M(L) = I THEN 240
   NEXT L
240 M(L) = M(I): M(I) = I
   FOR J = 1 TO n: TEMP = A(L, J): A(L, J) = A(I, J)
   A(I, J) = TEMP: NEXT J
270 NEXT I
END SUB
```

The data used in the listing is that for the IOA problem of Section 11.1.

3.6. Finite differences

The finite difference method has been around for about 150 years and it really comes into its own with the availability of computers as it is essentially a method of *numerical differentiation.* Thus any differential equation can immediately be expressed in finite difference form. Applying this at several points in a *domain* the resulting simultaneous equations can be solved using the techniques discussed in Sections 3.3 and 3.4.

Difference tables

Table 3.4 gives a finite difference table for $f(x) = x^3$, the results being those characteristic of this simple function (for example a point of inflexion at $x = 0$ and no turning points).

3. NUMERICAL METHODS

Table 3.4. Finite difference table for $f(x) = x^3$

n (of dx)	x	f(x)	\multicolumn{4}{c}{Differences}			
			first	second	third	fourth
0	-3	-27				
			19			
1	-2	-8		12		
			7		6	
2	-1	-1		6		0
			1		6	
3	0	0		0		0
			1		6	
4	1	1		6		0
			7		6	
5	2	8		12		
			19			
6	3	27				

The even numbered differences can be related to particular values of *n* and *x* but the odd numbered differences cannot. Then for the first differences we can therefore relate each value shown in the table to the start, the middle or the end of the interval to which it corresponds, resulting in the definitions:

$\Delta f_n = f_{n+1} - f_n$ or the *forward difference* for point n   (3.35)

$\delta f_{n+1/2} = f_{n+1} - f_n$ or the *central difference* for the interval   (3.36)

$\nabla f_{n+1} = f_{n+1} - f_n$ or the *backward difference* for point n+1   (3.37)

Then the values of the first differences do not alter (and are as in Table 3.4, for example) but their point of reference alters.

Generally central differences are the *natural* choice and they are also more accurate, involving a *truncation error* of the order of dx^2 whereas forward and backward differences involve a truncation error of order dx.

In some cases, however, forward differences result in simpler mathematical models of certain types of problems and are therefore preferred.

3. Numerical Methods

Central difference formulas

Denoting $\delta x = h$ the central difference formulas for the second and fourth differences can be deduced from Equation 3.36, giving

$$(df/dx)_{n+1/2} = f'_{n+1/2} = (f_{n+1} - f_n)/h \tag{3.38}$$

$$\begin{aligned}f''_n &= (f'_{n+1/2} - f'_{n-1/2})/h = [(f_{n+1} - f_n)/h - (f_n - f_{n-1})/h]/h \\ &= (f_{n+1} - 2f_n + f_{n-1})/h^2\end{aligned} \tag{3.39}$$

$$\begin{aligned}f^{IV}_n &= (f''_{n+1} - 2f''_n + f''_{n-1})/h^2 = [f_{n+2} - 2f_{n+1} + f_n - 2(f_{n+1} - 2f_n + f_{n-1}) + f_n - 2f_{n-1} + f_{n-2}]/h^4 \\ &= (f_{n+2} - 4f_{n+1} + 6f_n - 4f_{n-1} + f_{n-2})/h^4\end{aligned} \tag{3.40}$$

and these formulas can be extended into two or more dimensions, for example.

Conclusion

The finite difference method (FDM) is a very important one and it was also the predecessor of the finite element method (FEM) which plays an important part in the present book.

3.7. Numerical integration

Numerical integration has important applications in modern mathematical analysis. In the economics an obvious example might be calculation of the areas under supply and demand curves to determine the associated revenue. At present we shall restrict attention to one dimensional integration, but like analytical integration, numerical integration is readily extended to deal with two or more dimensions.

Mid-ordinate, trapezoidal and Simpson rules

Figure 3.3 shows the two most basic rules for numerical integration. With the first of these, the mid-ordinate rule, the area under the curve $y = f(x)$ is estimated as

$$I = h \sum_{i=1}^{n} y_i \tag{3.41}$$

that is, as the sum of the rectangles of width h and height y_i, the height of the curve at the middle of each strip, there being n such strips.

3. NUMERICAL METHODS

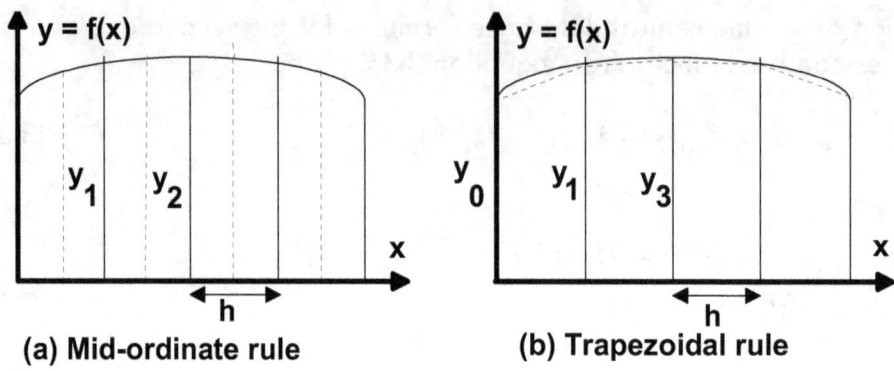

Figure 3.3. Simple numerical integration rules

The trapezoidal rule, on the other hand, averages the ordinates on each side of each strip, equivalent to calculating the area of a trapezoid. Then for n such strips we obtain the formula

$$I = (h/2)[y_0 + y_n + 2 \sum_{i=1}^{n-1} y_i] \tag{3.42}$$

so that summation of ordinates involves halving the first and last and adding the remaining (internal ordinates).

This rule gives a linear approximation (in each strip) to $y = f(x) = a_1 + a_2 x + a_3 x^2 - -$ (in general), so that the *truncation error* is of the order of the square of h which we denote as $O(h^2)$.

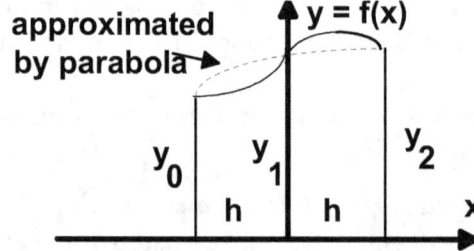

Figure 3.4
Simpson's rule.

Figure 3.4 illustrates the idea of Simpson's rule. Here a pair of strips is used to exactly integrate the quadratic approximation shown (dashed line). Then we can write the exact integral of this quadratic curve as

$$I = \int_{-h}^{h} (a + bx + cx^2) dx = [ax + bx^2/2 + cx^3/3]_{-h}^{h} = 2ah + 2ch^3/3 \tag{3.43}$$

3. Numerical Methods

The numerical integration is written as

$$\sum_{i=0}^{2} w_i f(x_i) (2h) \tag{3.44}$$

where w_i are *weights* for each point, $f(x_i)$ is the ordinate at each point and $2h$ is the *subdomain size*. Then, noting that $w_0 = w_2$ from symmetry the numerical result can be written as

$$\begin{aligned} I &= [w_0(a - bh + ch^2) + w_1(a) + w_0(a + bh + ch^2)](2h) \\ &= 2ah(2w_0 + w_1) + 2ch^3(2w_0) \end{aligned} \tag{3.45}$$

As the results of Equations 3.43 and 3.45 must be identically equal it quickly follows from term by term comparison of the right hand sides that $w_0 = 1/6$ and $w_1 = 1 - 2w_0 = 4/6$ so that the formula for integration of the double strip shown in Figure 3.4 is

$$I = (2h/6)(y_0 + 4y_1 + y_2) \tag{3.46a}$$

so that combining several such strip pairs Simpson's formula can be written in the mnemonic form

$$I = (h/3)[y_{first} + y_{last} + 4\Sigma y_{odd} + 2\Sigma y_{even}] \tag{3.46b}$$

even numbered ordinates generally being involved in two adjoining 'double strips' so that a factor of two is attached to the summation of these, the factor four for the 'middle' ordinates in the strip pairs following from Equation 3.46a.

Because of symmetry considerations, in fact, Simpson's rule exactly integrates a cubic function as is easily shown by adding a term dx^3 before integrating in Equation 3.42. Therefore it has a truncation error $O(h^4)$ and is thus much more accurate than the trapezoidal rule but is no more difficult to use.

3. NUMERICAL METHODS

Gauss quadrature

This exploits the symmetry property observed with Simpson's rule to generate a series of numerical integration rules. The first is the two point rule which exactly integrates a cubic function. The *optimum* integration point coordinates (-s and s) and weights w are given by

$$I = (2h)[wf(x=-s) + wf(x=s)]$$
$$= (2hw)(a - bs + cs^2 - ds^3) + (2hw)(a + bs + cs^2 + ds^3)$$
$$= (2hw)(2a + 2cs^2)$$

(3.47)

This result should be identically equal to that of Equation 3.43 and thus comparing them term by term it quickly follows that $w = \frac{1}{2}$ (as expected by symmetry with only two weights) and $s^2 = h^2/3$ or $s = +/- (h/\sqrt{3})$ for a double strip like that shown in Figure 3.4.

Hence Gauss quadrature for this double strip is written as

$$I = \Sigma w_i f(s_i)(2h) = (2h)\{f(-1/\sqrt{3})/2, f(1/\sqrt{3})/2\}$$

(3.48)

and integration for several such double strips is accomplished in the same way as with Simpson's rule. Once again the truncation error is $O(h^4)$ but now this is accomplished with two rather than three points.

Example
As a simple example suppose that we wish to calculate

$$I = {_0\int^{\pi/2}} \cos(x)dx = 1$$

(3.49)

using two strips (or one double strip) using the four rules discussed:

[1] Mid-ordinate rule (with three ordinates)

$$I = (\pi/6)[\cos(15^0) + \cos(45^0) + \cos(75^0)] = 1.0115 \quad (\text{error} = 0.0115)$$

[2] Trapezoidal rule (2 strips/3 ordinates)

$$I = (\pi/8)[\cos(0) + 2\cos(45^0) + \cos(90^0)] = 0.9481 \quad (\text{error} = -0.0519)$$

[3] Simpson's rule (1 double strip/3 ordinates)

$$I = (\pi/12)[\cos(0) + 4\cos(45^0) + \cos(90^0)] = 1.0023 \quad (\text{error} = 0.0023)$$

[4] Two point Gauss rule (1 double strip/2 ordinates)

$$I = (\pi/4)[\cos(45^0 - 45^0/\sqrt{3}) + \cos(45^0 + 45^0/\sqrt{3})] = 0.9985 \quad (\text{error} = -0.0015)$$

and the two point Gauss rule clearly gives the most accurate result.

In like fashion to the two point rule, Gauss rules for from 3 to 100 points have been calculated, an N point rule exactly integrating a polynomial of order *(2N - 1)* so that is has a truncation error of $O(h^{2N})$.

Conclusion

Numerical integration is a straightforward process and of the basic rules Simpson's rule is the preferable. Generally, however, the Gauss rules are 'optimal' and though these involve coordinates with irrational values this is no obstacle in the computer age.

3.8. Lagrangian interpolation

Numerical integration has many important applications. In the present section Lagrangian interpolation of values of a function at two or more points is discussed. We restrict attention to one dimensional interpolation but extension to two or more dimensions is straightforward.

Lagrange interpolation formula

The Lagrange interpolation formula for interpolation of N equally spaced values of a function $u = f(x)$ is

$$u = \sum_{i=1}^{N} f_i \, u_i \quad \text{where} \quad f_i = \sum_{k=1 (k \neq i)}^{N} (x - x_k)/(x_i - x_k) \tag{3.50}$$

using *interpolation functions* f_i corresponding to each point value u_i.

Figure 3.5
Linear interpolation

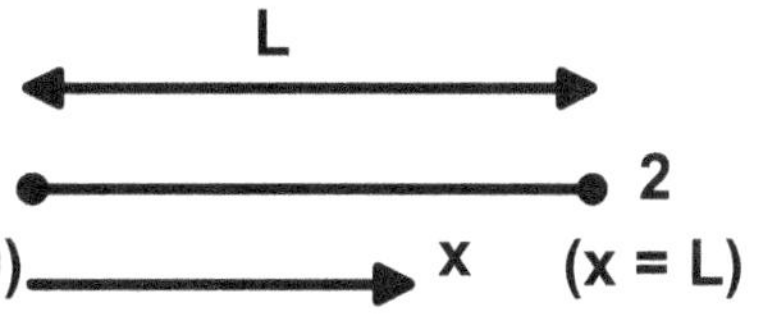

3. NUMERICAL METHODS

Applying Equation 3.50 to the linear interpolation of Figure 3.5 gives

$$f_1 = (x - x_2)/(x_1 - x_2) = (x - L)/(-L) = 1 - x/L \qquad (3.51a)$$
$$f_2 = (x - x_1)/(x_2 - x_1) = (x - 0)/L = x/L \qquad (3.51b)$$
or $\quad u = (1 - x/L)u_1 + (x/L)u_2 \qquad (3.52)$

and writing the interpolation of Equation 3.52 in terms of a *dimensionless coordinate* $s = x/L$ which varies from zero to one we obtain

$$u = (1 - s)u_1 + (s)u_2 = \Sigma f_i u_i = \{f\}^t\{u\} \qquad (3.53)$$

where $\{f\}$ is a vector of interpolation functions and $\{u\}$ is the vector of point of *nodal* values of the function $u = f(x)$.

The linear interpolation could have been established by inspection, of course, but it provides a useful introduction to the Lagrange formula. Then use of this to form the interpolation functions for higher order interpolation functions follows without difficulty.

Figure 3.6 shows three equally spaced points for which we seek to establish a quadratic interpolation. Rather than use the Lagrange formula we shall use matrix inversion to establish the interpolation functions because this approach can be applied to interpolations of different types of variables, as we shall see in Section 3.9.

Figure 3.6 Quadratic interpolation

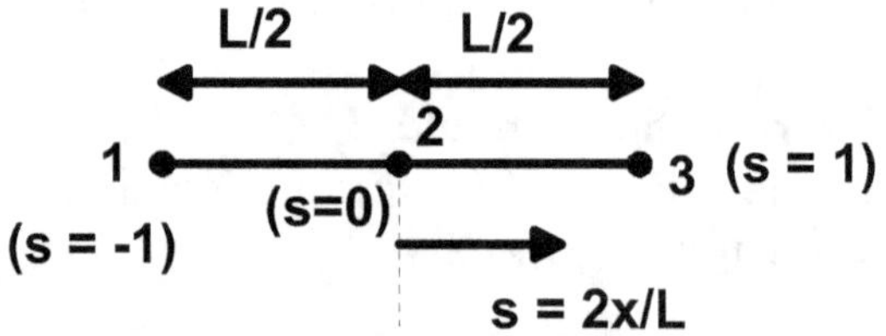

Again using a dimensionless coordinate (now originating at the centre of the domain) we write a quadratic interpolation polynomial

$$u = a_1 + a_2 s + a_3 s^2 = \{M\}^t\{s\}$$
$$= [1, \ s, \ s^2] \begin{Bmatrix} a_1 \\ a_2 \\ a_3 \end{Bmatrix} \qquad (3.54)$$

where $\{M\}$ is a vector of *modes* and $\{a\}$ is a vector of their *amplitudes*.

3. NUMERICAL METHODS

Then substituting the nodal values of u on the LHS of Equation 3.54 and their corresponding dimensionless coordinates (s) on the RHS we obtain

$$\{u\} = \begin{Bmatrix} u_1 \\ u_2 \\ u_3 \end{Bmatrix} = \begin{bmatrix} 1 & -1 & 1 \\ 1 & 0 & 0 \\ 1 & 1 & 1 \end{bmatrix} \begin{Bmatrix} a_1 \\ a_2 \\ a_3 \end{Bmatrix} = A\{a\} \quad (3.55)$$

Inverting the matrix A the amplitudes are obtained as

$$\{a\} = \begin{Bmatrix} a_1 \\ a_2 \\ a_3 \end{Bmatrix} = \begin{bmatrix} 0 & 1 & 0 \\ -1/2 & 0 & 1/2 \\ 1/2 & -1 & 1/2 \end{bmatrix} \begin{Bmatrix} u_1 \\ u_2 \\ u_3 \end{Bmatrix} = A^{-1}\{u\} \quad (3.56)$$

Then combining Equations 3.54 and 3.56 we obtain

$$u = \{M\}^t\{a\} = \{M\}^t A^{-1}\{u\} = \{f\}^t\{u\} \quad (3.57)$$

so that the required interpolation functions are given by

$$\{f\}^t = \{M\}^t a = [1, s, s^2] \begin{bmatrix} 0 & 1 & 0 \\ -1/2 & 0 & 1/2 \\ 1/2 & -1 & 1/2 \end{bmatrix} \quad (3.58)$$

giving the final interpolation as

$$u = (1/2)(s^2 - s)u_1 + (1 - s^2)u_2 + (1/2)(s^2 + s)u_3 = \Sigma\, f_i u_i \quad (3.59)$$

The reader should check this result by putting $s = -1, 0, 1$ into Equation 3.59 when the required results $u = u_1, u_2, u_3$ are obtained.

This interpolation is, of course, much more accurate than linear interpolation when curved functions are involved. Extension of the inversion procedure to establish a cubic Lagrangian interpolation for four points is straightforward.

3. NUMERICAL METHODS

3.9. Hermitian interpolation

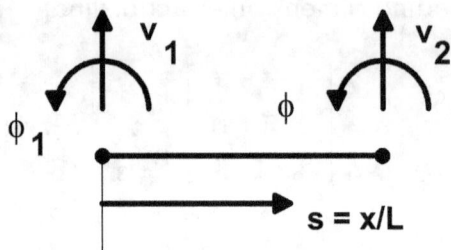

Figure 3.7
Cubic Hermitian interpolation

Figure 3.7 shows two nodes with *freedoms* v_1 and v_2 in a translational variable v and also two rotational freedoms ϕ_1 and ϕ_2 where

$$\phi = dv/dx = (dv/ds)(ds/dL) = (1/L)(dv/ds) \qquad (3.60)$$
$$\text{or } \phi* = dv/ds = L\phi$$

and ϕ is the derivative or slope of v and $\phi*$ is the *dimensionless derivative* of v with respect to the dimensionless coordinate s and this is the more useful form for the present purposes as it allows us to form a dimensionless interpolation matrix A^{-1} using the inversion procedure used in Section 3.8.

Then writing and differentiating a cubic interpolation polynomial gives

$$v = a_1 + a_2 s + a_3 s^2 + a_4 s^3 = \{f\}^t \{a\} \qquad (3.61)$$
$$\phi* = dv/ds = a_2 + 2a_3 s + 3a_4 s^2 \qquad (3.62)$$

and substituting nodal values on the left and right sides we obtain

$$\{v, \phi*\} = \begin{Bmatrix} v_1 \\ \phi_1* \\ v_2 \\ \phi_2* \end{Bmatrix} = \begin{bmatrix} 1 & 0 & 0 & 0 \\ 0 & 1 & 0 & 0 \\ 1 & 1 & 1 & 1 \\ 0 & 1 & 2 & 3 \end{bmatrix} \begin{Bmatrix} a_1 \\ a_2 \\ a_3 \\ a_4 \end{Bmatrix} = A\{a\} \qquad (3.63)$$

Then inverting A gives the interpolation functions as

$$\{f\}^t = \{M\}^t A^{-1} = [1, s, s^2, s^3] \begin{bmatrix} 1 & 0 & 0 & 0 \\ 0 & 1 & 0 & 0 \\ -3 & -2 & 3 & -1 \\ 2 & 1 & -2 & 1 \end{bmatrix}$$

$$(3.64)$$

so that the final interpolations for v and its derivatives can be written as

$$v = f_1 v_1 + L f_2 \phi_2 + f_3 v_2 + L f_4 \phi_4 = f_1 v_1 + f_2 \phi_1^* + f_3 v_3 + f_4 \phi_2^*$$

where $f_1 = (1 - 3s^2 + 2s^3)$, $f_2 = (s - 2s^2 + s^3)$, $f_3 = (3s^2 - 2s^3)$, $f_4 = (s^3 - s^2)$

(3.65)

and

$$\phi = dv/dx = (1/L)(dv/ds) = (1/L)(d\{f\}^t/ds)\{v, \phi\}$$

$$= (6s^2 - 6s)v_1/L + (1 - 4s + 3s^2)\phi_1 + (6s - 6s^2)v_2/L + (3s^2 - 2s)\phi_2$$

(3.66)

The reader should check these results by putting $s = 0$ and 1 into Equations 3.65 and 3.66 when $v = v_1, v_2$ or $\phi = \phi_1, \phi_2$ should be obtained.

Conclusion

Both Lagrangian and Hermitian interpolations are much used in mathematical modelling of physical systems. They might also be of interest in econometric problems where values and their rates of change are known. In addition the inversion procedure used to establish the cubic Hermitian interpolation can, with little modification, be used to fit cubic *splines* in a 'piecewise' fashion to model complicated curves and shapes (essentially the known values and slopes are used to determine the amplitudes {a} of Equation 3.61.

3. NUMERICAL METHODS

3.10. Statistical Correlation

The *Pearson correlation coefficient* is widely used to compare two sets of observations. If the coefficient (or c.c.) is close to one the two sets are strongly correlated, if it is zero they are not related and if it is close to minus one then the two sets of data are negatively correlated. It is calculated from the covariance between the two data sets as

$$c.c. = r_{xy} = Cov(xy)/S_x S_y \qquad (3.67)$$

$$\text{where } Cov(xy) = n \Sigma xy - \Sigma x \Sigma y \qquad (3.68)$$
$$S_x = \sqrt{(n\Sigma x^2 - (\Sigma x)^2)} \qquad (3.69)$$
$$S_y = \sqrt{n\Sigma y^2 - (\Sigma y)^2} \qquad (3.70)$$

are the covariance and standard deviations of the two distributions.

As an example Table 3.5 shows the expected marks *(x)* for a group of students and the actual marks *(y)* obtained in a test and the next three columns are used to calculate the value of the correlation coefficient according to Equations 3.67 - 3.70.

Table 3.5. Correlation coefficient calculation

x	y	x^2	y^2	xy
8	10	64	100	80
7	8	49	64	56
3	2	9	4	6
5	6	24	36	30
7	9	49	81	63
2	2	4	4	4
4	5	16	25	20
Totals: 36	42	216	314	259

Then we finally obtain the correlation coefficient as

$$r_{xy} = [7(259) - 36(42)] / [(\sqrt{7(216) - 36^2}) \sqrt{7(314) - 42^2} = 0.98$$

$$(3.71)$$

and hence the expected and actual marks are strongly correlated.

3. NUMERICAL METHODS

The Pearson product-moment correlation coefficient is easy to calculate, though some experience is needed in order to ensure that proper judgments are made.

The *Chi-squared test* is based on the skew Chi-squared distribution and is also called the *goodness of fit* or the *O-E test*. As an example of this, columns 2 and 3 of Table 3.5 compare a normal distribution with the distribution of 100 student test scores. Then the data and calculation of the χ^2 variate $\Sigma(O - E)^2/E$ where O and E respectively denote observed and expected results is shown in Table 3.6, where M = mean and S = standard deviation (O) or variance (E).

Table 3.6. Calculation of Chi-squared value.

Range	O (Observed)	E (Normal)	$(O - E)^2/E$
< M - S	10	16	2.25
(M - S) - M	20	34	5.76
M - (M + S)	50	34	7.53
> M + S	20	16	1
Sum	100	100	16.54

Then we obtain the observed value of the Chi-squared variate as

$$\chi^2_{obs} = 16.54 \qquad (3.72)$$

and this is compared with the result for $v = (n - 1) = 3$ *degrees of freedom* and $\alpha = 0.05$ from standard statistical tables which is

$$\chi^2_{test} (0.05, 3 \; d.f) = 7.81 \qquad (3.73)$$

and as the observed result exceeds the test result the test is failed so that the student marks are not normally distributed.

The test is said to have been failed at the *95% significance level* (i.e. with variable $\alpha = 0.05$ in the tables) and this is the criterion usually used with this test.

Finally note also that data plots are useful to obtain an idea of scatter and that spreadsheet programs can be used to carry out *linear regression* of two data sets to see if they have similar linearity compared to the independent variable.

3.11. References

Bajpai AC, Mustoe LR, Walker D, *Engineering Mathematics*, Wiley, Chichester. 1974.

Crandall SH. *Engineering Analysis: A Survey of Numerical Procedures*. McGraw-Hill, New York, 1956.

Lee JAN, *Numerical Analysis for Computers*, Reinhold, New York, 1966.

Mohr GA, *Finite Elements for Solids, Fluids, & Optimization*, OUP, Oxford, 1992.

Mohr GA, Numerical procedures for input-output analysis, *Applied Mathematics & Computation* 101 (1999) 89-98.

Newbold P, Bos T, *Introductory Business Forecasting*, South-Western, Cincinnati OH, 1990.

Paul RS, Hauessler EF, *Introductory Mathematical Analysis for Students of Business and Economics*, Reston Publ., Reston VA, 1985.

Premienkiecki JS, *Theory of Matrix Structural Analysis*, McGraw-Hill, New York, 1968.

Southwell RV, *Relaxation Method in Theoretical Physics*, OUP, Oxford, 1946.

Chapter 4

FINITE ELEMENT NETWORK MODELS

DC networks are modeled as a collection of discrete *elements* connecting the nodes of the circuit. For these simple *element matrices* are able to be formed and deployed in a *system matrix* for the complete network. The resulting matrix problem is then solved to determine the potentials at each node, from which the current flow in each element can then be calculated. A *dual* form of the problem which uses *loop flows* rather than nodal potentials as variables is then considered.

4.1. Linear one dimensional elements

The simplest possible finite elements have one *degree of freedom* at each of two nodes i,j, for example a temperature T taking values T_i and T_j at each node, as shown in Figure 4.1.

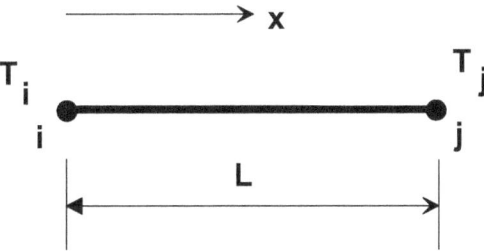

Figure 4.1. Two freedom linear element.

The temperature T at any point in the element is given by the linear interpolation

$$T = \{f\}^t\{T\} = f_1 T_1 + f_2 T_2 = (1 - x/L)T_1 + (x/L)T_2 \qquad (4.1)$$

where $\{f\}$ is a vector of *interpolation functions* and $\{T\}$ is a vector of values at corresponding nodes.

4. FINITE ELEMENT NETWORK MODELS

The equation governing steady state anisotropic heat flow in two dimensions is

$$\partial(\kappa_x \partial T/\partial x)/\partial x + \partial(\kappa_y \partial T/\partial y)\partial y + G = 0 \tag{4.2}$$

where $T = T(x,y)$ is the temperature distribution, κ_x and κ_y are the thermal conductivity's in each axial direction and G is the heat generation per unit volume.

Reducing the problem to one dimension with $G = 0$, substituting an interpolation for T, integrating over the element volume and using Galerkin weighting (with the interpolation functions) we obtain

$$A\kappa \int \{f\}\{f_{xx}\}^t \, dx \, \{T\} = \{0\} \tag{4.3}$$

where A is the cross-sectional area of the element. Applying integration by parts to this result gives

$$A\kappa \int \{f_x\}\{f_x\}^t \, dx \, \{T\} = A\kappa\{f\}\,\partial T/\partial x \,| \tag{4.4}$$

Then using the linear interpolation (of two nodes) of Eqn 4.1 we have

$$\{f\} = \{1 - x/L,\ x/L\} \text{ and } \{f_x\} = \{-1/L,\ 1/L\} \tag{4.5}$$

and substituting Equations 4.5 into Equation 4.4 we obtain

$$(A\kappa/L)\begin{bmatrix} 1 & -1 \\ -1 & 1 \end{bmatrix}\begin{Bmatrix} T_1 \\ T_2 \end{Bmatrix} = A\kappa \begin{Bmatrix} \partial T/\partial x_1 \\ \partial T/\partial x_2 \end{Bmatrix} \tag{4.6}$$

noting that the presence of the interpolation on the RHS of Equation 4.4 indicates simply that the nodal values of the variable interpolated are used for this boundary term. The resulting terms on the RHS of Equation 4.6 are the *inter element reactions* or fluxes and these sum to zero between elements.

4. FINITE ELEMENT NETWORK MODELS

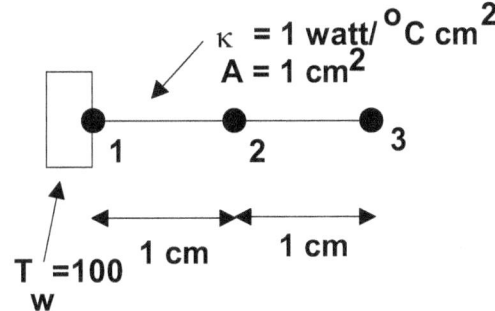

Figure 4.2.
One dimensional heat flow.

Figure 4.2 shows a simple 1-D heat flow example with only two elements. Then using Equation 4.6 for each element and 'assembling' the element matrices according to their node numbers the equations for the system are:

$$\begin{bmatrix} 1 & -1 & 0 \\ -1 & 2 & -1 \\ 0 & -1 & 1 \end{bmatrix} \begin{Bmatrix} T_1 \\ T_2 \\ T_3 \end{Bmatrix} = \begin{Bmatrix} 0 \\ 0 \\ 0 \end{Bmatrix} \quad (4.7)$$

The specified temperature at the wall ($T_w = T_1 = 1000$) is enforced by multiplying the first column by it, transposing the result to the RHS and then removing the first equation, yielding the reduced equations:

$$\begin{bmatrix} 2 & -1 \\ -1 & 2 \end{bmatrix} \begin{Bmatrix} T_2 \\ T_3 \end{Bmatrix} = \begin{Bmatrix} 100 \\ 0 \end{Bmatrix} \quad (4.8)$$

giving the expected results $T_2 = T_3 = 100$ and, if we had put $T_3 = 0$, then the result would have been $T_2 = 50$, again the expected result.

The problem is, though almost trivial, a good example of FEM at its simplest though some of the mathematics involved when we begin with a differential equation will worry some readers. As with the DC network problem of the following section, however, results such as Equation 4.8 are in fact obvious with very little experience.

4. Finite Element Network Models

4.2. FEM modeling of DC networks

In the following section we introduce a simple example of FEM, namely analysis of current flow in a direct current (DC) network. Here we can form the element matrix by writing an equation for flow conservation at each node. This, however, corresponds to the more mathematical approach of Section 4.1.

The element equations

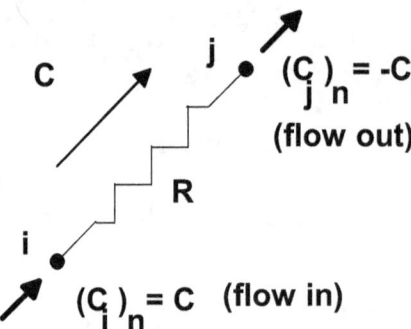

Figure 4.3.
Typical element n with nodes i and j.

Figure 4.3 shows a typical element n with resistance R and connecting nodes i and j. Assuming flow into a node is positive we can use Ohm's law (that is drop in voltage or *potential* δV = current x resistance = CR) to write

$$G\delta V = GV_i - GV_j = C = (C_i)_n \tag{4.9}$$

$$-GV_i + GV_j = -C = (C_j)_n \tag{4.10}$$

where $G = 1/R$ is the *conductance* of the element. Combining Equations 4.9 and 4.10 into matrix form we obtain

$$\begin{bmatrix} G & -G \\ G & G \end{bmatrix} \begin{Bmatrix} V_i \\ V_j \end{Bmatrix} = \begin{Bmatrix} (C_i)_n \\ (C_j)_n \end{Bmatrix} \tag{4.11}$$

or $k_e \{V\} = \{C_n\}$ (4.12)

where k is the element *conductance matrix*.

4. Finite Element Network Models

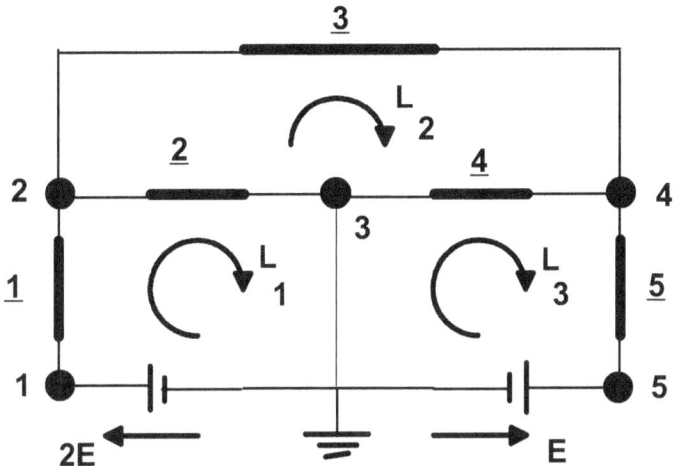

Figure 4.4. DC network: element numbers underscored.

For the simple network of Figure 4.4, deploying the entries from the element matrices in the system matrix according to the element node numbers, this takes the form

$$C = \begin{bmatrix} G_1 & -G_1 & 0 & 0 & 0 \\ -G_1 & G_1+G_2+G_3 & -G_2 & -G_3 & 0 \\ 0 & -G_2 & G_2+G_4 & -G_4 & 0 \\ 0 & -G_3 & -G_4 & G_3+G_4+G_5 & -G_5 \\ 0 & 0 & 0 & -G_5 & G_5 \end{bmatrix} \quad (4.13)$$

and note that that as currents at a node must sum to zero (i.e. no 'leakage', this being Kirchhoff's current law) the summed RHS or 'load' vector of Equation 4.11 will be zero, or we have a 'nothing happening' problem until we deal with the boundary conditions shortly.

This 'summation' or assembly of the element matrices can in this case be simply coded in a program as:

C(I,I) = C(I,I) + G   (4.14a)
C(I,J) = C(I,J) - G   (4.14b)
C(J,I) = C(J,I) - G   (4.15a)
C(J,J) = C(J,J) + G   (4.15b)

where I, J are the node numbers for the element being dealt with and G is its conductance.

4. Finite Element Network Models

Solution of the system equations

Then to solve the system equations we first apply the boundary conditions $V_1 = 2E$, $V_3 = 0$ and $V_5 = 1$ using the following procedure:

1. Multiply the columns corresponding to these values by these boundary values and transpose the results to the right side.

2. Zero the corresponding rows and columns on the left side, leaving a one on the diagonal.

3. Place the boundary condition values on the right side.

Doing this in our example problem we obtain

$$\begin{bmatrix} 1 & 0 & 0 & 0 & 0 \\ 0 & G_1+G_2+G_3 & 0 & -G_3 & 0 \\ 0 & 0 & 1 & 0 & 0 \\ 0 & -G_3 & 0 & G_3+G_4+G_5 & 0 \\ 0 & 0 & 0 & 0 & 1 \end{bmatrix} \begin{Bmatrix} V_1 \\ V_2 \\ V_3 \\ V_4 \\ V_5 \end{Bmatrix} = \begin{Bmatrix} 2E \\ G1 \\ 0 \\ G5 \\ E \end{Bmatrix} \quad (4.16)$$

If the element resistances are $R_1 = 1$, $R_2 = 4$, $R_3 = 1$, $R_4 = 5$, $R_5 = 1$ and $E = 1$, the solution for the nodal potentials is $V_1 = 2$, $V_2 = 1.367$, $V_3 = 0$, $V_4 = 1.076$ and $V_5 = 1$.

The current flows in the elements are given by

$$C_{ij} = (V_i - V_j)/R_{ij} \quad (4.17)$$

giving $C_{12} = 0.633$, $C_{23} = 0.342$, $C_{24} = 0.291$, $C_{34} = -0.215$, $C_{45} = 0.076$.

Note in passing that this simple example can be solved by applying Kirchhoff's current law, that is, that the algebraic sum of the current inflows at a node is zero, at nodes 2 and 4, giving

$$(2E - V_2)/R_{12} - V_2/G_{23} + (V_4 - V_2)/G_{24} = 0 \quad (4.18)$$

$$(E - V_4)/R_{45} - V_4/G_{34} + (V_2 - V_4)/G_{45} = 0 \quad (4.19)$$

which corresponds to the second and fourth rows in 4.16.

4. FINITE ELEMENT NETWORK MODELS

4.3. Program for DC networks

The following QBASIC program solves DC network problems. The first data line is the number of nodes (NP), elements (NE) and points at which voltage is specified (NS). Then the element node numbers and conductances are read and used to form the system matrix. Next the specified voltages (the boundary conditions) are read and the system matrix and RHS load vector modified accordingly. Finally the nodal current flows (none here) are read, reading of these being terminated by a 0,0 data line.

The simple Gauss-Mohr reduction procedure introduced in Section 3.4 is used in lines 240 - 340 to solve for the nodal voltages, after which the element currents are calculated using Equation 4.17. In this simple program the element data is not stored and thus is read again after the RESTORE statement of line 390. The data is for the problem of Figure 4.3, giving the results stated in the preceding section.

Note that the program includes calculation of *boundary reactions*. For this purpose boundary condition rows are not 'zeroed' but kept and (boundary row) x nodal voltages = boundary reactions calculated in lines 380 - 386, in our example problem of Figure 4.3 giving the current inflows at nodes 1, 3 and 5 as $C_1 = 0.633$, $C_3 = -0.557$ and $C_5 = -0.076$.

```
5 REM FEM model of distribution networks
7 RESTORE 1000
10 DIM C(20, 20), V(20), IB(20): A$ = "#": B$ = "######.###"
20 READ NP, NE, NS
100 FOR K = 1 TO NE
110 READ I, J, r
115 IF r = 0 THEN 170
130 C(I, I) = C(I, I) + 1 / r
140 C(I, J) = C(I, J) - 1 / r
150 C(J, I) = C(J, I) - 1 / r
160 C(J, J) = C(J, J) + 1 / r
170 NEXT
180 FOR K = 1 TO NS
190 READ N, S: IB(N) = 1
200 FOR I = 1 TO NP
205 IF IB(I) = 1 THEN 220
210 V(I) = V(I) - S * C(I, N)
220 NEXT I
230 V(N) = S: NEXT
232 READ NQ, Q
234 IF NQ = 0 THEN 238
235 IF IB(NQ) = 1 THEN 232
```

4. Finite Element Network Models

```
236 V(NQ) = V(NQ) + Q: GOTO 232
238 REM
240 FOR I = 1 TO NP
245 IF IB(I) = 1 THEN 340
250 X = C(I, I): V(I) = V(I) / X
260 FOR J = I + 1 TO NP
270 C(I, J) = C(I, J) / X: NEXT
280 FOR K = 1 TO NP
285 IF IB(K) = 1 THEN 330
290 IF K = I THEN GOTO 330
300 X = C(K, I): V(K) = V(K) - X * V(I)
310 FOR J = I + 1 TO NP
320 C(K, J) = C(K, J) - X * C(I, J): NEXT J
330 NEXT K
340 NEXT I
350 PRINT "Node    Potential"
360 FOR I = 1 TO NP
370 PRINT USING A$; I; : PRINT USING B$; V(I): NEXT I
375 PRINT "Flows"
380 FOR I = 1 TO NP
381 IF IB(I) <> 1 THEN 386
382 Q = 0: FOR K = 1 TO NP
383 Q = Q + C(I, K) * V(K): NEXT
385 PRINT USING A$; I; : PRINT USING B$; Q
386 NEXT I
390 RESTORE 1010
391 TC = 0: TQ = 0
392 FOR K = 1 TO NE: READ I, J, r: F = 0: IF r = 0 THEN 394
393 F = (V(I) - V(J)) / r
394 PRINT USING A$; I; J; : PRINT " Route flow = ";
PRINT USING B$; F: TC = TC + F * r: TQ = TQ + F: NEXT
396 PRINT "TC = ", TC, " TQ = ", TQ
1000 DATA 5,5,3
1010 DATA 1,2,1
1020 DATA 2,3,4
1030 DATA 2,4,1
1040 DATA 3,4,5
1050 DATA 4,5,1
1060 DATA 1,2
1065 DATA 3,0
1070 DATA 5,1
1080 DATA 0,0
```

4. FINITE ELEMENT NETWORK MODELS

4.4. The dual problem for DC networks

The solution in Section 4.2 for the nodal potentials in Figure 4.4 was the *primal problem* for the DC network. The *dual* DC network problem is obtained by using the *loop flows* L_1, L_2, L_3 shown in Figure 4.4 as variables for the problem.

Now using Kirchhoff's voltage law, that, is that the sum of the voltage drops around a closed loop is zero, we obtain for the three equations

$$2E - R_{12}L_1 - R_{23}(L_1 - L_2) = 0$$

$$-R_{24} - R_{34}(L_2 - L_3) - R_{23}(L_2 - L_1) = 0 \quad (4.20)$$

$$-R_{45}L_3 - R_{34}(L_3 - L_2) - E = 0$$

Solving these we obtain

$$L_1 = 0.633, \ L_2 = 0.291 \text{ and } L_3 = 0.076, \quad (4.21)$$

the first and third results corresponding to the flows to and from the first and last nodes in the primal problem and the second result being the flow in the third element of the primal problem.

The foregoing program can also be used to solve the dual problem by using the loops as reference entities, rather than the nodes, also denoting the region outside the circuit as loop 4, for which the boundary condition $L_4 = 0$ is set. Then the element data for the first element is its shared loop numbers 1, 4 followed by its conductance of unity. Thus the complete data for the problem is

4000 DATA 4,5,1
4010 DATA 1,4,1
4020 DATA 1,2,0.25
4030 DATA 2,4,1
4040 DATA 2,3,0.2
4050 DATA 3,4,1
4060 DATA 4,0
4070 DATA 1,2, 3,-1
4080 DATA 0,0

The final data in line 4070 are the loads of the forcing potentials affecting loops 1 and 3, in the second instance having a negative sign because it opposes L_3 in direction. Note that line 7 of the program must change to RESTORE 4000 and line 390 to RESTORE 4010.

The solutions for the loop flows are those of Equations 4.21, the boundary reaction for $L_4 = 0$ is -1, corresponding to the difference between the two forcing potentials. The 'flows' calculated for the three elements are in fact voltage drops, respectively 0.633, 1.367, 0.291, 1.076 and 0.076 taking the elements in their order of numbering in Figure 4.3. These results correspond to the nodal potential solutions obtained for the primal problem.

In practice the primal problem is the most useful model as the data has a more natural nodal basis and the program output is the quantities of interest, namely the nodal potentials and the element and boundary flows.

Note too in passing that the primal DC network problem corresponds to the *distribution problem* of Operations Research/Management Science. Indeed this was discovered by the author using a more basic version of the foregoing program.

Data was input from the optimum solution for a small distribution network, using the unit transport costs for each route in place of resistance as the element constitutive parameter, specifying the supplies and demands at each point as positive and negative flows respectively and setting the 'potential' at the last point as zero. The boundary reaction turned out equal to the demand at the last point and it turned out that the element route flows (of the optimum network) remained the same regardless of the unit costs specified for the routes.

This last result shows that optimal distribution networks have no *redundant* routes and are just sufficient to provide for all the supply and demand flows. Though the route costs play a part in determining the optimum network, once this has been obtained by eliminating the more costly routes, insofar as the supply and demand requirements allow, the route costs can take any value without affecting the optimum network flows. This means, in fact, that if changes in route costs are significant the problem should be resolved to see if the optimum solution has altered.

4.5. References

Chung TJ, *Finite Element Analysis in Fluid Dynamics*, McGraw-Hill, NY, 1978.

Crandall, SH, *Engineering Analysis: A Survey of Numerical Procedures*, McGraw-Hill, New York. 1956.

Irons BM, Ahmad S, *Techniques of Finite Elements*, Ellis Horwood, Chichester, 1980.

Jennings, A., *Matrix Computation for Engineers and Scientists*, Wiley, Chichester, 1977.

Mohr GA, Milner HR, *A Microcomputer Introduction to the Finite Element Method*, Pitman, Melbourne, 1986; Heinemann, London, 1987.

Mohr GA, *Finite Elements for Solids, Fluids, and Optimization*, OUP Oxford, 1992.

Mohr, GA, Finite element modeling of distribution problems, *Applied Mathematics & Computation*, vol. 105, p 69, 1999.

Mohr, GA, Optimization of primal and dual network models of distribution, *Computer Methods in Applied Mechanics & Engineering*, vol. 188, p 135, 2000.

Prezmieniecki, JS. *Theory of Matrix Structural Analysis*, McGraw-Hill, New York, 1967.

4. Finite Element Network Models

Chapter 5

LINEAR PROGRAMMING

This chapter introduces *Linear Programming (LP)*, that is, the solution of optimization problems with *design variables* governed by a set of simultaneous linear constraint equations with an objective function which is also linear. In management science there are many problems in which the variables are the magnitudes of use of various quantities which have fixed costs (at a given time) and these can expressed as LP problems and then solved by simple computer programs.

5.1. Introduction

Mathematical optimization of systems generally involves some or all of the following steps:

1. A mathematical *model* of the system is constructed. This may take the form of a governing differential equation, a governing equation or law which may be linear, quadratic etc. or simultaneous equations which may be formed by applying a governing DE or law at several points, each having coordinates or values in one or more problem variables.

2. The *objective* must be decided, for example minimum cost, maximum profit, maximum quantity produced or qualitative benefits to the community (to which we would normally assign a monetary value).

3. We then form an *objective* or *merit function* which would typically take the form:

$$\Sigma \text{ (costs)} = f(x, y - - -) \qquad (5.1a)$$

4. We then identify any *constraints* applying to variables in this objective function and these would typically take the form

$$x + y \le 100 \qquad (5.1b)$$

where x, y are numbers of components or their costs and 100 is a limit in supply of components or funds.

5. LINEAR PROGRAMMING

5. Then we would normally seek to express the problem in a form that can be dealt with by one of the standard techniques available, for example the *Linear Programming (LP)* method or the *steepest descent* method.

6. Having obtained an optimum (or at least improved) solution using such methods a *sensitivity analysis* is carried out in which the effects of changes in the values of the design variables x, y etc. (from the values for the optimum solution), their associated costs or the limit values involved in constraints are gauged by systematically varying these quantities and observing the changes in the objective function that result.

In a production plant operation, for example, we might desire the maximum quantity of production for given inputs, the minimum inputs for a given quantity of production, minimum production time or minimum cost per item produced.

Generally, in fact, we seek to maximize the *benefit/cost* ratio which might involve maximizing output, minimizing cost or both.

Conclusion

Mathematical optimization techniques involve a logical well ordered approach to problems. Once the problem has been 'set up' the number crunching techniques are relatively simple. For example linear programming problems can be solved using a slight variation in the Gauss-Jordan reduction routine given in Section 3.4.

5.2. Linear Programming

In the following section we introduce the linear programming (LP) problem. We begin with graphical solution of a problem with only two variables and this illustrates many of the characteristics of the LP problem.

Graphical solution of the LP problem

Figure 5.1 shows the linear programming problem:

$$\text{Min/Max} \quad z = 2x_1 + 7x_2 \tag{5.2}$$

where $z = f(x_1, x_2)$ is the objective or merit function in which z is the total cost and 2, 7 are the *unit costs*, subject to the constraints

(1) $\quad x_1 - 2x_2 \geq -14$ (5.3a)
(2) $\quad 5x_1 + 2x_2 \leq 50$ (5.3b)
(3) $\quad x_1 + 2x_2 \geq 18, \quad x_1, x_2 \geq 0$ (5.3c)

5. LINEAR PROGRAMMING

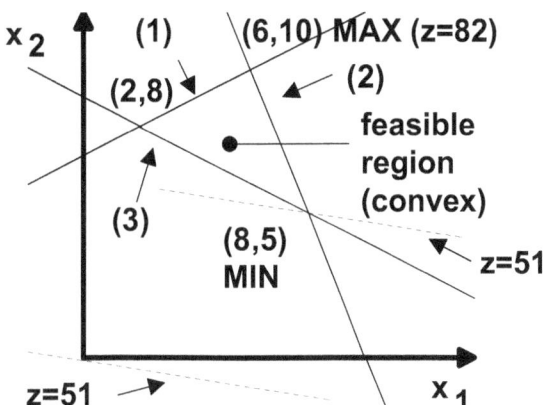

Figure 5.1
Graphical solution of a linear programming problem.

The variables x_1 and x_2 are assumed to be positive. Then, as shown in Figure 5.1, the feasible region is bounded by the three constraints and the vertex at which the line of Equation 5.2 first touches this gives the minimum point ($z = 51$) and the maximum is given by another vertex ($z = 82$).

This, then, is a key feature of the LP problem, namely that the solution is determined by the constraints and, indeed, it is these that really define the problem largely.

Poorly posed problems

Examples of poorly posed LP problems include:

1. If Equation 5.3c is replaced by

$$x_1 + 2x_2 \geq -1 \tag{5.4}$$

then the third constraint does not lie in the positive quadrant so that the minimum is the trivial solution $x_1 = x_2 = 0$.

2. If the objective function is

$$z = x_1 + 2x_2 \tag{5.5}$$

which is parallel to the third constraint then the minimum solution is indeterminate and lies on the line of Equation 5.3c between the vertices (2,8) and (8,5).

3. The problem is infeasible if all three constraints are such that the feasible region is not in the positive quadrant.

5. LINEAR PROGRAMMING

4. If the second constraint is, for example,

$$5x_1 + 2x_2 \geq -20 \qquad (5.6)$$

so that it passes to the left of point (2,8), the intersection of the other two constraints, then the feasible region is unbounded and there is no maximum solution to the optimization problem.

When there are many constraints, however, such difficulties are relatively unlikely but, of course, numerical methods of solution are then needed as in most cases there will be more than two variables.

Conclusion

The LP problem has a very simple graphical solution in the case of only two variables. Generally, however, numerical methods must be used and these are discussed in the following section.

5.3. The Simplex Method

The Simplex Method of solving LP problems was developed by Danzig circa 1947. In this slack variables y are added to inequality constraints and the problem is written:

$$\text{Min/Max} \quad z = \{c\}^t\{x\} \qquad (5.7)$$

$$\text{subject to} \quad A\{x\} + I\{y\} = \{b\} \qquad (5.8)$$

Then if we apply Gauss-Jordan reduction to Equation 5.8, pre multiplying both sides by a matrix B which is equal to the inverse of A, we obtain

$$I\{x\} + A^{-1}\{y\} = A^{-1}\{b\} \qquad (5.9)$$

where we write A^{-1} symbolically only. In fact this applies strictly only when the constraints are all equality constraints equal in number to the number of variables $\{x\}$ so that A is a square and hence invertible matrix, when the solution is the RHS of Equation 5.9.

Generally, however, there are some inequality constraints to which slack variables must be added. Then there are usually more variables than there are constraint equations and the solution procedure must determine which are the 'critical' or *active* constraints and solve to determine the optimum solution in terms of these.

5. Linear Programming

This means that, in practice, we replace A^{-1} in Equation 5.9 by a matrix B which is a matrix which *reduces* the augmented matrix *(A, I)* partially using Gauss-Jordan reduction on a column by column basis. Then variables which take a non zero value at any point in the solution process are said to be in the *basis,* noting that generally some variables will be zero, in particular slack variables associated with constraints intersecting at the optimum point.

This procedure then has useful application to problems of *constrained linear estimation* in which each variable has a range such as

$$x_i^* - \alpha \leq x_i \leq x_i + \beta \tag{5.10}$$

such constraints being a special case of the LP problem.

As an example of the Simplex Method consider the two variable problem

$$\text{Max} \quad z = 5x_1 + 4x_2 \tag{5.11}$$

subject to the constraints

$$2x_1 + x_2 \leq 6 \tag{5.12}$$

$$4x_1 + 5x_2 \leq 20 \tag{5.13}$$

Including two slack variables there are four variables and the optimum solution will involve non-zero values of two of these so that the number of possible solutions is

$$^4C_2 = 4!/(2!2!) = 6 \tag{5.14}$$

these being the points A, B, C, D, E, F shown in Figure 5.2, that is the intersections of the constraints and/or the axes, which are also constraints as all variables must be positive.

5. LINEAR PROGRAMMING

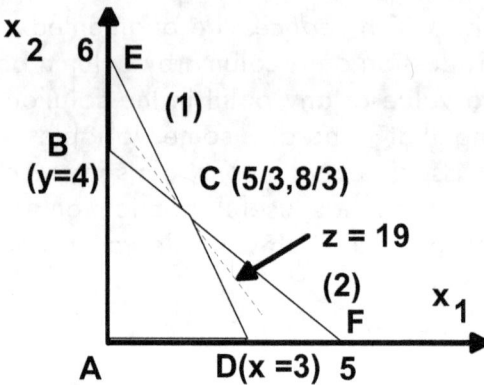

Figure 5.2
LP problem
with 2 variables.

Writing the simplex *tableau* of the problem as:

Table 5.1. Simplex tableau for Equations 5.11 - 5.13 (pivots underlined).

<u>2</u>	1	1	0	6	
4	5	0	1	20	
5	4	0	0	0	
1	1/2	1/2	0	3	
0	<u>3</u>	-2	1	8	
0	3/2	-5/2	0	-15	
1	0	5/6	-1/6	5/3	$x_1 = 5/3$
0	1	-2/3	1/3	8/3	$x_2 = 8/3$
0	0	-3/2	-1/2	-19	$z = 19$

Then the problem is solved by using the pivot selection rule:

1. The pivot column is chosen as that with the maximum positive cost. When no positive cost remains (in the bottom or objective function row) the required maximum has been obtained.

2. The pivot row is then chosen as that with the minimum value of b/a, b being a RHS value for a constraint and a being a coefficient in the pivot column.

Then in Table 5.1 the first tableau has max $c = 5$ and min $b/a = 3$, giving the underlined pivot = 2 shown. Using Gauss-Jordan reduction to reduce this column to 'unit' form with zeroes for all but the pivot position, we obtain the second tableau shown.

5. LINEAR PROGRAMMING

Then in the second tableau the max $c = 3/2$ and the min b/a for this column is 8/3, giving the underlined pivot shown (= 3). Then GJR with this pivot yields the third tableau shown. As no positive costs remain this gives the solution for the maximum, $z = 19$ with $x_1 = 5/3$ and $x_2 = 8/3$.

Note that choosing the row using the 'min b/a' rule is equivalent to moving along the axis for this variable (for the pivot column) until a constraint is first encountered, the resulting pivot choice being the 'safest', ensuring that we remain in the feasible region.

Reversed constraints

In the latter exercise we have only dealt with $\leq$ constraints (by adding slack variables). To deal with $\geq$ constraints the constraint is simply reversed in sign and once again we add slack variables.

Equality constraints

Equality constraints must be enforced. One way of ensuring this is adding an *artificial variable y^** and ensure that a pivot is chosen in the row for this constraint to force y^* out of the basis (i.e. to zero). Pivots must thereafter be disallowed in the column for y^*.

An alternative approach is to replace each equality constraint by a pair of $\leq$ and $\geq$ constraints, reversing the signs for the $\geq$ constraint as described above.

Sensitivity analysis

This involves varying some of the variables, their costs or the limits for the constraints to ascertain the effect upon the optimum solution.

In the case of changes in unit costs the amount of such change which does not alter the optimum solution is of particular interest. Generally, however, we will be at least equally interested in a possible new solution which is easily obtained by rerunning the computer program.

Another change, of course, is to add further constraints and once again the simplest approach is to add another data line to the computer program data for each of these.

Conclusion

Solution of LP problems using the tableau procedure described above is, of course, limited to cases with few variables, otherwise computer programs are required. To this point we have only applied the Simplex Method to maximization and pivoting rules that also deal with minimization are discussed in the next section.

Then section 5.5 deals with the dual LP problem. Here the original (design) and slack variables interchange roles. Note, however, that the dual LP problem can also be solved by tackling the original problem using dual pivoting rules.

5. Linear Programming

5.4. Alternative pivoting Rules for the Simplex Method

An alternative pivoting rule to the 'max c, min b/a" rule used in Section 5.3 is, for minimization, to *search* the whole A matrix for the *optimum pivot*, that is that pivot which gives the maximum change in the objective function but which does not cause any entry in the cost row (other than the last for z) to become negative (otherwise we would have overshot the minimum). Indicating the sign requirements for a,b,c in pivot search and selection we can write this and a *dual pivoting rule* for maximization as:

Min: $a_{ij} \to \max\{(-b)(+c)/(-a) \mid \text{all } c' > 0\}$ until all $b > 0$ (5.15)

Max: $a_{ij} \to \max\{(+b)(+c)/(+a) \mid \text{all } b' > 0\}$ until all $c < 0$ (5.16)

and these rules can be applied successively when required, that is, after obtaining the minimum solution, the second rule is applied to obtain the maximum solution.

In the first of these we choose pivots corresponding to negative RHS values as the presence of these indicates that we are not inside the feasible region and then the negative pivots used eliminate these negative RHS values. Once the minimum solution has been obtained the second pivot selection rule can be used to obtain the maximum solution, now choosing the pivot which gives the maximum change in the objective function but does not cause any RHS value to become negative (corresponding to leaving the feasible region).

Then using these rules for the example of Equations 5.2 - 5.3 we obtain:

Table 5.2. Application of dual pivoting rules.

-1	2	1	0	0	14	
5	2	0	1	0	50	
<u>-1</u>	-2	0	0	1	-18	
2	7	0	0	0	0	
0	4	1	0	-1	32	
0	<u>-8</u>	0	1	-5	-40	
1	2	0	0	-1	18	
0	3	0	0	2	-36	
0	0	1	1/2	3/2	12	$y_1 = 12$
0	1	0	-1/8	-5/8	5	$x_2 = 5$
1	0	0	1/4	1/4	8	$x_1 = 8$
0	0	0	3/8	31/8	-51	$z = 51$
0	0	2/3	1/3	1	8	$y_3 = 8$
0	1	5/12	1/12	0	10	$x_2 = 10$
1	0	-1/6	1/6	0	6	$x_1 = 6$
0	0	-31/12	-11/12	0	-82	$z = 82$

5. LINEAR PROGRAMMING

The solutions correspond to those obtained graphically in Section 5.2.

These dual pivoting rules remind us that the dual of the standard 'max c, min b/a' rule used in Section 5.3 can also be used to obtain minimum solutions. This is to choose the pivot row as that with the worst -b (constraint violation causing infeasibility) and then the column with the minimum c/|a| value, with a < 0 to eliminate this negative RHS value.

Then the standard rule ('max c, min b/a ') is used for maximization. Indeed the simpler rules result in the same pivot choices in the example of Table 5.2. In larger problems, however, the rules of Equations 5.15 and 5.16 will result in solution with fewer reductions though there is a tradeoff in savings in time doing reductions against time taken searching for and checking pivots.

The following listing is of a program using Equation 5.15 as the pivoting rule storing only the augmented matrix A of Equation 5.8, the using a *pointer matrix* B( ) to indicate which variables are in the *basis*, that is, non zero. The data is for the problem of Figure 5.2, that is with two *design variables* (D = 2) and three slack variables (S = 3) for the three constraints.

```
10 REM LP Program - MIN using Min(bc/a) rule
20 DIM A(9, 5), X(12), B(8), Z(4)
30 READ D, S: M = D + 1: N = S + 1
40 FOR I = 1 TO N: FOR J = 1 TO M: READ A(I, J): NEXT: NEXT
50 REM initialization of variables and pointer matrices
60 L = 0: V = D + S
70 FOR I = 1 TO D: X(I) = 0: NEXT
80 FOR I = M TO V: X(I) = A(I - D, M): NEXT
90 FOR I = 1 TO S: B(I) = D + I: NEXT
100 FOR I = 1 TO D: Z(I) = I: NEXT
110 I1 = 0: J1 = 0
120 IF L = 20 THEN 460
130 REM pivot selection
140 FOR J = 1 TO D: IF A(N, J) = 0 THEN 460
NEXT
150 FOR I = 1 TO S: IF A(I, M) < 0 THEN 170
NEXT
160 GOTO 460
170 Q = -1
180 FOR I = 1 TO S: FOR J = 1 TO D
190 IF A(I, J) = 0 OR A(I, M) > 0 THEN 280
200 T = A(N, J) * A(I, M) / A(I, J)
210 IF T <= Q THEN 280
```

```
220 FOR K = 1 TO D
230 IF J = K THEN 260
240 T1 = A(N, K) - A(N, J) * A(I, K) / A(I, J)
250 IF T1 < 0 THEN 280
260 NEXT K
270 I1 = I: J1 = J: Q = T
280 NEXT J: NEXT I
290 IF Q <= O THEN 460
300 REM Gauss Jordan reduction
310 IF I1 = 0 OR J1 = 0 THEN 460
320 L = L + 1
330 T = B(I1): X(T) = 0
340 B(I1) = Z(J1): Z(J1) = T
350 P1 = 1 / A(I1, J1): A(I1, J1) = 1
360 FOR J = 1 TO M: A(I1, J) = A(I1, J) * P1: NEXT
370 FOR I = 1 TO N
380 IF I = I1 THEN 420
390 T = A(I, J1): A(I, J1) = 0
400 FOR J = 1 TO M
410 A(I, J) = A(I, J) - A(I1, J) * T: NEXT
420 NEXT I
430 FOR I = 1 TO S
440 T = B(I): X(T) = A(I, M): NEXT
450 GOTO 110
460 PRINT L, " reductions required."
470 PRINT "Min = ", -A(N, M)
480 FOR I = 1 TO S: PRINT B(I), X(B(I)): NEXT
490 END
500 DATA 2,3, -1,2,14, 5,2,50, -1,-2,-18, 2,7,0
```

5.5. The dual LP problem

As an example consider the *primal* problem:

$$\text{Min/Max} \quad z = x_1 + 2x_2 + 4x_3 \tag{5.17}$$

subject to:

$$x_1 + x_2 + x_3 \leq 6 \tag{5.18}$$

$$2x_1 + 2x_2 + 4x_3 \geq 8 \tag{5.19}$$

$$2x_1 + x_2 \leq 4 \tag{5.20}$$

for which the resulting tableau and solution are given in Table 5.3.

5. LINEAR PROGRAMMING

Table 5.3. Successive solution for Min/Max of problem of Eqns 5.17 - 5.20.

1	1	1	1	0	0	6	
<u>-2</u>	-2	-4	0	1	0	-8	
2	1	0	0	0	1	4	
1	2	4	0	0	0	0	
0	0	-1	1	1/2	0	2	
1	1	2	0	-1/2	0	4	
0	-1	<u>-4</u>	0	1	0	-4	
0	1	2	0	1/2	0	-4	
0	1/4	0	1	1/4	-1/4	3	$y_1 = 3$
0	1/2	0	0	0	1/2	2	$x_2 = 2$
0	1/4	1	0	-1/4	-1/4	1	$x_3 = 1$
0	1/2	0	0	1	1/2	-6	Min
0	1	0	4	1	-1	12	
0	1/2	0	0	0	1/2	2	
0	1/2	1	1	0	-1/2	4	
0	-1/2	0	-4	0	3/2	-18	
2	2	0	4	1	0	16	$y_2 = 16$
2	1	0	0	0	1	4	$y_3 = 4$
1	1	1	1	0	0	6	$x_3 = 6$
-3	-2	0	-4	0	0	-24	Max

The pivots selected using the 'max -b, min c/-a' rule for MIN and its dual for the MAX are underscored in Table 5.3 and the solution proceeds without difficulty.

Now we will obtain a solution for the dual form of this problem and compare results. This will show that the costs and RHS entries are interchanged between the two problems and that the maximum of one is the minimum of the other.

If we state the primal LP problem as

$$\text{Min:} \quad z_P = \{c\}^T\{x\} \tag{5.21}$$

subject to $\quad A\{x\} \geq \{b\} \quad \{x\} \geq 0 \tag{5.22}$

then the dual LP problem is

$$\text{Max:} \quad z_D = \{b\}^T\{y\} \tag{5.23}$$

subject to $\quad A^T\{y\} \leq \{c\} \quad \{y\} \geq 0 \tag{5.24}$

5. LINEAR PROGRAMMING

As an example consider the problem of Equations 5.17 - 5.20. Reversing the signs of the first and third constraints the primal problem is:

$$\text{Min/max:} \quad z_P = x_1 + 2x_2 + 4x_3 \tag{5.25}$$

subject to

$$-x_1 - x_2 - x_3 \geq -6 \tag{5.26a}$$

$$2x_1 + 2x_2 + 4x_3 \geq 8 \tag{5.26b}$$

$$-2x_1 - x_2 \geq -4 \tag{5.26c}$$

Then 'tranposing' the problem according to Equations 5.21 - 5.24 the dual problem is obtained as

$$\text{Min/Max} \quad z_D = -6y_1 + 8y_2 - 4y_3 \tag{5.27}$$

subject to

$$-y_1 + 2y_2 - 2y_3 \leq 1 \tag{5.28a}$$

$$-y_1 + 2y_2 - y_3 \leq 2 \tag{5.28b}$$

$$-y_1 + 4y_2 \leq 4 \tag{5.28c}$$

Then the dual problem is solved using a simplex method tableau in Table 5.4. First the maximum solution is obtained using the 'max c, min b/a ' rule. Then, before minimization can proceed, the signs of the unit costs and the RHS constraint limits must be reversed. This is because the maximum solution is infeasible from the point of view of the minimum solution (which has already been overshot).

This is done in the fourth tableau in Table 5.4 and then the minimum of the dual problem is obtained using the 'worst -b, min c/ -a' rule.

Comparing Tables 5.4 and 5.3 we see that for the maximum of the dual problem ($z = 6$, corresponding to the minimum of the primal) we have $y_2 = 1$, $x_2 = 1/2$ and $y_3 = 1/2$. These corresponding to the cost values for the primal problem, demonstrating the information value of these.

Then for the minimum of the dual problem ($z = 24$, corresponding to the maximum of the primal) we have $y_1 = 4$, $x_2 = 2$ and $x_1 = 3$, again these corresponding to the cost values for the primal problem.

5. LINEAR PROGRAMMING

Table 5.4. Solution of the dual LP problem.

-1	<u>2</u>	-2	1	0	0	1	
-1	2	-1	0	1	0	2	
-1	4	0	0	0	1	4	
-6	8	-4	0	0	0	0	
-1/2	1	-1	1/2	0	0	1/2	
0	0	1	-1	1	0	1	
1	0	<u>4</u>	2	0	1	2	
-2	0	4	-4	0	0	-4	
-1/4	1	0	0	0	1/4	1	$y_2 = 1$
-1/4	0	0	-1/2	1	-1/4	1/2	$x_2 = 1/2$
1/4	0	1	-1/2	0	1/4	1/2	$y_3 = 1/2$
-3	0	0	2	0	1	-6	Max
<u>-1/4</u>	1	0	0	0	1/4	-1	Reverse
-1/4	0	0	-1/2	1	-1/4	-1/2	signs of
1/4	0	1	-1/2	0	1/4	-1/2	b's &c's
3	0	0	2	0	1	-6	
1	-4	0	0	0	-1	4	
0	-1	0	-1/2	1	-1/2	1/2	
0	1	1	<u>-1/2</u>	0	1/2	-3/2	
1	-4	0	0	0	-1	4	$y_1 = 4$
0	-2	-1	0	1	-1	2	$x_2 = 2$
0	-2	-2	1	0	-1	3	$x_1 = 3$
0	16	4	0	0	0	-24	Min

Thus the primal problem can be either minimized or maximized, or both, and complete information is obtained. The only advantage of the dual problem, therefore, is when it results in a more economical solution, perhaps when there are many constraints with few variables, for example, a situation which will be reversed when the problem is posed in its dual form.

Conclusion

The linear programming problem is an important one which has a simple graphical solution when there are only two variables and this illustrates the part which the constraints play in forming the solution.

Numerical solution can be achieved using Gauss-Jordan reduction applied to a tableau for the problem. The standard pivoting rule for maximization is the 'max c, min b/a' rule and for minimization the dual of this can be used, that is the 'worst $-b$, min $c/-a$' rule.

Two more complex pivoting rules are given in which the maximum permissible change in the objective function is found by searching the whole of the augmented A matrix. This may be a little tedious to apply manually but is readily incorporated into computer programs.

5. Linear Programming

5.6. Equality constraints

Thus far we have dealt with problems with inequality constraints (both $\leq$ and $\geq$). In the present section we include a simplex method example in which an equality constraint is dealt with by splitting it into two constraints (one $\leq$ and one ≥ 0). This artifice can be used to deal with equality constraints in the program in Section 5.4.

The problem is to minimize and maximize

$$z = 15x_1 + 5x_2 \tag{5.29}$$

subject to

$$x_1 + 2x_2 \leq 10 \tag{5.29a}$$
$$x_1 - 3x_2 = 0 \tag{5.29b}$$
$$x_1 + x_2 \geq 6 \tag{5.29c}$$

Table 5.5. Simplex tableau for Equations 5.29.

1	2	1	0	0	0	10	
1	-3	0	1	0	0	0	
-1	3	0	0	1	0	0	
-1	<u>-1</u>	0	0	0	1	-6	
15	5	0	0	0	0	0	
-1	0	1	0	0	2	-2	
4	0	0	1	0	-3	18	
<u>-4</u>	0	0	0	1	3	-18	
1	1	0	0	0	-1	6	
10	0	0	0	0	5	-30	
0	0	1	0	-1/4	<u>5/4</u>	5/2	
0	0	0	1	1	0	0	
1	0	0	0	-1/4	-3/4	9/2	$x_1 = 4.5$
0	1	0	0	1/4	-1/4	3/2	$x_2 = 1.5$
0	0	0	0	5/2	25/2	-75	MIN
0	0	4/5	0	-1/5	1	2	
0	0	0	1	<u>1</u>	0	0	
1	0	3/5	0	-2/5	0	6	
0	1	1/5	0	1/5	0	2	
0	0	-8	0	5	0	-100	
0	0	4/5	1/5	0	1	2	
0	0	0	1	1	0	0	
1	0	3/5	2/5	0	0	6	$x_1 = 6$
0	1	1/5	-1/5	0	0	2	$x_2 = 2$
0	0	-8	-5	0	0	-100	MAX

5. Linear Programming

Splitting the second constraint into two the simplex tableau obtained is shown in Table 5.5. First using the 'worst -b, min c/-a' rule the minimum solution is obtained ($x_1 = 4.5$, $x_2 = 1.5$ and $z = 75$) and then the standard 'max c, min b/a' rule is used to obtain the maximum solution ($x_1 = 6$, $x_2 = 2$ and $z = 100$).

Note that the last pivot is for the unusual case of minimum RHS value = 0 (the only other apparent alternative, the entry 1/5 two rows below in this column, results in an infeasible solution with a negative RHS entry).

Conclusion

The Simplex method program given in Section 5.8 is used to demonstrate successive use of dual pivoting rules but does not deal with equality constraints directly and hence the split constraint approach can be used, though at the expense of adding two constraints for each equality constraint. It is more efficient, however, to include equality constraints directly and force a pivot choice in each of their rows in the constraint matrix, thereafter disallowing return to that constraint. The pivot choice, of course, is then of the minimum cost for minimization problems, or the maximum cost for maximization problems, subject to the pivot sign constraints in the dual rules given in Section 5.4 and this approach is used in the program of Section 5.9.

5.7. Distribution Problems

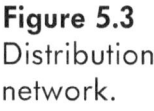
Figure 5.3
Distribution network.
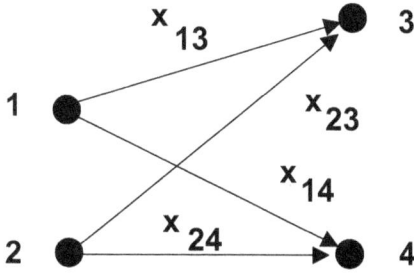

Figure 5.3 shows a simple distribution network with two supply points S_1 and S_2 and two demand points D_1 and D_2. The flows between the points are the x_{ij} values shown and the costs per unit for these flows are shown in Table 5.6 where the supplies and demands generated by the two points are also given.

5. LINEAR PROGRAMMING

Table 5.6. Distribution problem data.

Origin	Destination		Supply
	3	4	
1	2	1	30
2	1	2	60
Demand	40	50	90/90

Then the *distribution (or transportation) problem* is the optimization problem

$$\text{Min. } z = \Sigma \Sigma c_{ij} x_{ij} \tag{5.30}$$

subject to

$$x_{13} + x_{14} + 0 + 0 = 30 \tag{5.31a}$$

$$0 + 0 + x_{23} + x_{24} = 60 \tag{5.31b}$$

$$x_{13} + 0 + x_{23} + 0 = 40 \tag{5.32a}$$

$$0 + x_{14} + 0 + x_{24} = 50 \tag{5.32b}$$

where Equations 5.31 are the supply constraints and Equations 5.32 are the demand constraints.

Then the problem can be solved by:

1. The simplex method when the last constraint is omitted. This makes allowance for the fact that the sum of demands equals the sum of supplies so that this last constraint is not required. The data for the problem of Figure 5.4 is included in the program given in the following section.

2. Tabular methods such as the *Northwest Corner Method*, but computer methods such as the Simplex Method or the 'direct' method used in Section 5.9 are obligatory in practice.

5. LINEAR PROGRAMMING

5.8. Program for sequential MIN + MAX

The following program uses the 'worst -b/min c/-a' rule to find the minimum solution and then the standard 'max c/min b/a' rule to find a maximum solution.

Note that the program uses the short GJR coding given in Section 3.4 (in lines 180-230) as a basis for *partial* reduction of the matrix for each pivot choice.

The data is read in simply as a line giving # constraints (N), total # variables (M) and Q = 1,2,3 (see line 10 for explanation), followed by the constraints (in $\leq$ form and including their columns for slack variables and their RHSs) and finally the 'cost row'. That is, for simplicity the full simplex tableau is read in.

```
10 REM LP program: Q=1 for MAX, Q=2 for MIN & Q=3 for MIN then MAX
20 RESTORE 450
30 DIM A(10, 15): T = 10 ^ -6: READ N, M, Q
40 FOR I = 1 TO N + 1: FOR J = 1 TO M + 1: READ A(I, J): NEXT: NEXT
50 C1 = 0: FOR J = 1 TO M: C2 = A(N + 1, J)
60 IF C2 > C1 THEN C1 = C2: C = J
NEXT
70 IF C1 = 0 THEN 250
80 F = 0: B1 = 10 ^ 10
90 FOR I = 1 TO N
100 IF A(I, M + 1) < 0 THEN F = 1
110 IF ABS(A(I, C)) < T THEN 150
120 B2 = A(I, M + 1) / A(I, C)
130 IF B2 < 0 THEN 150
140 IF B2 < B1 THEN B1 = B2: R = I
150 NEXT I
160 IF F = 1 THEN GOSUB 330
170 IF F = 0 AND Q >= 2 THEN 250
180 X = A(R, C)
190 FOR J = 1 TO M + 1: A(R, J) = A(R, J) / X: NEXT
200 FOR I = 1 TO N + 1
210 IF I = R THEN 230
215 X = A(I, C)
220 FOR J = 1 TO M + 1: A(I, J) = A(I, J) - X * A(R, J): NEXT
230 NEXT I
240 GOTO 50
250 PRINT "Z = ", -A(N + 1, M + 1)
```

5. LINEAR PROGRAMMING

```
260 FOR I = 1 TO N: FOR J = 1 TO M
270 D = ABS(A(I, J) - 1)
280 IF D < T AND ABS(A(N + 1, J)) < T THEN K = J
NEXT J
290 PRINT "X"; : PRINT USING "##"; K; : PRINT " = ";
PRINT USING "######.###"; A(I, M + 1)
300 NEXT I
310 IF Q = 3 THEN Q = 1: GOTO 50
320 END
330 B1 = 0: FOR I = 1 TO N
340 B2 = -A(I, M + 1): IF B2 < 0 THEN 360
350 IF B2 > B1 THEN B1 = B2: R = I
360 NEXT I
370 C1 = 10 ^ 10
380 FOR J = 1 TO M
390 IF ABS(A(R, J)) < T THEN 430
400 IF A(R, J) > 0 THEN 430
410 C2 = -(A(N + 1, J) / A(R, J))
420 IF C2 < C1 THEN C1 = C2: C = J
430 NEXT J
440 RETURN
450 DATA 4,6,3
460 DATA 1,2,1,0,0,0,10
470 DATA 1,-3,0,1,0,0,0
480 DATA -1,3,0,0,1,0,0
490 DATA -1,-1,0,0,0,1,-6
500 DATA 15,5,0,0,0,0,0
510 DATA 6,10,3
520 DATA 1,1,0,0,1,0,0,0,0,0,30
530 DATA -1,-1,0,0,0,1,0,0,0,0,-30
540 DATA 0,0,1,1,0,0,1,0,0,0,60
550 DATA 0,0,-1,-1,0,0,0,1,0,0,-60
560 DATA 1,0,1,0,0,0,0,0,1,0,40
570 DATA -1,0,-1,0,0,0,0,0,1,-40
580 DATA 2,1,1,2,0,0,0,0,0,0
```

The dimensioning limits to nine constraints and fourteen variables (line 30) and data is included for two problems:

[1] The problem of Section 5.6 (lines 450 - 500) which is solved for both the minimum and maximum without difficulty.

[2] The distribution problem of Sec. 5.7 using the 'split constraint artifice demonstrated in Sec. 5.6 (lines 510-580). The minimum solution is:

$x_{14} = 30$, $x_{23} = 40$, $x_{24} = 20$

so that the minimum total transportation cost is:

$z = 30(1) + 40(1) + 20(2) = 110$

and the maximum solution is:

$x_{13} = 30$, $x_{23} = 10$, $x_{24} = 50$

giving the maximum total cost $z = 170$.

As in the program given in Section 5.4, with a little additional coding the program can be modified to store only the matrix A of Equation 5.8, the RHS vector and one additional column matrix to store the new column formed in the 'I' part of the augmented matrix when a column is reduced in matrix A. This new column then replaces the reduced column (to 'unit form' with a unit entry and the rest zeroes) in the matrix A, keeping a record of which variables have entered the *basis* by storing their ordinal numbers in another 1D array.

5.9. Direct LP method program for distribution problems

The following program uses the 'direct' method of Mohr to solve distribution problems. In this a pivot is taken in each (constraint) row in turn in the column with the minimum value of $c_j/|a_{ij}|$ and GJR applied to this column, yielding an initial *infeasible* solution to the problem. The minimum solution is then obtained by choosing pivots using the 'worst -b, min c/-a' rule (again note $a < 0$ to eliminate the infeasible - b on the RHS).

Next the maximum solution is obtained (in lines 210 - 270) using the 'max c, min b/a' rule. Generally we require only the minimum solution, when line 140 alters to '140 IF I=0 THEN 280' (only with this option is the MIN printed).

```
10 REM Distribution Problem Program - for MAX
20 REM restore 500
30 DIM A(20, 20), B(20), NV(20): READ NC, NX: REM Read data
40 FOR I = 1 TO NC + 1: FOR J = 1 TO NX: READ A(I, J): NEXT: READ B(I):
NEXT
50 FOR I = 1 TO NC: C = 10 ^ 6
60 FOR J = 1 TO NX: IF ABS(A(I, J)) < .000001 THEN 80
70 F = A(NC + 1, J) / ABS(A(I, J)): IF F < C THEN C = F: COL = J
80 NEXT J
90 GOSUB 350: NEXT I
```

5. LINEAR PROGRAMMING

```
100 I = O: C = 0: FOR K = 1 TO NC: IF B(K) < C THEN I = K: C = B(K)
105 NEXT
110 C = 10 ^ 6: FOR J = 1 TO NX: IF A(I, J) >= 0 THEN 130
120 F = A(NC + 1, J) / ABS(A(I, J)): IF F < C THEN C = F: COL = J
130 NEXT
140 IF I = 0 THEN 210
150 GOTO 190
160 FOR J = 1 TO NX
170 F = A(NC+1,J)-A(I, J)*A(NC+1,COL) / A(I, COL): IF F < 0 THEN PRINT "OVER"
180 NEXT
190 GOSUB 350
200 IF I > 0 THEN 100
210 C = 0: FOR K = 1 TO NX: IF A(NC + 1, K) > C THEN J = K: C = A(NC + 1, K)
215 NEXT
220 IF J = NX + 1 THEN 280
230 T = 10 ^ 6: FOR K = 1 TO NC: IF A(K, J) <= 0 THEN 250
240 F = B(K) / A(K, J): IF F < T THEN I = K: T = F
250 NEXT: IF C = 0 THEN 280
260 COL = J: GOSUB 350
270 GOTO 210
280 FOR J = 1 TO NX
290 C = 0: FOR I = 1 TO NC: IF ABS(A(I, J)) < .000001 THEN C = C + 1
295 NEXT
300 IF C <> NC - 1 THEN 320
310 FOR I = 1 TO NC: IF ABS(A(I, J)) = 1 THEN K = I
315 NEXT: NV(K) = J
320 NEXT J
330 FOR I = 1 TO NC + 1
335 PRINT "  X"; : PRINT USING "##"; NV(I); :
336 PRINT " = "; : PRINT USING "#########"; B(I): NEXT
340 END
350 P = A(I, COL): B(I) = B(I) / P
360 FOR J = 1 TO NX: A(I, J) = A(I, J) / P: NEXT
370 FOR K = 1 TO NC + 1: IF K = I THEN 410
380 M = A(K, COL): B(K) = B(K) - M * B(I)
390 FOR J = 1 TO NX
400 A(K, J) = A(K, J) - M * A(I, J): NEXT J
410 NEXT K
420 RETURN
```

5. LINEAR PROGRAMMING

430 DATA 5,9
440 DATA 1,1,1,0,0,0,0,0,0,110
450 DATA 0,0,0,1,1,1,0,0,0,160
460 DATA 0,0,0,0,0,0,1,1,1,150
470 DATA 1,0,0,1,0,0,1,0,0,140
480 DATA 0,1,0,0,1,0,0,1,0,200
490 DATA 50,100,100,200,300,200,100,200,300,0
500 DATA 8,20
510 DATA 1,1,1,1,1,0,0,0,0,0,0,0,0,0,0,0,0,0,0,0,90
520 DATA 0,0,0,0,0,1,1,1,1,1,0,0,0,0,0,0,0,0,0,0,75
530 DATA 0,0,0,0,0,0,0,0,0,0,1,1,1,1,1,0,0,0,0,0,35
540 DATA 0,0,0,0,0,0,0,0,0,0,0,0,0,0,0,1,1,1,1,1,25
550 DATA 1,0,0,0,0,1,0,0,0,0,1,0,0,0,0,1,0,0,0,0,40
560 DATA 0,1,0,0,0,0,1,0,0,0,0,1,0,0,0,0,1,0,0,0,35
570 DATA 0,0,1,0,0,0,0,1,0,0,0,0,1,0,0,0,0,1,0,0,70
580 DATA 0,0,0,1,0,0,0,0,1,0,0,0,0,1,0,0,0,0,1,0,30
590 DATA 1.5,6.4,1.8,4,3.5,1.6,2.6,1.9,3.1,5.8,5.3,3.5,2.4,1.3,2.2
600 DATA 50,50,50,50,50,0

The data lines 430-490 are for the problem described by the data table:

	Unit costs			Supplies
( ) = node #	50	100	100	110 (1)
	200	300	200	160 (2)
	100	200	300	150 (3)
Demands	140 (4)	200 (5)	80 (6)	

for which the solution (MIN) is route flows 15 = 110, 25 = 80, 26 = 80, 34 = 140 and 35 = 10 (others zero) with total cost 670,000.

The MAX solution is route flows 14 = 110, 25 = 160, 34 = 30, 35 = 40 and 36 = 80 with total cost 885,000.

The final data lines are for the problem of Table 9.3, for which the solutions are as given there.

Conclusion

The simple LP program given is a useful introduction, particularly as it gives both the MIN and MAX solution.

The 'direct' method program given for distribution problems also gives both the MIN and MAX solutions. From the customer or demand point of view we should prefer the MIN solution to our distribution problem, but from the company profit of supply point of view we might well be interested in the MAX solution.

5. LINEAR PROGRAMMING

5.10. References

Ackoff RL (ed.), *Progress in Operations Research*, vol. 1, Wiley NY, 1961.

Ackoff RL, Sasieni MW, *Fundamentals of Operations Research*, Wiley NY, 1968.

Battersby, A, *Mathematics in Management*, Penguin, Harmondsworth UK, 1966.

Bersekas DP, *Constrained Optimization and Lagrange Multiplier Methods*, Academic Press, New York, 1982.

Budnick FS, Mojena R, Vollmann TE, *Principles of Operations Research for Management*, Irwin, Homewood IL, 1977.

Churchman CW, Ackoff RL, Arnoff EL, *Introduction to Operations Research*, Wiley NY, 1968.

Enrick NL, *Management Operations Research*, Holt Rinehart & Winston, NY, 1965.

Hillier FS, Lieberman GJ, *Introduction to Operations Research*, 3rd edn, Holden Day, Oakland CA, 1980.

Kaufman A, Faure R, *Introduction to Operations Research*, Academic, London, 1968.

Makower MS, Williamson E, *Operations Research*, 3rd edn, Hodder & Stoughton, Sevenoaks, Kent, 1975.

Mohr GA, *Finite Elements for Solids, Fluids, and Optimization*, OUP, Oxford, 1992.

Mohr GA, Optimization of primal and dual network models of distribution, *Computer Methods & Applied Mechanics in Engng*, vol. 188, p 135, 2000.

Mohr GA, Cook PL, Dual pivoting rules for the Simplex Method, *Int. J Arts & Sciences* 2 (2001) 49-60.

Rust BW, Burrus WR, *Mathematical Programming and the Numerical Solution of Linear Equations*, Elsevier, New York, 1972.

Sasieni M, Yaspan A, Friedman L, *Operations Research*, Wiley, NY, 1959.

Schmenner, RW, *Production/Operations Management: Concepts and Situations*, 4th edn, McMillan, NY, 1990.

Singh J, *Operations Research*, Penguin, UK, 1971.

Theil H, Boot JCG, Kloek T, *Operations Research and Quantitative Economics*, McGraw-Hill, NY, 1965.

Wang C, *Computer Methods in Advanced Structural Analysis*, Intext, New York, 1973.

Whittle P, *Optimization under Constraints*, Wiley, London, 1971.

Chapter 6

NONLINEAR PROGRAMMING

This chapter provides a short introduction to nonlinear optimization problems. First the *steepest descent* method is introduced for an unconstrained problem. Next the *sequence of unconstrained minima technique (SUMT)* is used to deal with problems with constraints.

6.1. Classical theory of optimization

The classical theory of optimization is based on the elementary calculus of curves, that is a stationary or turning point in $y = f(x)$ is given by $dy/dx = 0$ and this is a relative maximum when $d^2y/dx^2 < 0$. We picture this as the slope dy/dx being positive or up to the left of the T.P. and changing to negative or down to the right of the T.P. so that dy/dx is decreasing and hence its derivative d^2y/dx^2 is negative.

Multivariate problems

In speaking of the calculus of curves we are dealing with *univariate problems*. In the case of multivariate problems stationary points with respect to several variables x_i are defined by

$$\partial f/\partial x_i = 0 \quad i = 1 \to n \tag{6.1}$$

and in optimization problems this is our objective. Here the derivatives are *partial derivatives* with respect to each of the x_i and these are simply obtained by differentiating $f(x_1, x_2 - -)$ with respect to each of the x_i in turn, treating the function as if the particular x_i were the only variable, which for the purposes of calculating a partial derivative it is.

Then if a point is stationary with respect to all the problem variables x_i it is a relative minimum if

$$|H| = |\partial^2 f/\partial x_i \partial x_j| > 0 \quad \partial^2 f/\partial x_i \partial x_j \neq 0, \; i,j = 1 \to n \tag{6.2}$$

where H is a *Hessian* matrix of second order partial derivatives. The point is thus a relative maximum when $|H| < 0$ and is a *saddle point* when $|H| = 0$.

Including constraints

Inequality constraints are written in the form

$$c_j(x_i) + y_j = 0 \quad i = 1 \to n, \; j = 1 \to m \qquad (6.3)$$

where the y_j are *slack variables*.

Then the extrema of $f(x)$ are the turning points of the *Lagrangian function*

$$\phi(x, \lambda) = f(x) + \sum_{j=1}^{m} \lambda_j c_j(x_i) \qquad (6.4)$$

where $\{\lambda\}$ are *Lagrange multipliers*. The extrema are thus unconstrained solutions of

$$\{\partial f/\partial x_i + \sum_{j=1}^{m} \lambda_j \partial c_j/\partial x_i = 0 \mid c_j + y_j = 0\} \quad j = 1 \to m, \; i = 1 \to n \qquad (6.5)$$

Then when the Lagrangian function is a minimum for variations in $\{x\}$ it is a maximum for variations in $\{\lambda_i\}$ (if some $y \neq 0$, and this second problem is called the *dual problem*), that is we have a *saddle point* in the Lagrangian function.

Conclusion

Formal statement of optimization of multivariate problems appears a little formidable at first but simple examples such as that given in Section 2.7 do much to overcome the difficulty. The steepest descent method introduced in the following section is based on Newton's method (see Section 3.1) and is conceptually very simple.

6.2. Unconstrained nonlinear problems

Nonlinear problems are governed by the fundamentals stated in Section 6.1 and when there are only one or two variables analytical calculus can be used as demonstrated in Chapter 2. Generally, however, numerical methods must be used, as for LP problems. Most of these have a search character so that techniques such as those discussed in Sections 3.1 and 3.2 are useful.

Univariate problems

For problems involving very complicated expressions with only one variable, for example, search with a computer program of only a handful of lines can be useful. Here trial values are used until the function to be optimized passes a turning point. Then bisection or interpolation can be used to home in upon the solution.

6. Nonlinear Programming

The method of steepest descent

For multivariate problems the method of steepest descent is one of the most fundamental methods available. This is a *first order gradient method* which is based on allowing a *perturbation*

$$|\delta x| = \sqrt{(\Sigma\, \delta x^2)} \tag{6.6}$$

in the vector of (design) variables, resulting in the objective function altering by an amount

$$\delta f = \Sigma\, (\partial f/\partial x_i)(\delta x_i) + \lambda(\Sigma(\delta x^2 - \Delta^2)) \tag{6.7}$$

where Δ is the optimum perturbation, that is, that for which

$$\partial(\delta f)/\partial(\delta x_i) = 0 = \partial f/\partial x_i + 2\lambda\,(\delta x_i) \quad i = 1 \to n \tag{6.8}$$

from which it follows that

$$\{\delta x_i\} = -\{\partial f/\partial x_i\}/2\lambda = -(\text{constant})\{g\} \tag{6.9}$$

so that the greatest change in the objective function results from search in the direction of the gradient vector $\{g\}$.

The method is comparable to Newton's method for finding the roots of equations (see Section 3.1). Indeed for nonlinear optimization of multivariate problems the *second order gradient methods* in which the search direction is given by an equation of the form

$$\{\delta x_i\} = -H^{-1}\{g\} \tag{6.10}$$

have their mathematical basis in Newton's method. The modern numerical methods, however, begin by assuming $H = I$ (the unit matrix) and gradually form an improved approximation for the Hessian matrix using products of the changes in the gradient vector $\delta\{g\}$.

6. NONLINEAR PROGRAMMING

Numerical calculation of the gradient vector

In practice numerical methods are usually used to calculate the gradient vector approximately, perturbing each variable in turn by an amount δx_i and noting the change in the objective function δf_i. Then the gradient vector is estimated by the first order finite difference approximations

$$\{g\} = \{\delta f_i / \delta x_i\} \tag{6.11}$$

this being a simple example of the 'vector search methods', many of which use a combination of $\{g\}$ and the vector normal to it as a search direction.

An example of steepest descent

As a simple example of the steepest descent method suppose we wish to minimize the function

$$f = (x_1 - 2)^2 + (x_2 - 1)^2 \tag{6.12}$$

The minimum is very obvious but assuming otherwise the steepest descent search procedure is written using a step length S as

$$\begin{Bmatrix} x_1 \\ x_2 \end{Bmatrix} = \begin{Bmatrix} x_1 \\ x_2 \end{Bmatrix}_{n-1} - S \begin{Bmatrix} \partial f / \partial x_1 = 2x_1 - 4 \\ \partial f / \partial x_2 = 2x_2 - 2 \end{Bmatrix} \tag{6.13}$$

where here the required partial derivatives are known explicitly (but in general would be calculated by the perturbation process of Equation 6.11).

Then beginning at the point (3,3) with $S = 0.2$ Equation 6.13 becomes:

$$\begin{Bmatrix} x_1 \\ x_2 \end{Bmatrix} = \begin{Bmatrix} 3 \\ 3 \end{Bmatrix} - 0.2 \begin{Bmatrix} 2 \\ 4 \end{Bmatrix} = \begin{Bmatrix} 2.6 \\ 2.2 \end{Bmatrix} \tag{6.14}$$

yielding $f = 1.80$. Continuing with gradually increased step lengths the results shown in Table 6.1 are obtained.

Table 6.1. Steepest descent example

S	x_1	x_2	f
0	3	3	5
0.2	2.6	2.2	1.8
0.4	2.2	1.4	0.2
0.6	1.8	0.6	0.2
0.8	1.4	-0.2	1.8
0.5	2	1	0

6. NONLINEAR PROGRAMMING

Here with $s = 0.6$ we might suspect something but we proceed with $s = 0.8$ just to make sure. Now it is clear that a turning point has been passed, if not earlier, and bisection is used with $S = 0.5$ which, in this simple case, yields the correct solution.

Though this problem appears trivial it makes a useful computer exercise if the gradient vector is calculated numerically using perturbations in x_1 and x_2.

In the following section, however, the same example is given with the addition of constraints. Then penalty factors are used in sequence to obtain a solution and Section 6.4 gives a computer program which carries out the numerical solution.

Conclusion

The steepest descent method is a fundamental and powerful method of numerical solution of nonlinear optimization problems. The required gradient vector is easily calculated using perturbations in each of the variables in turn to give a finite difference approximation of the search direction. In the simple example given only one search direction was needed but generally several must be used successively.

6.3. Constrained nonlinear problems

Constrained nonlinear optimization problems are sometimes solved by stepwise application of the Simplex Method but this is a relatively tedious process. In the present section we describe the SUMT or *Sequence of Unconstrained Minima Technique* in which constraints are factored by *penalty factors* and added to the objective function. Then search techniques are used with a gradually increased value of the penalty factor to locate the optimum solution with increasing accuracy.

Exterior point methods

In these calculations begin from an exterior point (from the feasible region) and we seek to minimize the function

$$F(x) = f(x) + \beta \Sigma \mid c_i(x) \mid^2 + \beta \Sigma [e_i(x)]^2 \qquad \beta \to \infty \qquad (6.15)$$

where $\mid \ \mid$ denotes a *step function* which is zero when the inequality constraints $c_i(x)$ are not violated, $e_i(x)$ denotes an equality constraint and β is a penalty factor.

Then the SUMT technique involves solving the problem as though it were unconstrained using, for example, the steepest descent method with a sequence of gradually increasing values of the penalty factor.

6. Nonlinear Programming

If we begin with $\beta = 0$, for example, we would first obtain the unconstrained minimum. Then as $\beta \to \infty$ the constraints will take control of the solution if appropriate (in view of the use of a step function for the inequality constraints).

Interior point methods

With these SUMT is first applied to the task of minimizing

$$C = \Sigma\, s_i + \Sigma\, [e_j(x)]^2 \tag{6.16}$$

where s_i are slack variables associated with the inequality constraints. This finds a feasible point and then we seek to minimize the function

$$F(x) = f(x) + \beta\, \Sigma[1/c_i(x)] + \beta^{-1/2} \Sigma\, |\,e_j(x)\,|^2 \quad \beta \to \infty \tag{6.17}$$

and now the inverted form of the term for the inequality constraints provides a *response surface* which prevents access to infeasible regions.

Many such slight variations of the SUMT approach have been suggested but we shall restrict attention to the basic form of Equation 6.14.

An example problem

Suppose we add two constraints to the problem of Equation 6.12, giving the constrained nonlinear optimization problem

$$\text{Min:} \quad f = (x_1 - 2)^2 + (x_2 - 1)^2 \tag{6.18}$$

subject to the constraints

$$1 - x_1^2/4 - x_2 \geq 0 \tag{6.19a}$$

$$x_1 - 2x_2 + 1 = 0 \tag{6.19b}$$

Then the SUMT problem is stated as

$$\text{Min:} \quad F = f(x_1, x_2) + \beta\,|\,1 - x_1^2/4 - x_2\,|^2 + \beta(x_1 - 2x_2 + 1)^2 \quad \beta \to \infty \tag{6.20}$$

Then using steepest descent with

$$\{x\}_n = \{x\}_{n-1} - S\,\{\partial F/\partial x_1,\, \partial F/\partial x_2\} \tag{6.21}$$

the solution progresses towards the optimum in the typical fashion shown in Figure 6.1.

6. NONLINEAR PROGRAMMING

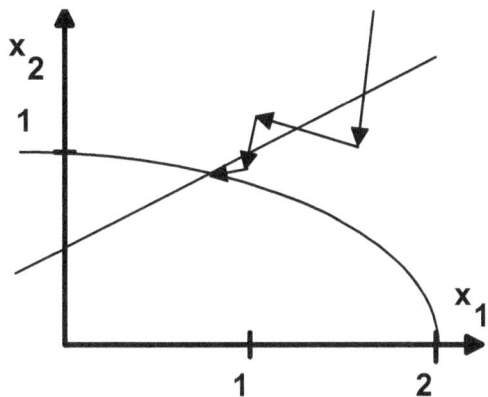

Figure 6.1.
Progress of steepest descent method on example problem.

Here the solution is beginning near (2,2), close to the unconstrained optimum at (2,1), and cross-crosses the equality constraint in a relatively inefficient way. This is because the steepest descent direction is influenced by the parabolic constraint and a component tangential to this will be involved in the search direction.

Improved procedures which incorporate the predictor-corrector method of Section 3.2, therefore, have been devised. In these the search directions are averaged with those used in the previous search and this sort of approach does much to smooth out the convergence shown in Figure 6.1.

In the method proposed by Mohr, for example, allowance is made for the scaling effect of the penalty factors in writing the predictor step as:

$$\{x^*\}_n = \{x\}_{n-1} - (1/2)S\{(\beta_n/\beta_{n-1})(g_{n-1})_{av} + g_{p0}\} \tag{6.22}$$

where β_n, β_{n-1} are the current and previous penalty factors

$(g_{n-1})_{av}$ is the gradient vector used for the last corrector step

g_{p0} is the gradient vector calculated at the beginning of this predictor step

and the corrector step is calculated as

$$\{x\}_n = \{x\}_{n-1} - S\{g_n\}_{av} = \{x)_{n-1} - (1/2)S\{g_{pe} + g_{p0}\} \tag{6.23}$$

where g_{pe} is the gradient calculated at the end of the predictor step.

Then the 'adjust the aim' approach of predictor-corrector methods is clearly evident in the last term of Equation 6.23.

6. NONLINEAR PROGRAMMING

Conclusion

The steepest descent method in conjunction with SUMT is an example of once state of the art optimization techniques for nonlinear problems with constraints.

For simple problems with few variables and constraints it may be of wider interest and the strategy involved is certainly an interesting one. In Section 6.4 a short computer program is used to solve the problem of Equations 6.17 - 6.19 and plot the 'landing on the moon' result shown in Figure 6.1.

6.4. Steepest descent exercise

As an exercise we tackle the SUMT problem of Equations 6.17 - 6.19 using steepest descent. Restating the problem for clarity we have:

$$\text{Min: } f = (x_1 - 2)^2 + (x_2 - 1)^2 \tag{6.24}$$

subject to the constraints:

$$1 - x_1^2/4 - x_2 \geq 0 \tag{6.25a}$$

$$x_1 - 2x_2 + 1 = 0 \tag{6.25b}$$

Then the SUMT problem is

$$\text{Min: } F = f(x_1, x_2) + \beta \mid 1 - x_1^2/4 - x_2 \mid^2 + \beta(x_1 - 2x_2 + 1)^2 \quad \beta \to \infty \tag{6.26}$$

and the gradients of this augmented function are given by

$$g_1 = 2x_1 - 4 + 2\beta C(-x_1/2) + 2\beta(x_1 - 2x_2 + 1)$$
$$g_2 = 2x_2 - 2 + 2\beta C(-1) - 4\beta(x_1 - 2x_2 + 1) \tag{6.27}$$

where $C = (1-x_1^2/4-x_2)$ and if $c > 0$ then we put $C = 0$ as this constraint is not violated. These gradients are then used to obtain solutions by trial search [with additional programming this can be automated, for example using bisection (see Section 3.1)].

Better results are obtained, however, by using perturbations of each *design variable* in turn (by about 5 or 10%) and calculating approximate gradients from the *finite difference* approximations:

$$g_i = (F_2 - F_1)/\delta x_i \quad \text{for each variable } i$$

6. Nonlinear Programming

This is done in following program and the simple coding can be generalized to deal with many variables and problems in any context.

Then by using only two searches with $\beta = 1$ (with searches $S = 0.082$ and $S = 0.14$) and also two searches with $\beta = 100$ ($S = 0.0047$ and $S = 0.00035$) a reasonably good solution can be obtained as

$$x_1 = 0.7321 \text{ and } x_2 = 0.8660 \text{ with } F = 1.6242$$

whereas the exact solution is $x_1 = \sqrt{3} - 1$, $x_2 = \sqrt{3}/2$ and $F = 13.75 - 7\sqrt{3}$.

If exact gradients are used for $\beta = 1, 10, 100, 1000, 10^4, 10^5, 10^6$ six or so searches can be used with each β to obtain a no more accurate result.

This is because use of FD gradients is comparable to using a *predictor-corrector method* (the greater accuracy of which was demonstrated in Section 3.2). This is because using exact gradients is like following tangents on a curve looking for a turning point. The results can be 'miles off'. The approximate FD gradients, however, act like a 'chord approximation' and give much better results, the chord (at reasonable intervals) giving a much better idea where a curve is going than the slope.

A short program

The following short program uses Equations 6.24 and 6.25 to evaluate the objective function and the constraint violations for our example problem.

To commence the coordinates of the starting point are input in line 20, for our example using 2, 2.

For each trial search the penalty value is input first (B in line 40) and then the trial search length (S in line 90), successive searches 'overwriting' the previous one. Thus when the objective function F (printed in line 110) is seen to 'turn' (i.e. increase) repeat the previous trial and then use (B = current, S = 0) to terminate that search. Continue with the next search (at least two with any B), using a new value of B when search is approaching a 'steady result' or make it 'policy' to use, say, 4 searches with each B. Repeat the process with the next B (preferably 100 times the last one, not 10). When (if) the solution seems OK/converged use $S = 0$ to terminate the last search (as usual) and then $B = 0$ to terminate the program, when progress of the solution is plotted for our example problem.

Exercise

Try the 4 step solution with B/S as noted above, i.e., with two searches only for B = 1 and B = 100, beginning with S = 0.082 for first search.

Note that these search lengths are termination values with which a search of many shorter steps was conducted to arrive at these values. Note too that solution plotting is included in the program – if this is not required the last statement in line 45 should end with THEN 195.

6. NONLINEAR PROGRAMMING

The four search lengths for this exercise are noted in line 240 of the program, so that inputs to obtain the optimum solutions are:

x1,x2 = 2,2 (line 20)
B = 1; S = 0.082; S = 0;   B = 1; S = 0.14; S = 0 (lines 40 and 90)
B = 100; S = 0.0047; S = 0;   B = 100; S = 0.00035; S = 0 (lines 40 and 90)
and B = 0 to end computation/start plot (last statement in line 45).

```
10 DIM C(10, 10): I = 0: M = 1.05
20 PRINT "input x1,x2": INPUT x1, x2: C(1, 1) = x1: C(1, 2) = x2
40 PRINT "input b": INPUT B
45 I = I + 1: C(I, 1) = x1: C(I, 2) = x2: S1 = 0: IF B = 0 THEN 155
60 GOSUB 200: F1 = F: x1 = x1 * M: GOSUB 200: F2 = F: x1 = x1 / M
70 G1 = (F2 - F1) / (x1 * (M - 1))
80 x2 = x2 * M: GOSUB 200: F2 = F: x2 = x2 / M: G2 = (F2 - F1) / (x2 * (M - 1))
90 PRINT "Input S ": INPUT S: IF S = 0 THEN 40
100 x1 = x1 + (S1 - S) * G1: x2 = x2 + (S1 - S) * G2
110 GOSUB 200: PRINT x1, x2, "F= ", F
150 S1 = S: GOTO 90
155 SCREEN 2: x = 200 * C(1, 1): y = 150 - 100 * C(1, 2): LINE (x, y)-(x, y)
156 FOR J = 1 TO I: x = C(J, 1): y = C(J, 2)
157 x = 200 * x: y = 150 - 100 * y
158 LINE -(x, y): NEXT J
159 x = 0: y = 50: LINE (x, y)-(x, y)
160 FOR Z = 0 TO 2 STEP .01
170 x = Z: y = 1 - x * x / 4: x = 200 * x: y = 150 - 100 * y
180 LINE -(x, y): NEXT Z
190 LINE (0, 100)-(400, 0): LINE (0, 150)-(600, 150): LINE (0, 150)-(0, 0)
192 LOCATE 22: PRINT x1, x2, "F =", F
195 END
200 G = 1 - x1 * x1 / 4 - x2: E = x1 - 2 * x2 + 1: IF G > 0 THEN G = 0
210 FU = (x1 - 2) ^ 2 + (x2 - 1) ^ 2
220 F = FU + B * G * G + B * E * E
230 RETURN
240 REM search x 4: .082 & .14; .0047 & .00035
```

Conclusion
The foregoing program and the problem it solves are both short and simple but demonstrate a general approach that can be applied to an almost unlimited range of optimization problems, for example FEM models of distribution and traffic flow networks, as shown in Chapters 7 and 8.

6. NONLINEAR PROGRAMMING

6.5. Conjugate gradient method

As noted in Section 6.3, the steepest descent method searches tend to have an inefficient criss-cross pattern, and implementation of a predictor corrector approach with the steepest descent method developed by Mohr is described.

Many other gradient techniques have been described and in most of these a 'compound' gradient approach is used as the search direction. One of the earliest examples is the *conjugate gradient method* in which the modified gradient vector is given by

$$\{g\}^* = \{g\} - \{g\}^t\{g\}\{h\}/\{h\}^t\{h\} \qquad (6.28)$$

where $\{h\}$ is the gradient vector used in the previous search.

As an example consider the problem

$$\text{Min. } f = (x_1 - 3)^2 + (x_2 - 3)^2 + (x_3 - 3)^2 \qquad (6.29)$$

subject to the constraints

$$1 + (x_1 - 1)^2/2 + (x_2 - 2)^2/2 - x_3 \geq 0 \qquad (6.30a)$$

$$6 - x_1 - x_2/2 - x_3 = 0 \qquad (6.30b)$$

$$3 + x_1 x_2/4 - x_3 \leq 0 \qquad (6.30c)$$

First, Table 6.2 shows the results obtained for this problem using the method of steepest descent, starting at point (1,1,1) and using M = 1.01 to obtain a reasonably good approximate solution (with M = 1.1 only five searches were needed but the result was less accurate).

The 'exact' solution was the average solution obtained using exact gradients, alternative starting points, M = 1.01 and $\beta = 10^n$, n = 1,2,3,4,5, resulting in a process of 20 or more searches. This solution satisfies Equation 6.28 and almost Equations 6.27 and 6.29 as equalities. so that using x_2 = 0.4604 in Equations 6.28 and 6.29 as simultaneous (=) equations gives the other values of this 'exact' solution. Note that the largest F value for this solution was for $\beta = 10^5$, not $\beta = 100$ for the other results, and thus this is a good result.

The approximate solution is satisfactory and note in passing that the solution (3, 0, 3) satisfies the constraints, giving F = f = 9, a good example of an approximate solution which might be useful in practice.

6. Nonlinear Programming

Table 6.2. Results for problem of Equations 6.26 - 6.29

β	Sβ	x_1	x_2	x_3	F
Steepest descent					
1	0.14	2.3796	1.8907	3.1658	4.2631
	0.10	2.6412	1.9222	2.9720	3.6909
100	0.58	2.3891	0.5509	3.0373	23.8181
	0.22	2.5046	0.5330	3.2666	7.3386
	0.095	2.5056	0.5084	3.2512	6.9825
	0.21	2.4943	0.4925	3.2510	6.9281
	0.83	2.4840	0.4751	3.2756	6.7697
Conjugate gradient					
1	0.14	2.3796	1.8907	3.1658	4.2631
	0.10	2.6132	1.9041	2.9281	3.7179
100	0.61	2.4244	0.4941	3.1196	14.2246
	0.20	2.5036	0.5550	3.2548	7.9206
	0.074	2.5027	0.5243	3.2330	7.3565
	0.52	2.4889	0.4757	3.2775	6.7516
'Exact'	$\beta = 10^5$	2.4839	0.4604	3.2859	6.7977

Next the results using the conjugate gradient method of Equation 6.25 are given. The early results are similar and a good approximate solution is obtained with one less search.

The coding for this solution is:

```
10 N = 3: DIM X(N), G(N), H(N): REM SUMT program
15 M = 1.01
20 FOR I = 1 TO N: READ X(I): NEXT: DATA 1,1,1
30 INPUT "i/p B", B: D = M - 1: IF B = 99 THEN END
35 FOR I = 1 TO N: H(I) = 0: NEXT
40 S1 = 0: F1 = 0: GOSUB CALC: FA = F
45 REM Gosub EXACT:Goto 65
50 FOR I = 1 TO N: X(I) = X(I) * M: GOSUB CALC
60 X(I) = X(I) / M: G(I) = (F - FA) / (X(I) * D): NEXT
65 GOSUB CONJG
70 INPUT "i/p S ", S: IF S = 0 THEN 40
75 IF S = 99 THEN 30
77 S = S / B
80 FOR I = 1 TO N: X(I) = X(I) + (S1 - S) * G(I): NEXT
90 GOSUB CALC: DF = F - F1: PRINT X1, X2, X3, " f,df = ", F, DF
100 S1 = S: F1 = F: GOTO 70: END
```

6. NONLINEAR PROGRAMMING

```
110 CALC: X1 = X(1): X2 = X(2): X3 = X(3)
120 C = 1 + (X1 - 1) ^ 2 / 2 + (X2 - 2) ^ 2 / 2 - X3: IF C > 0 THEN C = 0
130 E = 6 - X1 - X2 / 2 - X3
140 L = 3 + X1 * X2 / 4 - X3: IF L < 0 THEN L = 0
150 U = (X1 - 3) ^ 2 + (X2 - 3) ^ 2 + (X3 - 3) ^ 2
160 F = U + B * (C * C + E * E + L * L): RETURN
170 EXACT: G(1) = 2 * (X1 - 3) + 2 * B * (X1 - 1) * C - 2 * B * E + B * X2 * L /2
180 G(2) = 2 * (X2 - 3) + 2 * B * (X2 - 2) * C - B * E + B * X1 * L / 2
190 G(3) = 2 * (X3 - 3) - 2 * B * C - 2 * B * E - 2 * B * L
200 RETURN
210 CONJG: X = 0: Y = 0
220 FOR I = 1 TO N: X = X + G(I) * G(I)
230 Y = Y + H(I) * H(I): NEXT
240 IF Y = 0 THEN 260
250 FOR I = 1 TO N: G(I) = G(I) - X * H(I) / Y: NEXT
260 FOR I = 1 TO N: H(I) = G(I): NEXT
270 RETURN
```

The coordinates of the starting point and value of M are set in the program. Computation starts with request for the penalty value B, followed by search length S. Gradually increasing values of S are input until a turning point is passed, when the approximate value of S for the turning point is input, followed by a zero S to terminate the search, except where this is to be the last search with the current B value, when S = 99 is input. Then to terminate the program S = 99 and B = 99 are input.

Note that by omitting line 65 the first steepest descent results of Table 6.2 are obtained. Note also that a subroutine to compute the exact gradients is included.

Conclusion

Solutions for any given nonlinear optimization problem are not guaranteed by any particular numerical technique.

Such procedures as steepest descent, however, are very simple and very widely applicable. They can be attached to finite element programs, for example, to optimize finite element models of a wide variety of physical problems.

6.6. References

Bersekas DP, *Constrained Optimization and Lagrange Multiplier Methods*, Academic Press, New York, 1982.

Box Mj, Davies D, Swann WH, *Nonlinear Optimization Techniques*, ICI Monograph No. 5, Oliver & Boyd, Edinburgh, 1969.

Bracken J, McCormick GP, *Selected Applications of Nonlinear Programming*, Wiley, New York, 1968.

Budnick FS, Mojena R, Vollmann TE, *Principles of Operations Research for Management*, Irwin, Homewood IL, 1977.

Fiacco AV, McCormick GP, The sequential unconstrained minimization technique for nonlinear programming, *Management Science*, 10 (1964) 360-372.

Hillier FS, Lieberman GJ, *Introduction to Operations Research*, 3rd edn, Holden Day, Oakland CA, 1980.

Mohr GA, *Finite Elements for Solids, Fluids, and Optimization*, OUP, Oxford, 1992.

Mohr GA, Optimization of critical path models using finite elements, *Australian Civil Engineering Transactions*, CE36 (1994) 123-126.

Mohr GA, Finite element optimization of structures, part I (solids problems), *Computers & Structures* 53 (1994) 1217-1220.

Mohr GA, Finite element optimization of structures part II (fluids problems), *Computers & Structures* 53 (1994) 1221 - 1224.

Mohr GA, Approximate nonlinear optimization of numerical models, *Int. J. Arts & Sciences* 2 (2001) 14-22.

Mohr GA, Optimization and finite element modeling of input-output analysis problems, *Int. J. Arts & Sciences* 2 (2001) 23-29.

Mohr GA, A predictor-corrector method for constrained nonlinear optimization, *Int. J Arts & Sciences* 2 (2001) 38-48.

Whittle P, *Optimization under Constraints*, Wiley, London, 1971.

Chapter 7

FINITE ELEMENT DISTRIBUTION MODELS

The finite element method is applied to distribution problems in the same way as for DC networks in Chapter 4, resulting in useful models for such networks. Then the steepest descent method is applied to optimize these finite element models, using it to adjust the values of *element access* parameters A_i. At the beginning of each search these are set equal to the element route costs and when during search an element with a negative flow is encountered it is eliminated and a new gradient vector for search is calculated and employed.

7.1. Finite element distribution models

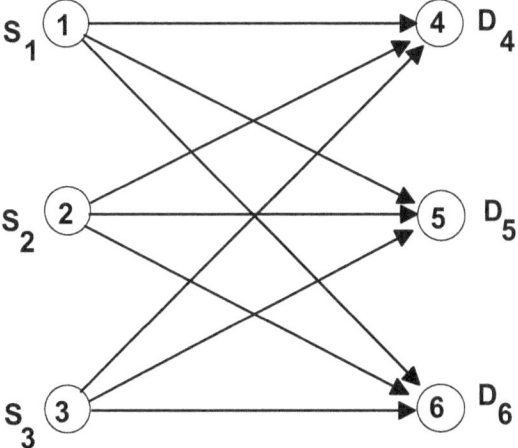

Figure 7.1. Distribution network.

Figure 7.1 shows a distribution network for which the data is given in Table 7.1.

7. FINITE ELEMENT DISTRIBUTION MODELS

Table 7.1. Distribution problem data.

Unit costs			Supplies
5	10	10	110 [1]
20	30	20	160 [2]
10	20	30	150 [3]
140 [4]	200 [5]	80 [6]	
Demands			

Using the program given at the close of Chapter 5 the optimum solution (giving minimum total transportation cost, $T = 6700$) has route flows:

$$15 = 110, \quad 25 = 80, \quad 26 = 80, \quad 34 = 140, \quad 35 = 10 \tag{7.1}$$

and the number of non zero route flows = (# supply points + # demand points) -1, as is always the case in this type of problem.

Writing this solution in matrix form as

$$A\{q\} = \begin{bmatrix} 1 & 0 & 0 & 0 & 0 \\ 0 & 1 & 1 & 0 & 0 \\ 0 & 0 & 0 & 1 & 1 \\ 0 & 0 & 0 & 1 & 0 \\ 1 & 1 & 0 & 0 & 1 \\ 0 & 0 & 1 & 0 & 0 \end{bmatrix} \begin{Bmatrix} q_{15} \\ q_{25} \\ q_{26} \\ q_{34} \\ q_{35} \end{Bmatrix} = \begin{Bmatrix} 110 \\ 160 \\ 150 \\ 140 \\ 200 \\ 80 \end{Bmatrix} \tag{7.2}$$

each route flow can be expressed, using *Mohr's First Law of Distribution*, as a function of the 'potentials' V_i, V_j at each node,

$$q_{ij} = (V_i - V_j)/c_{ij} \tag{7.3}$$

Taking all $c_{ij} = 1$, we can write the *basis transformation*

$$\{q\} = \begin{Bmatrix} q_{15} \\ q_{25} \\ q_{26} \\ q_{34} \\ q_{35} \end{Bmatrix} = \begin{bmatrix} 1 & 0 & 0 & 0 & -1 & 0 \\ 0 & 1 & 0 & 0 & -1 & 0 \\ 0 & 1 & 0 & 0 & 0 & -1 \\ 0 & 0 & 1 & -1 & 0 & 0 \\ 0 & 0 & 1 & 0 & -1 & 0 \end{bmatrix} \begin{Bmatrix} V_1 \\ V_2 \\ V_3 \\ V_4 \\ V_5 \\ V_6 \end{Bmatrix} = T\{v\} \tag{7.4}$$

7. FINITE ELEMENT DISTRIBUTION MODELS

Substituting Equation 7.4 into Equation 7.2, first reversing the signs of the bottom three rows of A (note that now $A = T^t$), we obtain

$$K\{V\} = AT\{V\} = \begin{bmatrix} 1 & 0 & 0 & 0 & -1 & 0 \\ 0 & 2 & 0 & 0 & -1 & -1 \\ 0 & 0 & 2 & -1 & -1 & 0 \\ 0 & 0 & -1 & 1 & 0 & 0 \\ -1 & -1 & -1 & 0 & 3 & 0 \\ 0 & -1 & 0 & 0 & 0 & 1 \end{bmatrix} \begin{Bmatrix} V_1 \\ V_2 \\ V_3 \\ V_4 \\ V_5 \\ V_6 \end{Bmatrix} = \begin{Bmatrix} 110 \\ 160 \\ 150 \\ -140 \\ -200 \\ -80 \end{Bmatrix} = \{Q\}$$

(7.5)

which is exactly the same result (for K) as is obtained by summing element matrices of the form

$$k_{ij} = (1/c_{ij}) \begin{bmatrix} 1 & -1 \\ -1 & 1 \end{bmatrix} \qquad (7.6)$$

(with all c_{ij} =1) for the optimum network (i.e. with only the five flows of Equation 7.1).

So it transpires that we can use the program given for DC networks in Chapter 4 to model distribution problems, in other words in exactly the same way as for DC networks by replacing resistance (R) by route unit cost c_{ij}. Then the 'loads' are the nodal supplies and demands (with inflow taken as positive), specified as such for each node, and the boundary condition is simply $V = 0$ at the last node (6 here) as a datum for V.

Modeling the optimum network (5 routes) it is found that the routes can now have any unit costs and the flows remain the same. If all $c_{ij} = 10$ the nodal potentials are

$V_1 = 300$, $V_2 = 1600$, $V_3 = -600$, $V_4 = -2000$, $V_5 = -800$, $V_6 = 0$ (7.7)

(the latter being the boundary condition) and the 'reaction' at node 6 = -80, as expected. That we can have any costs here corresponds to a *statically determinate structure* in structural mechanics. Here we shall call it a *minimum system*.

If all 9 original routes (with the costs of Table 7.1) are included, however, the solution is that shown in Table 7.2, with total cost $T = 7313$.

7. Finite Element Distribution Models

Table 7.2. Flow in FEM distribution model

	4	5	6
1	23.4	77.9	8.7
2	52.3	56.9	50.8
3	64.3	65.2	20.5

We now have a very useful means of modeling distribution problems, and using the steepest descent method they can then be optimized, as shown in the following section.

Indeed the FEM model can be used to obtain 'better than optimal' solutions. In Figure 7.1 using only the routes of Equation 7.1 and increasing supply at node 1 by 20 units, we obtain route flows

$$14 = 130, \ 25 = 60, \ 26 = 100, \ 34 = 140, \ 35 = 10$$

and total cost T is still = 6700, a more efficient result.

Note that the here the boundary flow at node 6 increases to 100 to take this supply increase. Alternatively, if we specify demand of 160 at node 4, the solution has a 'back flow' and is

$$14 = 130, \ 25 = 80, \ 26 = 80, \ 34 = 160, \ 35 = -10$$

Conclusion

We have here an important but simple new application of the powerful finite element method. Chapter 8 provides a further and similar example, that is, application to traffic flow networks.

7.2. Optimizing FEM distribution models

The FEM distribution models developed in Section 7.1 can be optimized using the method of steepest descent. The merit function is the sum of the route 'cost flows':

$$f = T = \Sigma \ c_{ij} q_{ij} \tag{7.8}$$

Defining an *element access* parameter A_{ij}, with initially $A_{ij}^0 = c_{ij}$ at the beginning of each search, using perturbations of each A_{ij}^0 the gradient vector is given by

$$\{g_{ij}\} = \{\delta f / \delta A_{ij}\} \tag{7.9}$$

where $\delta A_{ij} = (M - 1) A_{ij}$

with M a move limit for which the value 1.1 is used for the present application, solving the equations $K\{V\} = \{Q\}$ at each perturbation to determine δf.

7. FINITE ELEMENT DISTRIBUTION MODELS

Then trial search is conducted with a gradually increasing *search length S*, using

$$A_{ij}' = A_{ij}^0 - S\{g\} \qquad (7.10)$$

seeking a turning point in *f*.

If during search a negative route flow is detected we set $c_{ij} = A_{ij} = 0$ for that route and omit it from the model, also setting a flag which returns to calculation of a new gradient vector, the model having changed. Note that such element omission is disallowed during calculation of the gradient vector using Equation 7.9.

Dual models and maximization

Now, quite remarkably, our simple model permits two immediate variations:

1. Simply by using a positive sign in Equation 7.10 we can obtain maximum solutions.
2. Simply by using c_{ij} in place of $(1/c_{ij})$ as the constitutive parameter for the element matrices we obtain the *dual model*.

Now we can obtain both MIN and MAX solutions for FEM (primal) distribution models and for dual distribution models as well.

Then for the analysis of the dual model (that is with c_{ij} in place of $1/c_{ij}$) we obtain the route flows shown in Table 7.3, these having a total cost *T = 7930*.

Table 7.3. Route flows in dual FEM distribution model.

	4	5	6
1	29.3	51	29.7
2	68..7	80.3	11
3	42	68.7	39.3

In place of the nodal voltage values we have 'nodal currents' (i.e. dual variables of the 'voltage/resistance' type). The values for the dual of the optimum primal network corresponding to Equations 7.1 are

$$\{C^*\} = \{12.333, 4, 1.833, -12.167, 1.333, 0\} \qquad (7.11)$$

for which the route flows are calculated using Equation 7.3 with c_{ij} replaced by its inverse, giving the expected values of Equation 7.1.

7. Finite Element Distribution Models

Thus the nodal current values at nodes 2 and 5 are given by

$$C^*_2 = C^*_6 + q_{26}/c_{26} \tag{7.12}$$
$$C^*_3 = C^*_2 - q_{25}/c_{25} \tag{7.13}$$

and so on.

The four possible optimum results for the problem of Figure 7.1 are summarized in Table 7.4. Note that some flows are midway between the two possible 'exact' MIN and MAX solutions possessed by this problem shown in the table, these having been obtained using the direct LP method program given in Section 5.9. As noted in Section 5.2, this is because the optimum solution lies on one side of the simplex, not at a node.

Table 7.4. Solutions for primal and dual problem of Fig. 7.1.

Primal MIN					
S*	0	0.4	0.7	0.7	
T	7,313	7198	6981	6700	
flows	0, 110, 0 / 45, 35, 80 / 95, 55, 0				
Exact (1)	0, 110, 0 / 0, 80, 80 / 140, 10, 0				
Dual MIN					
S*	0	0.3	0.9	0.6	
T	7930	7792	7226	6700	
flows	0, 110, 0 / 69.3, 10.7, 80/ 70.7, 79.3, 0				
Exact (2)	0, 110, 0 / 80, 0, 80 / 60, 90, 0				
Primal MAX					
S*	0	2.0	2.7	1.9	1.6
T	7317	7335	7770	7570	8850
flows	110, 0, 0 / 0, 160, 0 / 30, 40, 80				
Exact (1)	110, 0, 0 / 30, 130, 0 / 0, 70, 80				
Dual MAX					
S*	0	0.4	0.7	1.1	
T	7930	8112	8495	8850	
flows	110, 0, 0/ 27.1, 132.9, 0/2.9, 67.1, 80				
Exact (2)	110, 0, 0 / 0, 160, 0 / 30, 40, 80				

7. Finite Element Distribution Models

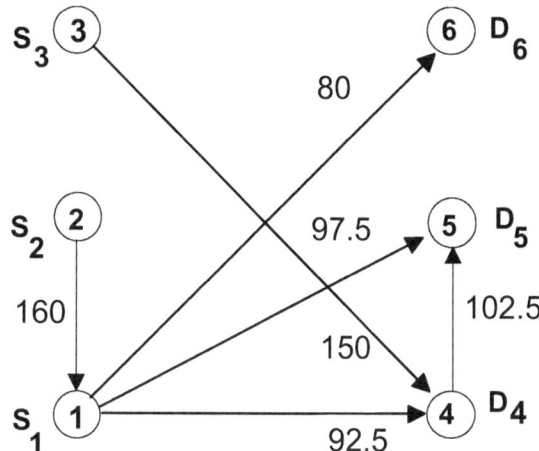

Figure 7.2. Solution for modified network.

As already noted, use of FEM, of course, allows much more general models to be studied. If in Figure 7.1, for example, additional (one-way) routes 12, 21, 23, 32, 45, 54, 56, 65 are included with unit cost of 5, the resulting minimum solution is shown in Figure 7.2.

Here points 1 and 4 have become transfer points to avoid the more costly direct routes from node 2. The total cost is reduced to 5050 (from 6700), an excellent example of the use of FEM models to obtain alternative solutions.

The search lengths used to obtain this result were

$S^* = 0, 0.15, 0.20, 0.30, 0.30, 0.30, 0.80, 0.01$

and, 'overstepping' with 0.30 (rather than 0.20) in the third search, the search lengths are

$S^* = 0, 0.15, 0.30, 0.30, 0.80, 0.01$

and again the total cost is only 5050 and the network is simplified with the changes $q_{15} = 0$, $q_{14} = 190$ and $q_{45} = 200$.

This is a reminder of the 'cross-cross' behaviour of steepest descent searches, the reason that improved methods such as *conjugate gradient* methods have been devised and the predictor-corrector method described in Section 6.3 is another way of overcoming the problem.

7. Finite Element Distribution Models

7.3. Program for optimization of FEM distribution models

The exact solutions of Table 7.4 were obtained using the following program. This is an extension of the program given in Chapter 4 for DC networks and data input is the same as for this.

Search (line 115) is conducted by simply using gradually increasing trial search lengths. When an element is omitted (for having negative flow) this is signaled by an additional output line (giving the value of T) and we know to begin a new search. When no more members can be omitted, that is we have a *minimum system,* the solution will not change with further search.

Key program variables are:

NP,NE,NS	number of nodes, elements and boundary conditions nodes
M	perturbation magnitude for gradient calculation (= 1.1 in line 10)
RC( )	element unit costs
RA( )	element 'access' parameters = unit costs at beginning of search
C( )	system matrix
Q( )	nodal 'loads'
V( )	nodal 'potentials' (after solution)
IB( )	boundary condition flags =1 for boundary condition node
NN( )	element node numbers
SPEC( )	specified potential values for boundary condition nodes (here = 0 for last node)
G( )	gradient values for each element (determined by steepest descent)
TC	total cost for the network flows

```
5 REM FEM model of distribution networks
10 M = 1.1: Y = .1: REM Lines 115, 152 & 352 are 'case change' lines
15 DIM C(20, 20), V(20), IB(20)
20 DIM RC(20), NN(20, 2), RA(20), SPEC(20), Q(20), G(20)
25 RESTORE 500
30 READ NP, NE, NS
35 FOR k = 1 TO NE
40 READ i, j, R: RC(k) = R: RA(k) = R
45 NN(k, 1) = i: NN(k, 2) = j: NEXT
50 FOR i = 1 TO NS: READ N, s: SPEC(N) = s: IB(N) = 1: NEXT
55 READ NQ, F: IF NQ = 0 THEN GOTO 65
60 Q(NQ) = F: GOTO 55
65 S1 = 0: FOR i = 1 TO NE: RA(i) = RC(i): NEXT: FLAG = 0: GF = 1: s = 0
70 cflag = 1: GOTO 135
72 F1 = TC: PRINT TC: Z = 0
75 Z = Z + 1: IF Z > NE THEN GOTO 102
77 IF RA(Z) = 0 THEN GOTO 100
80 RA(Z) = RA(Z) * M: cflag = 2: GOTO 135
82 RA(Z) = RA(Z) / M
85 REM If M <> 1 Then GoTo 90
```

7. Finite Element Distribution Models

```
87 REM G(z) = 0: GoTo 100
90 G(Z) = (TC - F1) / ((M - 1) * RA(Z))
95 REM
100 GOTO 75
102 GF = 0
105 PRINT "I/P S": INPUT s: IF s = 99 THEN GOTO 295
107 PRINT "S = "; s; " ";
110 FOR i = 1 TO NE: IF RA(i) = 0 THEN GOTO 125
115 RA(i) = RA(i) + (S1 - s) * G(i): REM + for min, - for max
125 NEXT
130 cflag = 3: GOTO 135
132 S1 = s: F1 = TC: IF FLAG = 1 THEN GOTO 65
133 GOTO 105
135 FOR i = 1 TO NP: V(i) = 0: FOR j = 1 TO NP: C(i, j) = 0: NEXT: NEXT
140 FOR k = 1 TO NE
145 R = RA(k): i = NN(k, 1): j = NN(k, 2)
150 IF R = 0 THEN GOTO 175
152 R = R / 1: REM r/1 for primal
155 C(i, i) = C(i, i) + 1 / R
160 C(i, j) = C(i, j) - 1 / R
165 C(j, i) = C(j, i) - 1 / R
170 C(j, j) = C(j, j) + 1 / R
175 NEXT
180 FOR k = 1 TO NP: IF IB(k) <> 1 THEN GOTO 215
185 F = SPEC(k)
190 FOR i = 1 TO NP
195 IF IB(i) = 1 THEN GOTO 205
200 V(i) = V(i) - F * C(i, N)
205 NEXT i
210 V(N) = F
215 NEXT
220 FOR i = 1 TO NP: V(i) = V(i) + Q(i): NEXT
225 FOR i = 1 TO NP
230 IF IB(i) = 1 THEN GOTO 285
235 X = C(i, i): IF X = 0 THEN X = 10 ^ -6
237 V(i) = V(i) / X
240 FOR j = i + 1 TO NP
245 C(i, j) = C(i, j) / X: NEXT
250 FOR k = 1 TO NP
255 IF IB(k) = 1 THEN GOTO 280
260 IF k = i THEN GOTO 280
265 X = C(k, i): V(k) = V(k) - X * V(i)
270 FOR j = i + 1 TO NP
275 C(k, j) = C(k, j) - X * C(i, j): NEXT j
280 NEXT k
285 NEXT i
290 GOTO 345
295 PRINT "Node    Potential"
300 FOR i = 1 TO NP
305 PRINT i, V(i): NEXT i
```

```
310 PRINT "Flows"
315 FOR i = 1 TO NP
320 IF IB(i) <> 1 THEN GOTO 340
325 F = 0: FOR k = 1 TO NP
330 F = F + C(i, k) * V(k): NEXT
335 PRINT i, F
340 NEXT i
345 TC = 0: TQ = 0
350 FOR k = 1 TO NE: R = RC(k): F = 0: A = RA(k): IF A = 0 THEN GOTO 370
352 A = A / 1: REM a/1 for primal
355 i = NN(k, 1): j = NN(k, 2): F = (V(i) - V(j)) / A
360 IF GF = 1 THEN GOTO 370
365 IF F >= 0 THEN GOTO 370
367 RA(k) = 0: RC(k) = 0: FLAG = 1
370 IF s <> 99 THEN GOTO 374
372 PRINT NN(k, 1), NN(k, 2), " route flow = ", F: GOTO 375
374 IF s <> 0 THEN PRINT CINT(F * 100) / 100;
375 TC = TC + F * R: TQ = TQ + F: NEXT
380 IF s = 0 THEN GOTO 385
382 PRINT " TC = "; TC; " TQ = "; TQ
385 IF FLAG = 1 THEN GOTO 65
386 IF s = 99 THEN GOTO 400
387 IF cflag = 1 THEN GOTO 72
388 IF cflag = 2 THEN GOTO 82
399 IF cflag = 3 THEN GOTO 132
400 END
500 DATA 6,9,1
505 DATA 1,4,5
510 DATA 1,5,10
515 DATA 1,6,10
520 DATA 2,4,20
525 DATA 2,5,30
530 DATA 2,6,20
535 DATA 3,4,10
540 DATA 3,5,20
545 DATA 3,6,30
550 DATA 6,0
555 DATA 1,110
560 DATA 2,160
565 DATA 3,150
570 DATA 4,-140
575 DATA 5,-200
580 DATA 0,0
```

The data appended is for the problem of Figure 7.1, for which the solution shown in Table 7.1 can be obtained with the searches used in Table 7.4.

7. Finite Element Distribution Models

Note that these S^* are the optimum search lengths which were determined by trial with a gradually increasing S until a member is eliminated. Use of excessively large S will abort the process so a certain amount of trial is required.

When a very small initial search length of circa 0.0001 produces little change in the objective function, and any larger search length produces an unchanged solution, then the solution has converged. Then the program is terminated by input of a search length of 99, when the final results for the route flows and other data is output.

An alternative method of seeking approximate optimum FEM distribution models iteratively is given in Chapter 9 where the results for other FEM distribution models using both the steepest descent and iterative methods are also given.

7.4. Inventory problems modeled as distribution problems

These are distribution problems where the S & D points are periods of time: ACME Co. makes a chemical for which demand is seasonal and production follows this approximately. The sales forecast is: 1st quarter 60,000 mg; 2nd quarter 97,000 mg; 3rd quarter 118,000 mg; 4th quarter 95,000 mg [total = 370,000].

Production scheduled is: 51,000, 80,000, 119,000 and 100,000 for the respective quarters [total = 350,000 so that 20,000 mg must be bought from outside at $70 per 1000 mg - but this price is falling at an estimated $1 per quarter].

Internal production cost is $50 per 1000 mg - to this is added $1 for storage for a quarter if kept for later sale and $2 for two quarters storage, when $10 is also needed for filtering and re-testing of the material. If kept for three quarters some reprocessing is required and cost, including storage, is $30 per 1000 mg.

If orders are held over for one quarter cost in administration and loss of customers is $5 (per 1000 mg), for two quarters this is $9 and $13 for three.

Thus the S & D Tableau is, with costs as $/1000 mg and sales/production in units of 1,000 mg:

Costs /1,000 mg	1st quarter	2nd quarter	3rd quarter	4th quarter	Production capacity (S)
1st quarter	50 [51]	51	62	80	51 (S1)
2nd quarter	55	50 [80]	51	62	80 (S2)
3rd quarter	59	55 [1]	50 [118]	51	119 (S3)
4th quarter	63	59 [5]	55	50 [95]	100 (S4)
Buy outside	70 [9]	69 [11]	68	67	20 (S5)
Sales forecast	60 (D1)	97 (D2)	118 (D3)	95 (D4)	Total: 370

7. Finite Element Distribution Models

Note that we would expect to buy outside in the fourth quarter when that is cheapest but that is not the optimum solution. Interpretation of the solution is also a little confusing - essentially flows above the diagonal in the table are 'holds' and those below are 'delay in filling order.'

```
600 DATA 8,20
610 DATA 1,1,1,1,0,0,0,0,0,0,0,0,0,0,0,0,0,0,0,0,51
620 DATA 0,0,0,0,1,1,1,1,0,0,0,0,0,0,0,0,0,0,0,0,80
630 DATA 0,0,0,0,0,0,0,0,1,1,1,1,0,0,0,0,0,0,0,0,119
640 DATA 0,0,0,0,0,0,0,0,0,0,0,0,1,1,1,1,0,0,0,0,100
650 DATA 0,0,0,0,0,0,0,0,0,0,0,0,0,0,0,0,1,1,1,1,20
660 DATA 1,0,0,0,1,0,0,0,1,0,0,0,1,0,0,0,1,0,0,0,60
670 DATA 0,1,0,0,0,1,0,0,0,1,0,0,0,1,0,0,0,1,0,0,97
680 DATA 0,0,1,0,0,0,1,0,0,0,1,0,0,0,1,0,0,0,1,0,118
685 REM Data 0,0,0,1,0,0,0,1,0,0,0,1,0,0,0,1,0,0,0,1,95
690 DATA 50,51,62,80,55,50,51,62,59,55,50,51,63,59,55,50,70,69,68,67,0
```

The data required for the program of Section 5.9 is as shown above. Note that for the minimum solution line 140 alters to '140 IF I=0 THEN 280'.

The solutions are shown in [ ] in the table, giving a total revenue of $18,939 (x1000).

As with the problem of Figure 7.1, the problem can be modelled as a finite element one, the immediate advantage being the system modeling that this allows, and thence study of changes to the system, before optimization of the system is even considered.

7.5. References

Battersby, A, *Mathematics in Management*, Penguin, Harmondsworth UK, 1966.

Budnick FS, Mojena R, Vollmann TE, *Principles of Operations Research for Management*, Irwin, Homewood IL, 1977.

Mohr GA, Milner HR, *A Microcomputer Introduction to the Finite Element Method*, Pitman, Melbourne, 1986; Heinemann, London, 1987.

Mohr, GA, Finite element modeling of distribution problems, *Applied Mathematics & Computation* 105 (1999) 69-76.

Mohr, GA, Optimization of primal and dual network models of distribution, *Computer Methods in Applied Mechanics & Engineering* 188 (2000) 135-144.

Chapter 8

FINITE ELEMENT TRAFFIC FLOW MODELS

The finite element method is applied to traffic flow networks in the much the same way as for distribution networks in Chapter 7, resulting in useful models for such networks. Again the steepest descent method is applied to *element access* parameters A_i, these being set equal to the element route parameters at the beginning of each search. When during search an element with a negative flow is encountered it is eliminated and a new gradient vector for search is calculated and employed for further search.

8.1. Finite element traffic flow models

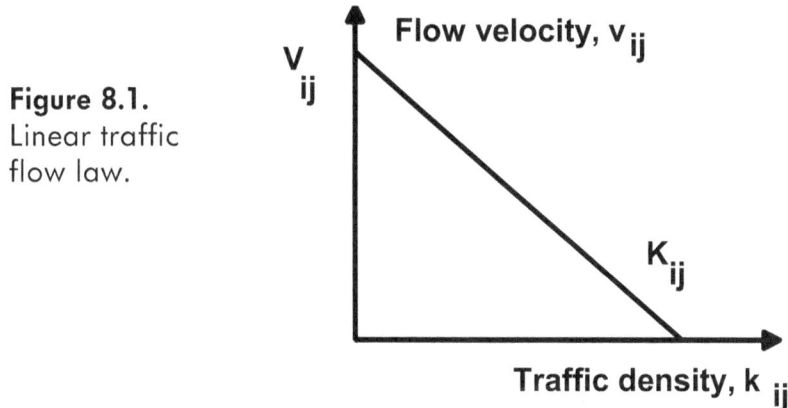

Figure 8.1. Linear traffic flow law.

The classical linear flow rule for traffic flow illustrated in Figure 8.1 is

$$v_{ij} = V_{ij}(1 - k_{ij}/K_{ij}) \tag{8.1}$$

where v_{ij} and k_{ij} are the element traffic velocity and density and V_{ij} and K_{ij} are respectively the element free flow velocity and jam density.

8. Finite Element Traffic Flow Models

The flow in the element is given by $q_{ij} = k_{ij}v_{ij}$, so that the equations for each element are:

$$\begin{Bmatrix} q_i \\ q_j \end{Bmatrix} = (K_{ij}V_{ij}/L_{ij}) \begin{bmatrix} 1 & -1 \\ -1 & 1 \end{bmatrix} \begin{Bmatrix} P_i \\ P_j \end{Bmatrix} \qquad (8.2)$$

where q_i, q_j are the inflows at each end, L_{ij} is the route length and P_i, P_j are arbitrary potentials at the element nodes.

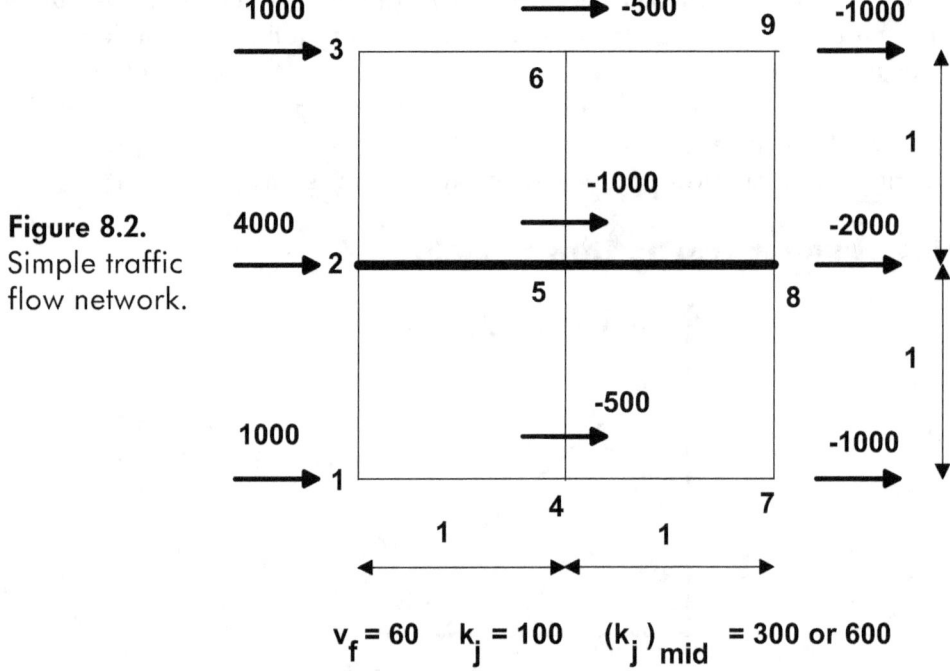

Figure 8.2. Simple traffic flow network.

$v_f = 60 \quad k_j = 100 \quad (k_j)_{mid} = 300 \text{ or } 600$

Thus the problem is analogous to that of a DC network, where now $L_{ij}/(K_{ij}V_{ij})$ plays the role of the element resistance, and to model a network the element matrices are deployed according to their node numbers to form a system matrix for the network.

Figure 8.2 shows a simple example network with the nodal flows shown, positive flows being inwards. The same free flow velocity $V_f = 60$ is assumed for all elements. A single boundary condition $P = 0$ is set at the last node as a datum and the in and out flows are the 'load' data.

8. FINITE ELEMENT TRAFFIC FLOW MODELS

The system equations are solved to determine the nodal potentials P_i from which the element flows are calculated using

$$q_{ij} = R_{ij}(P_i - P_j), \text{ where } R_{ij} = K_{ij}V_f/L_{ij} \tag{8.3}$$

Then solving the quadratic equation

$$q_{ij} = k_{ij}v_{ij} = k_{ij}V_f(1 - k_{ij}/K_j) \tag{8.4}$$

two roots k_a and k_b and their corresponding velocities v_a and v_b are obtained. In the present work the feasible root is the larger velocity v_b and using this the total travel time in the network is calculated as

$$T = \Sigma \mid q_{ij} \mid L_{ij}/ \mid v_b \mid \tag{8.5}$$

Table 8.1. Solutions for the route flows in Figure 8.2.

Route	(a) mid k_j = 300			(b) mid k_j = 600		
	flow	k_2	v_2	flow	k_2	v_2
12	-178.6	3.07	-58.16	60.4	1.02	59.39
23	178.6	3.07	58.16	-60.4	1.02	-59.39
14	1,178.6	26.85	43.89	939.6	19.44	48.34
45	-142.9	2.44	-58.54	-192.3	3.32	-58.01
36	1,178.6	26.85	43.89	939.6	19.44	48.34
56	142.9	2.44	58.54	192.3	3.32	58.01
25	3,642.9	84.54	43.09	4,120.9	79.11	52.09
58	2,357.1	46.49	50.7	2,736.3	49.73	55.03
47	821.5	16.37	50.18	631.9	11.96	52.82
69	821.5	16.37	50.18	631.9	11.96	52.82
78	-178.6	3.07	-58.16	-368.1	6.57	-56.06
89	178.6	3.07	58.16	368.1	6.57	-56.06
Total travel time	234.63 hours			213.44 hours		

The results are shown in Table 8.1. In case (b) we have upgraded the centre routes 25, 58 and the flow changes are as expected, the flows in these centre routes increasing and the total travel time in the system decreasing significantly.

8. FINITE ELEMENT TRAFFIC FLOW MODELS

8.2. Optimizing the network

To optimize such FEM models the method of steepest descent is used as in Chapter 7, first defining an 'element access' parameter A_{ij} and at the beginning of each search $A_{ij}^0 = K_{ij}V_f/L_{ij}$, again assuming the free flow velocity to be the same for all elements. The merit function is the total travel time of Equation 8.5. Using perturbations of each A_{ij}^0 in turn the gradient vector for search is given by:

$$\{q\} = \{\delta T / \delta A_{ij}\} \text{ where } \delta A_{ij} = (M - 1)A_{ij}^0 \qquad (8.6)$$

with M a move limit for which the value 1.1 is used in the present work.

Using this to search in the direction of steepest descent we write

$$\{A_{ij}^*\} = \{A_{ij}^0\} - S\{g\} \qquad (8.7)$$

using trial values of the step length S to locate a turning point in T.

If, during search, the magnitude of a route flow is less than a small value q_{min} then we set $A_{ij} = 0$ for that route and omit it from the model, also setting a flag which returns to calculation of a new gradient vector once the other route flows and thence T have been calculated. Note that such element omission is disallowed during calculation of the gradient vector.

Table 8.2. Steepest descent solution for optimum network in Fig. 8.2

Route	q_{ij}	K_{ij}	k_b	v_b
14	1000	100	21.132	47.321
36	1000	100	21.132	47.321
25	4000	600	76.393	52.36
58	3000	600	55.051	54.495
47	500	100	9.175	54.495
69	500	100	9.175	54.495
78	-500	100	9.175	-54.495
89	500	100	9.175	54.495

For the example of Figure 8.2, using $V_f = 60$ for all routes, $q_{min} = 10$ and successive searches $S = 0.9$, 200 and 0.00001, the resulting solution has only eight routes and is given in Table 8.2.

8. Finite Element Traffic Flow Models

The initial value of the total travel time was $T = 213.44$, and the final value is $T = 210.41$, a significant saving considering that four routes have also been omitted.

This result was verified using linear programming with simple 'split' constraints for each node. For node 1, for example, these are

$$-q_{12} + q_{13} + s_1 = 1000 \quad \text{and} \quad q_{12} - q_{13} + s_1 = -1000 \tag{8.8}$$

where s_1 is the first slack variable. The constraints for one node are omitted, as is customary for the distribution problem, because of the implicit constraint total inflows = total outflows. The same results are also obtained using the 'direct' LP method program given in Section 5.9.

8.3. Program for traffic flow network optimization

The following is a simple QBASIC program for FEM traffic flow models and their optimization. The data is for the problem of Figure 8.2. The first data line gives the number of nodes (NP), the number of elements (NE) and the number of boundary conditions (NS), here setting the potential at the last node to zero as a datum. Then lines of element data follow, giving the element node numbers, their jam densities and their route lengths (all = 1 here). Note that the free flow velocity is assumed to be the same value of 60 for all elements in line 22.

Next the boundary condition is set (at node 9). Then the nodal inflows are read, negative values being outflows, terminating this data by a 0,0 data line.

```
5 REM FEM model of traffic flow networks
10 M = 1.1: Y = .1: REM Lines 115, 150 & 350 are 'case change' lines
15 DIM C(20, 20), V(20), IB(20): A$ = "#####.#"
20 DIM RC(20), NN(20, 2), RA(20), SPEC(20), Q(20), G(20), EL(20), ER(20)
22 VF = 60
25 RESTORE 600
30 READ NP, NE, NS
35 FOR K = 1 TO NE
40 READ I, J, R, R1: ER(K) = R: EL(K) = R1
41 RR = ER(K) * VF / EL(K): RC(K) = RR: RA(K) = RR
45 NN(K, 1) = I: NN(K, 2) = J: NEXT
50 FOR I = 1 TO NS: READ N, S: SPEC(N) = S: IB(N) = 1: NEXT
55 READ NQ, F: IF NQ = 0 THEN 65
60 Q(NQ) = F: GOTO 55
65 S1 = 0: FOR I = 1 TO NE: RA(I) = RC(I): NEXT: FLAG = 0: GF = 1: S = 0
70 GOSUB 135: F1 = TC: PRINT TC
```

8. Finite Element Traffic Flow Models

```
75 FOR Z = 1 TO NE: IF RA(Z) = 0 THEN 100
80 RA(Z) = RA(Z) * M: GOSUB 135: RA(Z) = RA(Z) / M
90 G(Z) = (TC - F1) * RA(Z) * (M - 1)
100 NEXT: GF = 0
105 PRINT "IP S"; : INPUT S: IF S = 99 THEN 295
110 FOR I = 1 TO NE: IF RA(I) = 0 THEN 125
115 RA(I) = RA(I) + (S1 - S) * G(I): REM + for min, - for max
125 NEXT
130 GOSUB 135: S1 = S: F1 = TC: IF FLAG = 1 THEN 65
132 GOTO 105
135 FOR I = 1 TO NP: V(I) = 0: FOR J = 1 TO NP: C(I, J) = 0: NEXT: NEXT
140 FOR K = 1 TO NE
145 R = RA(K): I = NN(K, 1): J = NN(K, 2)
150 IF R = 0 THEN 175
155 C(I, I) = C(I, I) + R
160 C(I, J) = C(I, J) - R
165 C(J, I) = C(J, I) - R
170 C(J, J) = C(J, J) + R
175 NEXT
180 FOR K = 1 TO NP: IF IB(K) <> 1 THEN 215
185 F = SPEC(K)
190 FOR I = 1 TO NP
195 IF IB(I) = 1 THEN 205
200 V(I) = V(I) - F * C(I, N)
205 NEXT I
210 V(N) = F
215 NEXT
220 FOR I = 1 TO NP: V(I) = V(I) + Q(I): NEXT
225 FOR I = 1 TO NP
230 IF IB(I) = 1 THEN 285
235 X = C(I, I): IF X = 0 THEN X = 10 ^ -6
V(I) = V(I) / X
240 FOR J = I + 1 TO NP
245 C(I, J) = C(I, J) / X: NEXT
250 FOR K = 1 TO NP
255 IF IB(K) = 1 THEN 280
260 IF K = I THEN GOTO 280
265 X = C(K, I): V(K) = V(K) - X * V(I)
270 FOR J = I + 1 TO NP
275 C(K, J) = C(K, J) - X * C(I, J): NEXT J
280 NEXT K
285 NEXT I
290 GOTO 345
```

8. Finite Element Traffic Flow Models

```
295 PRINT "Node    Potential"
300 FOR I = 1 TO NP
305 PRINT I, V(I): NEXT I
310 PRINT "Flows"
315 FOR I = 1 TO NP
320 IF IB(I) <> 1 THEN 340
325 F = 0: FOR K = 1 TO NP
330 F = F + C(I, K) * V(K): NEXT
335 PRINT I, F
340 NEXT I
345 TC = 0: TQ = 0
350 FOR K = 1 TO NE: R = RC(K): F = 0: A = RA(K): IF A = 0 THEN 378
352 A = A / 1: REM a/1 for primal
355 I = NN(K, 1): J = NN(K, 2): F = (V(I) - V(J)) * A
360 IF GF = 1 THEN 371
365 IF ABS(F) >= 10 THEN 371
367 RA(K) = 0: RC(K) = 0: FLAG = 1: GOTO 378
371 B = -VF: A = VF / ER(K): D = SQR(B * B - 4 * A * ABS(F))
372 K1 = (-B + D) / (2 * A): K2 = (-B - D) / (2 * A): V1 = F / K1: V2 = F / K2
374 IF S <> 99 THEN 376
375 PRINT NN(K, 1); NN(K, 2); "flow = "; F; ER(K); K2; V2: GOTO 377
376 IF S <> 0 THEN PRINT USING A$; F;
377 TC = TC + ABS(F) * EL(K) / ABS(V2): TQ = TQ + F
378 NEXT
380 IF S = 0 THEN 385
PRINT "tc = "; TC; " tq = "; TQ
385 IF FLAG = 1 THEN 65
IF S = 99 THEN END
390 RETURN
600 DATA 9,12,1
610 DATA 1,2,100,1, 2,3,100,1, 1,4,100,1, 4,5,100,1, 3,6,100,1, 5,6,100,1
620 DATA 2,5,600,1, 5,8,600,1
630 DATA 4,7,100,1, 6,9,100,1, 7,8,100,1, 8,9,100,1
640 DATA 9,0
650 DATA 1,1000, 2,4000, 3,1000
660 DATA 4,-500, 5,-1000, 6,-500
670 DATA 7,-1000, 8,-2000
680 DATA 0,0
```

Running the program with a very small first step length (S) of 0.00001 and then terminating by inputting 99 when the next step length is requested (by the INPUT statement of line 105) will yield the results for case (b) in Table 8.1.

8. Finite Element Traffic Flow Models

Beginning again to seek an optimum, the step lengths

$$0.9,\ 200,\ 0.00001$$

give the optimum solution of Table 8.2. The first search concludes with $S = 0.9$ and two elements dropping out. Similarly for the second search and the final small step length (or any larger one) yields the final optimum solution.

Then 99 is input as a search length to conclude search and the final route flows and other results are output.

8.4. Alternative flow laws

There are many alternative flow laws to the classical linear law of Figure 8.1, for example the bilinear rule shown (without route number subscripts) in Figure 8.3.

Here v_p is a plateau speed dependent upon physical and legal constraints. For the rural traffic case shown $v_p = V$ and the traffic flow is given by

$$q = kv = (v/v_p)(Kv_p - vK + vk_p) \quad k \geq k_p \tag{8.9}$$

$$= (vKv_p - v^2K + av^2K)/v_p \quad k_p = aK\ (a < 1) \tag{8.10}$$

Differentiating with respect to v it is easily shown that the maximum flow is

$$Q_{max} = Kv_p/[4(1-\alpha)] \quad \text{with} \quad v = v_p/[2(1-\alpha)] \tag{8.11}$$

so that the peak flow is greater than that with the linear rule which is

$$q_{max} = KV/4,\ \text{when}\ v = V/2,\ k = K/2 \tag{8.12}$$

For the urban traffic case, taking $v_p = (1-\alpha)V$ in Equation 8.9 we obtain the same result for the flow rate as for the linear rule, namely

$$q = (v/V)(VK - vK) \tag{8.13}$$

8. Finite Element Traffic Flow Models

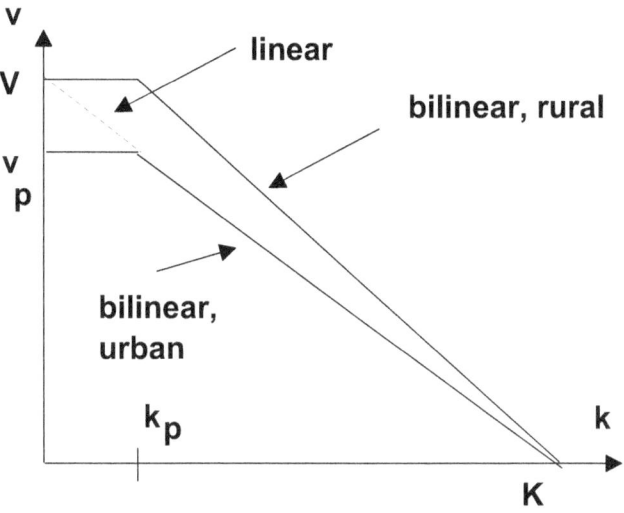

Figure 8.3. Bilinear traffic flow law

For the rural case, however, greater flow is predicted. More important, however, is that such rules can be used in conjunction with the FEM traffic flow models introduced here to study the effects of changes in speed limits in selected routes of a traffic network upon the flows in the entire network.

Conclusion

Traffic flow networks are easily modeled using the Finite Element Method, using the classical linear traffic flow rule to form the simple element matrices. Such models prove immediately useful in demonstrating the effects of changes to the network and can also be optimized using the same steepest descent procedure with initial element access parameters developed to optimize FEM distribution network models.

8.5. References

Mohr GA, Traffic flow theory, Caulfield Institute of Technology, exam paper VE63, 1978. Here question 2 involved assuming q_{ij} proportional to k_{ij}/L_{ij} and determining the flows in three parallel routes from this, almost the same as in Equation 8.3].

Mohr GA, A bilinear rule for macroscopic traffic flow, *Australian Road Research* 13 (1983) 38-40.

Mohr, GA, Finite element modeling of distribution problems, *Applied Mathematics & Computation* 105 (1999) 69-76.

Mohr, GA, Optimization of primal and dual network models of distribution, *Computer Methods in Applied Mechanics and Engineering* 188 (2000) 135-144.

Mohr, GA, Finite element modeling and optimization of traffic flow networks, *Transportmetrica,* vol. 1 (2005), pp 151-159.

Salter RJ, *Highway Traffic Analysis and Design*, MacMillan, London, 1976.

Chapter 9

FLOW RATIO DESIGN METHOD

Linear programming, despite the great attention paid to it in countless books on Operations Research/Management Science, can only deal with certain special and simple problems, such as 'mix' problems and distribution problems. Indeed it is not always possible to express the constraints explicitly as simultaneous equations, each involving more than one design variable. It is always possible to apply steepest descent in the manner used here for FEM distribution and traffic models to almost any mathematical model, but perturbation and resolution of the model to determine each entry in the gradient vector, along with resolution to reevaluate the merit function at each trial search step, is impractical in very large problems.

In this chapter the *Flow Ratio Design* (FRD) method of Mohr is applied to both FEM distribution and traffic flow models. This method is an *Optimality Criterion Method* (OCM) analogous to the *Fully Stressed Design* (FSD) method in structural mechanics in which components of 'statically indeterminate' structures are iteratively adjusted in size to satisfy stress limits. In FRD the 'cost' or 'resistance' of elements with higher than average flows is decreased, a very logical and desirable exercise in any system.

9.1. Optimality criterion methods

In *Optimality Criterion Methods* (OCM), analysis to determine the values of the variables of a mathematical model is iterated, adjusting chosen parameters of the model according to some *optimality criterion.* Generally such methods do not obtain an optimum solution in the mathematical sense but they do yield improved solutions which are often close to the optimum solution and, in some cases, may prove a more practical result.

Fully stressed design

In cost-benefit analysis the criterion of constant ratio of benefit r_i and cost c_i for all components i of a plan is well known.

Similar results apply elsewhere in mathematics, for example the pioneering paper by Michell (1904) in which it is shown that optimal building truss structures will have all their components equally stressed. The optimal solutions obtained by Michell involved structures consisting of orthogonal

9. FLOW RATIO DESIGN METHOD

sets of curves intersecting at right angles, but it has since been shown that with relaxed boundary conditions the solutions are trusses with straight members as generally used in practice.

Then in other types of structures this criterion is often used, this process being called *Fully Stressed Design* (FSD), and after each analysis of the structure to determine the member stresses the sizes of the members are adjusted according, for example, to the ratio

$$t_{i+1} = t_i(S_i/S^*) \qquad (9.1)$$

where t_i is the element thickness (the adjusted dimension) in the ith iteration, S_i its stress in this iteration and S^* is the upper stress limit. Then in many problems convergence to an approximately optimal solution is obtained after a few iterations.

This same approach is useful in many other contexts, but retaining the FSD case as an example, the steps are:

1. Establish an optimality criterion. In FSD this is that stress S = force/cross section area (for the example of a rod in tension or compression) should be approximately equal to some limiting value S^* for safety, in every part of the system.

2. Analyze the structure and determine the stress in every member.
Then: (a) where member stress > S^* increase the member cross section
       (b) where member stress < S^* decrease the member cross section

3. Continue repeating step (2) until member stresses are all approximately equal to S^* and/or the structure weight $W = \Sigma\, A_i L_i$ stops changing (converges), here denoting A_i = cross section areas of members and L_i = their length.

This approach is sometimes called the *stress ratio method* and with such methods of iterative solution many other slight refinements to help guide us towards a realistic and sensible solution can be included, such as the following:
   a)   *Move limits* which limit the changes in member areas (in the FSD example) allowed in any one step.
   b)   *Section limits* A_{min}, that is minimum and perhaps maximum allowed values of A.
   c)   *Convergence factors* which multiply the amount by which a member area is changed (compared to the value suggested by calculation).

9. FLOW RATIO DESIGN METHOD

Convergence factors

With some types of iterative numerical method an *over-convergence factor* greater than one is used. Common values range from 1.2 to 1.8, for example making the change in member area in FSD 1.5 times the amount suggested by its stress ratio *S/S** with a view to speeding up the solution.

In other rather more exceptional cases an *under convergence factor* less than one is used to prevent oscillation in the solution.

As an example consider the Gauss-Seidel iteration problem given in Section 3.3:

Solve: $2x_1 + x_2 = 7$
$x_1 + 2x_2 = 8$

For 'GSI' we rewrite these equations as $x_1 = (7 - x_2)/2$
$x_2 = (8 - x_1)/2$

and using a convergence factor = f a new value in x_1 is written as

$$x_1^* = x_1 + f(x_1' - x_1) = (1 - f)x_1 + fx_1'$$

where x_1^* = new value, x_1 = old value and x_i' = value calculated at this iteration using GSI.

Then using $f = 1.2$ we obtain the recurrence relations

$$x_1^* = -0.2x_1 + 0.6(7 - x_2)$$
$$x_2^* = -0.2x_2 + 0.6(8 - x_1)$$

and beginning with $x_1 = x_2 = 1$ we obtain the successive results

$x_1 = 3.4$ $x_2 = 2.56$
$x_1 = 1.984$ $x_2 = 3.0976$
$x_1 = 1.9446$ $x_2 = 3.0137$

giving a slightly faster convergence than without a convergence factor but from this point on we should put $f = 1$ (it is common procedure to gradually diminish a convergence factor as the solution proceeds).

In such a small example a slight improvement in convergence rate might not seem to matter much but in the case of large systems of simultaneous equations such as in finite element analysis of a substructure of an aircraft, for example, such slight improvements in solution efficiency are valuable.

9. FLOW RATIO DESIGN METHOD

Conclusion

Optimality criterion methods are a useful subset of the techniques used for (approximate) optimization. They are very easy to understand and can usually be added to an existing numerical model by looping it with adjustments based on comparison with the optimality criteria at the end of the loop.

In particular FSD is an example that is easy to visualize and understand and, indeed, the same analogy is useful in some other applications of optimality criterion (OCM) methods.

9.2. FRD for FEM distribution models

For distribution problems the element constitutive parameters are their unit costs and for minimization these are adjusted at each iteration using

$$c_{ij} = Rc_{ij} \text{ where } R = q_m/|q_{ij}|, \quad q_m \approx q_{av}/2, \quad q_{av} = \Sigma \ Q/N \quad (9.2)$$

where ΣQ is the total flow in the network of N routes and q_m is the 'median' flow. For maximization $c_{ij} = c_{ij}/R$ is used to adjust the element unit costs (iteratively).

Then to obtain the minimum solution lower and upper route cost limits

$$c_L = c_{av}/40 \rightarrow c_{av}/10, \quad c_U = 10^4 \text{ or } 10^6 \quad (9.3)$$

where $c_{av} = \Sigma \ c_{ij}/N$, are used.

For maximization the lower limit is chosen from 10 to 100% of the value used for minimization and the upper limit is chosen in the range $5*c_{av}$ to $100*c_{av}$, using the value 100 in the examples studied in the present work.

As noted in Chapter 7, c_{ij} is replaced by its inverse in Equation 9.2 in the dual problem.

Observing these limits iteration proceeds and some routes vanish as their c_{ij} values approach c_U, flows $q_{ij} < 0.001$ being set to zero prior to calculating the total distribution cost

$$T_0 = \Sigma |q_{ij}|(c_{ij})_0 \quad (9.4)$$

where $(c_{ij})_0$ are the initial unit costs for each route.

Note that the lower limit 0.001 for q_{ij} was used with 8 d.p. computation and a value of 0.01 gave the same results and might be needed with less accurate computation.

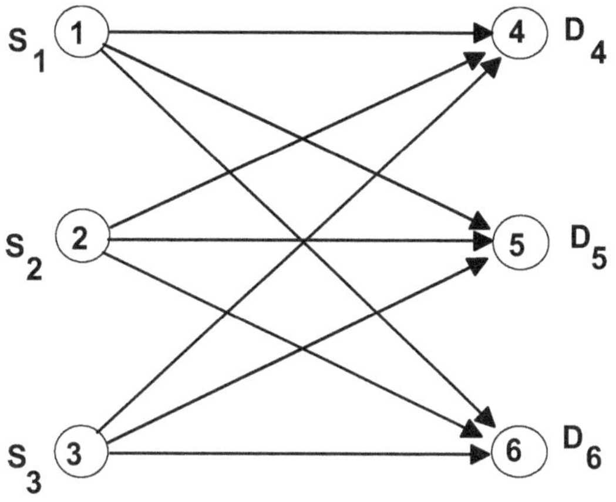

9. FLOW RATIO DESIGN METHOD

Figure 9.1. Distribution network

Table 9.1. Distribution problem data.

Unit costs			Supplies
5	10	10	110
20	30	20	160
10	20	30	150
140	200	80	
Demands			

Figure 9.1 shows an example distribution problem and Table 9.1 its data. Table 9.2 shows the route flows obtained using $q_m = 25$ compared to the exact LP solutions (columns 3 and 4).

Table 9.2. Results for the distribution problem of Figure 9.1.

Route	c_0	Min	Max	P_{min}	D_{max}	P_{max}	D_{min}
14	5	0	110	0	0.09	32.50	32.50
15	10	110	0	110	109.81	52.50	52.50
16	10	0	0	0	0.1	25.00	25.00
24	20	80/0	0/30	80	69.82	55.42	55.42
25	30	0/80	160/130	0	90.1	75.42	75.42
26	20	80	0	80	0.08	29.17	29.17
34	10	60/140	30/0	60	70.08	52.08	52.08
35	20	90/10	40/70	90	0.09	72.08	72.08
36	30	0	80	0	79.82	25.83	25.83
T_0		6700	8850	6700	8297.9	7629.2	7629.2
I				12	21	80	150

9. FLOW RATIO DESIGN METHOD

For minimization we have

$$c_{av} = 155/9 \approx 17 \text{ and we take } c_L = 1 \approx c_{av}/20 \qquad (9.5)$$

and $c_L =$ is in the middle of the range suggested in Equation 9.3.

Then after $I = 12$ iterations (of the primal FEM model) the exact minimum solution (P_{min} in Table 1) is obtained, the final element costs being $c_{ij} = c_L = 1$ for routes with non-zero flows and for the vanishing routes

$$c_{14} = c_{25} = c_{16} = c_{36} = 10^4 \qquad (9.6)$$

so that, indeed, in these $q_{ij} \simeq 0$.

For the dual minimum, D_{min} on the other hand, all the final $c_{ij} = c_L = 1$ except that $c_{16} \gg 1$ initially but $c_{16} \rightarrow c_L$ slowly with iteration (and $c_{16} \simeq 4$ when $I = 150$). Here an 'intermediate' solution with no zero flows is found, this being the saddle point between the primal and dual solutions.

For maximization the same q_m value is used and the cost limits are:

$$c_L = 0.1 \text{ (10\% the value for MIN)}, \quad c_U = 100 \qquad (9.7)$$

The dual maximum solution D_{max} is only a lower bound to the exact solution (column 4) and the final element costs are $c_{ij} = c_L$ for routes with $q_{ij} = 0$ and $c_{ij} = c_U$ for routes with 'non-zero' flows.

For the primal maximum P_{max} the saddle point solution is obtained again, here with all final element costs $c_{ij} = c_U$ except that $c_{16} \simeq 0$ initially but $c_{16} \rightarrow c_U$ slowly with iteration (and $c_{16} \simeq 25$ at $I = 80$).

Note that for this saddle point solution $T_0 =$ is here close to the average of the initial (at i = 1) primal and dual solutions after one iteration, that is

$$(P_1 + D_1)/2 = (7313.5 + 7929.6)/2 = 7621.6 \qquad (9.8)$$

Note also that use of a median value for q_m here was found by trial to provide satisfactory results, particularly in the case of the primal minimum problem which is that of usual interest. Doubtless improved results for the dual maximum can be obtained with alternative values for q_m (and perhaps c_U). Doubtless also, the 'dual' appearance of the saddle point solution is the result of use of this median value q_m, an intriguing result.

9. FLOW RATIO DESIGN METHOD

9.3. Distribution network with dummy routes

Table 9.3. Results for 4 x 5 problem

Route	c_0	Min	Max	P_{min}	D_{max}	P_{max}	D_{min}
15	1.5	0	0	30.5	0.00	16.50	16.50
16	6.4	0	35	0	34.99	14.31	14.33
17	1.8	70	25	45.5	21.68	24.94	24.94
18	4.0	0	30	0	11.67	14.31	14.33
19	3.5	20	0	14.0	21.67	19.94	19.91
25	1.6	40	0	9.5	0.00	13.50	13.50
26	2.6	35	0	35.0	0.00	11.31	11.33
27	1.9	0	25	24.5	28.34	21.94	21.94
28	3.1	0	0	6.0	18.33	11.31	11.33
29	5.8	0	50	0	28.33	16.94	16.9
35	5.3	0	35	0	34.98	5.00	5.01
36	3.5	0	0	0	0.01	5.00	5.02
37	2.4	0	0	0	0.01	12.50	12.5
38	1.3	30	0	24	0.00	5.00	5.02
39	2.2	5	0	11.0	0.01	7.50	7.46
45	50.0	0	5	0	5.02	5.00	5.00
46	50.0	0	0	0	0.00	4.38	4.39
47	50.0	0	20	0	19.98	10.62	10.62
48	50.0	0	0	0	0.00	-0.62	-0.61
49	50.0	25	0	25.0	0.00	5.62	5.58
T_0		1651	2162	1653.4	2095.8	1923.5	1920.9
I				10	12	70	40

Table 9.3 shows the route flows obtained using $q_m = 5$ for a 4 x 5 problem with supply flows (i = 1,2,3,4) of 90, 75, 35, 25 and demand flows (j = 5,6,7,8,9) of -40, -35, -70, -3-, -50. Here demand exceeds supply by 25 units and a dummy supply point 4 with route costs of 50 is introduced to model this situation.

Here for flow ratio minimization $c_L = 0.1 \simeq c_{av}/40$ was used and the result (column 5) is close to the exact solution.

For maximization $c_L = 10\%$ of the value for minimization is again used, and also for the other two problems in Table 9.4. The dual maximum is a lower bound and P_{max} and D_{min} are almost identical and their T_0 values are close to the average of the exact extremal solutions.

9. FLOW RATIO DESIGN METHOD

Note here the small negative flow for route 48 and in this route flow cycles between values of 0 and 1 in iteration to obtain the saddle point solution.

Note too that the initial solution for the dual of this problem results in several negative flows (and consequently $D_1 = 4630.4$) and that generally in other problems negative route flows may be introduced, sometimes temporarily, by flow ratio iteration, particularly if q_m is not close to $q_{av}/2$ when alternative solutions to those found here may be obtained.

Table 9.4. Summary of results for four distribution problems

Problem:	1 (3x3)	2 (3x4)	3 (3x4)	4 (4x5)
Exact:				
Min	6700	330	743	1651
Max	8850	760	1548	2162
Steepest descent:				
Min	6700	340	779	1651
Max	8850	760	1548	2160.5
FRD:				
Min	6700	340	798	1653.3
Max:	8298	680	1530	2095.8

Table 9.3 compares extremal total cost (T_0) solutions for the problems of Tables 9.1 and 9.3 and two other 3x4 problems obtained using the present flow ratio procedure with the exact solutions and those obtained using the steepest descent procedure with 'element access' parameters introduced in Chapters 7 and 8.

Overall the simple FRD approach gives good results. Generally we will require only the minimum (primal) solutions in practice and, as the FRD method used here shows, this occurs when all (non-zero) route flows have equal cost.

This is an important result, corresponding to the 'constant strain' character of (optimal) Michell structures.

A corresponding constant 'r/c' ratio result is widely used in cost-benefit analysis. The flow ratio approach used in the present work, therefore, emphasizes the wide applicability of such criteria.

9. FLOW RATIO DESIGN METHOD

9.4. Application of FRD to traffic flow problems

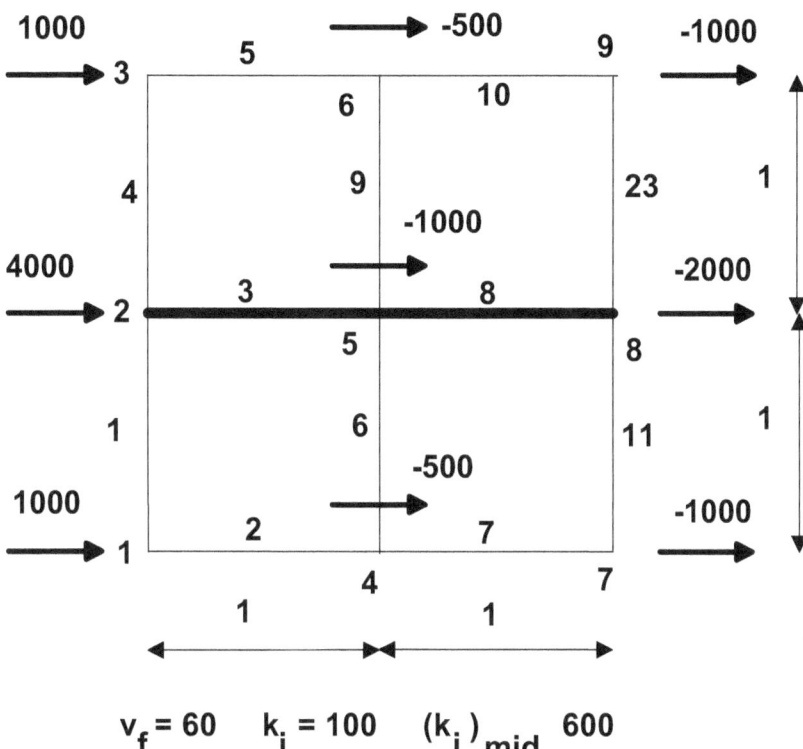

Figure 9.2. Traffic flow network example.

For traffic flow networks the constitutive parameter is $R_{ij} = K_{ij} V_{ij}/L_{ij}$.
Returning to the example problem of Figure 9.2, K_{ij} is variable and this is updated using:

$$K_{ij}^* = K_{ij}(|q_{ij}|/q_m) \qquad (9.9)$$

For this network the total flow is 6000 with 12 routes, giving $q_{av} = 500$ and this value is used for q_m. Then, using lower and upper limits $(K_{ij})_L = 100$, $(K_{ij})_U = 10000$ and omitting routes with $|q_{ij}| < q_{min} = 100$, the solution of Table 9.5 is obtained for the route flows after seven iterations.

The route flows are the same as in Table 8.2, but the densities and velocities differ, and thence the total travel time $T = 186.87$ is less than obtained using steepest descent because FRD allows the element jam densities to vary (as the only variable part of the element parameter R_{ij}). The values thus are close to or equal to the limiting values, an interesting but somewhat impractical solution.

9. Flow Ratio design Method

Table 9.5. FRD solution for the optimum network in Figure 1.

Route	q_{ij}	K_{ij}	k_b	v_b
14	1000	10000	16.595	59.900
36	1000	10000	16.595	59.900
25	4000	10000	67.117	59.597
58	3000	10000	50.253	59.698
47	500	143.72	8.882	56.292
69	500	143.72	8.882	56.292
78	-500	100	9.175	-54.495
89	500	100	9.175	54.495

Thus to obtain the results of Table 8.2 for the element densities and velocities they must be calculated using the original values of the route parameters R_{ij}, the flow values shown in Table 9.5 (the same as the flow values in Table 8.2) and Equation 8.4.

9.5. Program for FRD of distribution problems

The following working listing is for flow ratio optimization of FEM distribution models. Note that upper/lower case are mixed somewhat as the program was converted to QBASIC from MegaBasic, the latter using automatic assignation of upper and lower case according to context.

Key variables are:

NP,NE.NS.NQ	number of nodes, elements, boundary nodes, nodal loads
QM	the mean element flow parameter of Equation 9.2
RL, RU	the lower and upper route cost limits of Equation 9.3
NN( )	the element node numbers
RI( )	the initial element unit costs
ER( )	the element unit costs as they vary during iteration
C( )	the system matrix
Q( )	the nodal 'loads'
V( )	the nodal 'potentials' obtained after solution
IB( )	boundary condition flags = 1 for boundary condition nodes
SP( )	specified values at boundary condition nodes
F	element/route flow
TQ, TCI	system total flows and costs

9. Flow Ratio design Method

Lines 8 - 117 define and input data. Iterative solution commences at line 120, the system matrix being assembled in line 122 - 170 and specified boundary condition values and loads are introduced in lines 172 - 238.

Then solution for the nodal potentials V( ) is obtained in lines 240 - 340.

In lines 375 - 386 the boundary 'reaction' flows are calculated (here only that at the last node at which zero potential is always specified). In lines 391 - 398 the route flows F are calculated and for significant flows (> 0.001) their unit costs are adjusted according to Equation 9.2 in line 394.

In lines 394 and 395 route costs outside the limit values are set to these.

In line 399 any number is input to continue iteration and 99 is input to terminate iteration. For this problem the solution has converged after 12 iterations.

The listing is for minimization of the primal problem. For maximization set MINM = 2 in line 9 so that the element costs are factored in inverse fashion in line 394. For the dual problem set FPD = 2 in line 9 so that the element parameter is inverted in the statements following lines 125 and 392.

```
5 REM FEM model of distribution networks
7 RESTORE 600
8 QM = 25: RL = 1: RU = 10000
9 MINM = 1: FPD = 1: REM MINM =1/2 for Min/Max: FPD = 1/2 for primal/dual
IF MINM = 2 THEN RU = 100
IF MINM = 2 THEN RL = RL / 10
10 DIM C(20, 20), V(20), IB(20), NN(20, 2), ER(20), SP(20), Q(20), RI(20)
20 READ NP, NE, NS, NQ: ITN = 0
100 FOR K = 1 TO NE: READ I, J, R
110 NN(K, 1) = I: NN(K, 2) = J: ER(K) = R: RI(K) = R: NEXT
115 FOR K = 1 TO NS: READ N, S: IB(N) = 1: SP(N) = S: NEXT
117 FOR K = 1 TO NQ: READ Z, Q(Z): NEXT
120 FOR I = 1 TO NP: FOR J = 1 TO NP: C(I, J) = 0: NEXT: NEXT: ITN = ITN + 1
122 FOR K = 1 TO NE: I = NN(K, 1): J = NN(K, 2): R = ER(K)
125 IF R = 0 THEN 170
IF FPD = 2 THEN R = 1 / R
130 C(I, I) = C(I, I) + 1 / R
140 C(I, J) = C(I, J) - 1 / R
150 C(J, I) = C(J, I) - 1 / R
160 C(J, J) = C(J, J) + 1 / R
170 NEXT
172 FOR I = 1 TO NP: V(I) = 0: NEXT
180 FOR K = 1 TO NP
190 IF IB(K) <> 1 THEN 230: S = SP(K)
200 FOR I = 1 TO NP
205 IF IB(I) = 1 THEN 220
```

9. Flow Ratio design Method

```
210 V(I) = V(I) - S * C(I, K)
220 NEXT I
225 V(K) = S
230 NEXT
232 FOR K = 1 TO NP
235 IF IB(K) = 1 THEN 238
236 V(K) = V(K) + Q(K)
238 NEXT
240 FOR I = 1 TO NP
245 IF IB(I) = 1 THEN 340
250 X = C(I, I): V(I) = V(I) / X
260 FOR J = I + 1 TO NP
270 C(I, J) = C(I, J) / X: NEXT
280 FOR K = 1 TO NP
285 IF IB(K) = 1 THEN 330
290 IF K = I THEN GOTO 330
300 X = C(K, I): V(K) = V(K) - X * V(I)
310 FOR J = I + 1 TO NP
320 C(K, J) = C(K, J) - X * C(I, J): NEXT J
330 NEXT K
340 NEXT I
350 PRINT "Node    Potential"
360 FOR I = 1 TO NP
370 PRINT I, V(I): NEXT I
375 PRINT "Flows"
380 FOR I = 1 TO NP
381 IF IB(I) <> 1 THEN 386
382 Z = 0: FOR K = 1 TO NP
383 Z = Z + C(I, K) * V(K): NEXT
385 PRINT I, Z
386 NEXT I
391 TC = 0: TQ = 0: TCI = 0
392 FOR K = 1 TO NE: I = NN(K, 1): J = NN(K, 2): R = ER(K)
IF FPD = 2 THEN R = 1 / R
393 IF R = 0 THEN 396:
F = (V(J) - V(I)) / R: IF ABS(F) < .001 THEN F = 0
IF ABS(F) < .001 THEN GOTO 396
FRF = QM / ABS(F): IF MINM = 2 THEN FRF = 1 / FRF
394 ER(K) = ER(K) * FRF: IF ER(K) > RU THEN ER(K) = RU
395 IF ER(K) < RL THEN ER(K) = RL
396 PRINT I; J; " route flow = "; F, " r = "; ER(K)
397 TCI = TCI + ABS(F) * RI(K): TC = TC + ABS(F) * R: TQ = TQ + ABS(F): NEXT
398 PRINT "tc = "; TC; " tq = "; TQ; " tci ="; TCI; " itn ="; ITN
399 INPUT Z: IF Z = 99 THEN END
GOTO 120
```

9. FLOW RATIO DESIGN METHOD

```
600 DATA 6,9,1,5
610 DATA 1,4,5
620 DATA 1,5,10
630 DATA 1,6,10
640 DATA 2,4,20
650 DATA 2,5,30
660 DATA 2,6,20
670 DATA 3,4,10
680 DATA 3,5,20
690 DATA 3,6,30
700 DATA 6,0
710 DATA 1,110
720 DATA 2,160
730 DATA 3,150
740 DATA 4,-140
750 DATA 5,-200
760 DATA 0,0

800 DATA 9,20,1,8
805 DATA 1,5,1.5, 1,6,6.4, 1,7,1.8, 1,8,4, 1,9,3.5
830 DATA 2,5,1.6, 2,6,2.6, 2,7,1.9, 2,8,3.1, 2,9,5.8
855 DATA 3,5,5.3, 3,6,3.5, 3,7,2.4, 3,8,1.3, 3,9,2.2
880 DATA 4,5,50, 4,6,50, 4,7,50, 4,8,50, 4,9,50
905 DATA 9,0
910 DATA 1,90, 2,75, 3,35, 4,25
930 DATA 5,-40, 6,-35, 7,-70, 8,-30, 0,0
```

The data of lines 600 - 760 is for the problem of Figure 9.1 and the data in the remaining lines is for the problem of Table 9.3.

The program is run by keying F5. Results for the first iteration are printed and an input ?. Enter a 1 (or any other number) to continue iteration. When convergence has been obtained a 99 is input to terminate computation.

Conclusion

The FRD method is very easy to program, literally requiring only a few lines of code to be added to iterate the FEM solution routine, recalculating the element parameters according to the ratio of their flows to the median flow. In the primal problem, for example, this reduces the cost of routes with larger flows, clearly a desirable procedure.

The primal MIN problem is that of usual interest and in this 'feasible' elements in the final FRD have costs equal to the lower cost limit, unfeasible elements having costs close to or equal to the upper cost limit.

9. Flow Ratio design Method

A fascinating result is the near equality of the primal MAX and dual MIN solutions to what appears to be a saddle point solution and this is, at least, of theoretical interest.

Finally, note that the suggestions for values of the lower and upper cost limits:

MIN: c_L about $c_{av}/20$ and $c_U = 10{,}000$ or $1{,}000{,}000$
MAX: c_L 10% of MIN value and $c_U = 100$

are a general guide only based on problems such as those of Table 9.4.

9.6. References

Kaufman A, Faure R, *Introduction to Operations Research, Mathematics in Science and Engineering vol. 47*, Academic Press, New York, 1968.

Michell AGM, The limits of economy in frame structures, *Phil. Mag.* series 6, 8 (1904) 589-597.

Mohr GA, Elastic and plastic predictions of slab reinforcement requirements, *Civil Engrg Trans Instn Engrs Australia* CE21 (1979) 16-20.

Mohr GA, *Finite Elements for Solids, Fluids, and Optimization*, Oxford University Press, Oxford, 1992.

Mohr GA, Finite element modeling of distribution problems, *Applied Mathematics & Computation,* 105 (1999) 69-76.

Mohr GA, Optimization of primal and dual network models of distribution, *Computer Methods & Applied Mechanics in Engng* 188 (2000) 135-144.

Mohr GA, Finite element solutions for optimal triangular plates, *Int. J. Mechanical Sciences* 41 (1999), p 1289-1300.

Mohr GA, Finite element solutions for optimal square plates, *Int. J. Mechanical Sciences* 42 (2000), p 2337-2345.

Mohr GA, Flow ratio design of primal and dual network models of distribution, *Australian and New Zealand Institute of Applied Mathematics Journal*, vol. 45 (2004), 573 - 583.

Rozvany GIN, Gollub W, Michell layouts for various combinations of line supports, part 1, *Int. J. Mechanical Sciences* 32 (1990) 1021-1043.

Spillers WR, Al Banna S, Optimization using iterative design techniques, *Computers & Structures* 3 (1973) 1263-1270.

Chapter 10

CRITICAL PATH METHOD

The Critical Path Method (CPM) is one of the most widely used methods for scheduling the sequence of *activities* of a project. The system matrix is now a *precedence matrix,* column K of which stores the number and *earliest finish* time of each element ending at node K and this is used to determine the *critical path*, that is the longest route through the network of elements, this being the earliest finish time for the project.

10.1. The Critical Path Method

The principal objective of the critical path method is to ensure greater profitability in construction. To this end we are mainly concerned with the controllable elements of the project which are time dependent, in particular the use of labour or labour-related services. Other costs such as interest charges or material costs, on the other hand, we usually have no control over but accurate estimation of unit costs and quantities required is still, however, important.

Flow charts

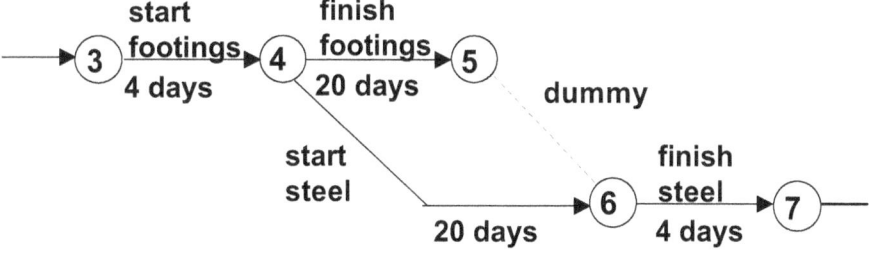

Figure 10.1. Flow chart using arrow notation.

Figure 10.1 shows part of a *flow chart* using classical 'arrow notation' (or *activity on* arrow) to show the way in which *activities* or *elements* of a project are connected. For each element a duration is shown and the footings element has been split into two parts to provide a more efficient schedule.

10. CRITICAL PATH METHOD

Element 56 is a *dummy element* which is needed to help enforce the proper sequence of work (and analysis using a computer program will not work without it as *node* 5 will be ignored in the backward pass of the program).

Figure 10.2. Precedence notation.

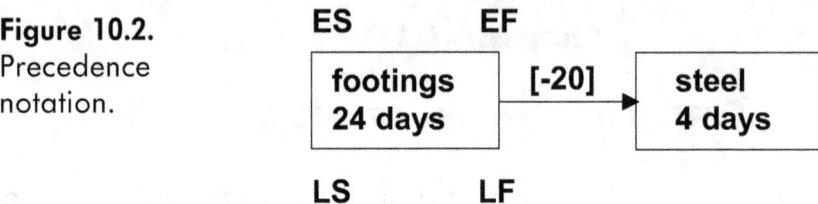

An alternative notation for flow charts is *precedence notation (activity on node)* and this is illustrated in Figure 10.2. Here a *lag factor* is used to more concisely describe the overlap in activities shown in Figure 10.1. In addition the earliest start and finish and latest start and finish times are sometimes shown on each element in the locations shown.

Precedence notation can be set up on a regular grid using standard preprinted sheets. The results are often much simpler and clearer and many fewer elements are used as a result of such artifices as lag factors as is seen by comparing Figures 10.1 and 10.2.

Figure 10.3. Precedence notation for multistorey building.

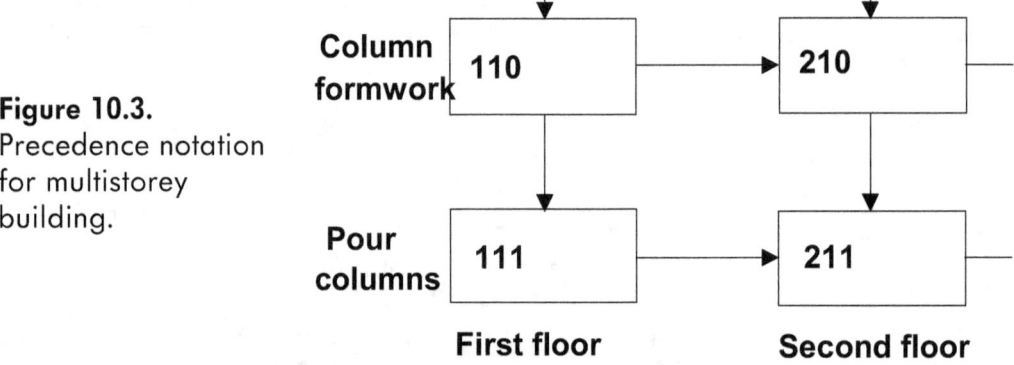

This approach is then of particular usefulness for multistorey buildings, for example, the columns of the chart being able to be used for repetition of elements at each floor level, as illustrated in Figure 10.3.

Then in Figure 10.3 the first digit of each element number is the floor number. Note in passing that multistorey buildings can also be scheduled effectively using the flow line technique described in Section 11.2.

10. CRITICAL PATH METHOD

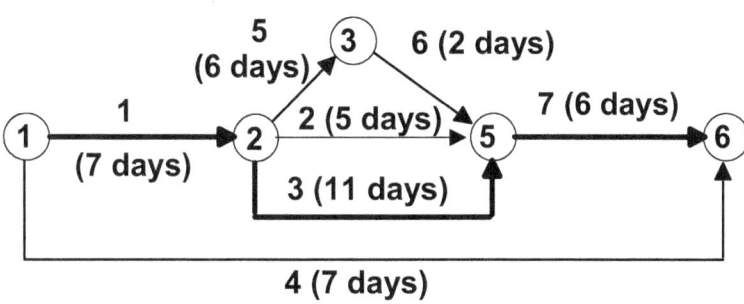

Figure 10.4. Example critical path network.

Figure 10.4 shows a simple network for which the critical path is shown by heavy lines. Here there is no node 4 but this could be inserted to provide a dummy element at the tail of element 3 so that elements 2 and 3 then have unique node numbers (as may be preferred by some computer programs).

Table 10.1. Determination of critical path

Node	Path times	Latest time
1	0	0
2	7	7
3	12	12
5	14,12,18	18
6	21,18,24,7	24

To determine the critical path Table 10.1 is constructed with all the path times leading to each node calculated. Then the latest of these times is the earliest start (ES) time for elements which follow this node.

The latest time for the last node is the longest (critical) path time for the project and thus the duration of the project. Then elements whose path times to any node in Table 10.1 are the latest such times for that node are *critical elements* and these lie on the critical path.

The operations of Table 10.1 are called a *forward pass* and when this is complete and the total project time is known a *backward pass* is commenced. In this we work back through the network subtracting element times for each element from the latest time for their end nodes to give the latest times for their start nodes. Comparing these with the node times established in Table 10.1 the earliest start and finish (ES and EF) and latest start and finish (LS and LF) times for each element are calculated.

10. CRITICAL PATH METHOD

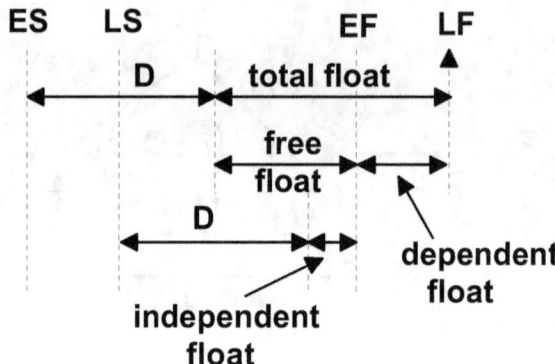

Figure 10.5.
Various types of float.

Then elements on the critical path have ES = LS and EF = LF, that is they have zero *slack* or *float*. Various types of float can be defined, as shown in Figure 10.5. These are:

1. *Total float.* This is the amount of delay an element may have without delaying the completion of the project.

2. *Free float.* This is the amount of delay an element may have without affecting following elements (including their float). This applies only to elements which are the last of an independent chain of events, for example element 6 in Figure 10.4.

3. *Dependent float.* This is part of the total float associated with the path upon which an element lies and usage of this float by an element reduces float available to following elements.

4. *Independent float.* This is an irreducible amount of float available which has been 'built in' to the analysis to allow for contingencies.

In practice independent float is perhaps best allowed by way of dummy activities. This clarifies the definition of float for which we can then write

$$\text{Total float (TF)} = \text{Free float (FF)} + \text{Dependent float (DF)} \qquad (10.1)$$

as shown in Figure 10.5.

Conclusion

The critical path method is a very widely used technique for project scheduling, perhaps because it is the natural, if not obvious, approach.

The critical path can be found using the tabular scheme of Table 10.1 and from this the ES, LS, EF and LF times for each element follow. Simple programs which also accomplish this are given later in the chapter.

10. CRITICAL PATH METHOD

10.2. Bar charts and resource scheduling

Bar charts, sometimes called *Gantt charts*, are the means by which the results of a CPM analysis are used to coordinate the progress of a project. Of particular importance, *resource scheduling*, in which bars are shifted judiciously in order to smooth out fluctuations in resource usage can be accomplished with the aid of bar charts.

Application of bar charts

Once an analysis of a network has been carried out to determine the critical path and then the ES, LS, EF and LF times for each element these are used to construct a bar chart.

Typically classical CPM computer printouts used such notation as:

XXX	critical element
VVV	non-critical element
000	free float
DDD	dependent float
SS	Saturday or Sunday (no work)
H	public holiday

and so on, so that a great deal of information is set to a calendar.

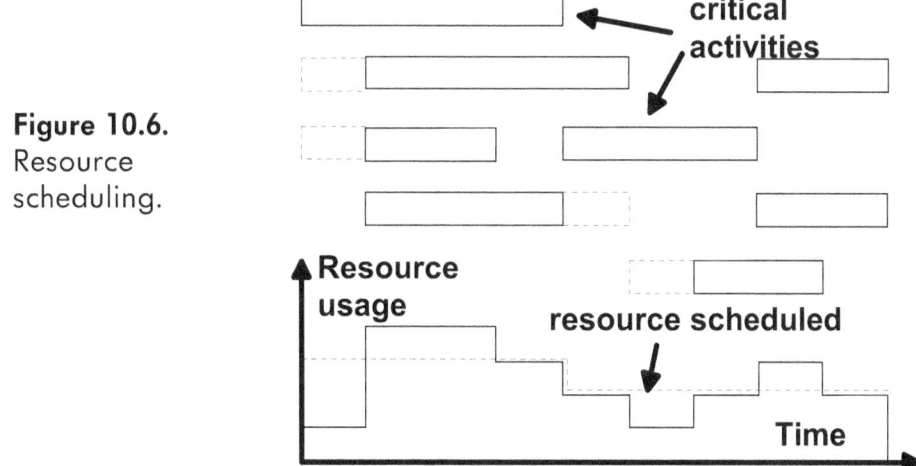

Figure 10.6. Resource scheduling.

Figure 10.6 shows an example of a bar chart for the use of a particular resource (hence many possible bar charts can be constructed for different resources, including materials and labour, and for parts of the project). Then, as shown by the dashed lines, bars can be shifted in order to smooth out resource usage and this process is referred to as *resource scheduling*.

Clearly use of the resource has been leveled out, three units being used for an initial period and two units for the remainder.

10. CRITICAL PATH METHOD

Conclusion

Bar charts and applications such as resource scheduling are an important part of project scheduling using CPM. They are also important in managing the day to day running of a project.

Note too that schedules are frequently altered as the result of actual times taken for elements of a project. When the CPM analysis is repeated at a number of stages with this new information the general process involved is referred to as *dynamic programming*. Further examples of dynamic programming are given in most books on Operations Research.

10.3. Crashing a project

In critical path analysis 'crashing' a project refers to compressing elements on the critical path as much as possible. Generally this will raise the costs of these elements but the total cost of the project may be reduced as a result of savings in overheads and other fixed costs such as interest rates payable on finance for the project, avoidance of penalties for late completion and bonuses for early completion.

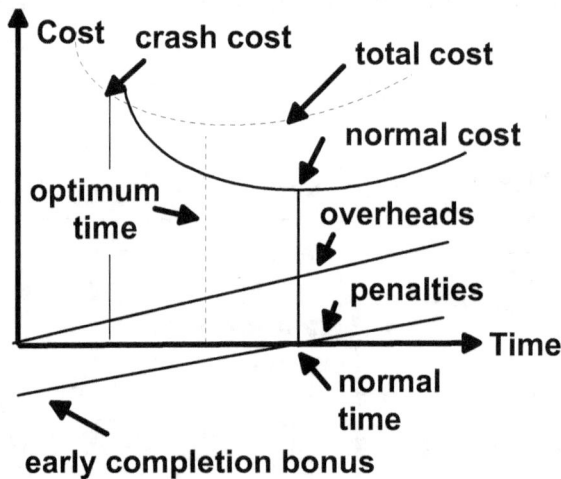

Figure 10.7.
Effect of overheads and penalties on project cost.

Figure 10.7 shows an example. The normal project time is that for the minimum cost neglecting overheads etc. When overheads and penalties are taken into account, however, the total cost curve gives a minimum somewhere between the crash and normal project times. Hence, whilst a project might only be crashed fully when there is considerable pressure to do so, some degree of compression of times on the critical path is generally worthwhile.

10. CRITICAL PATH METHOD

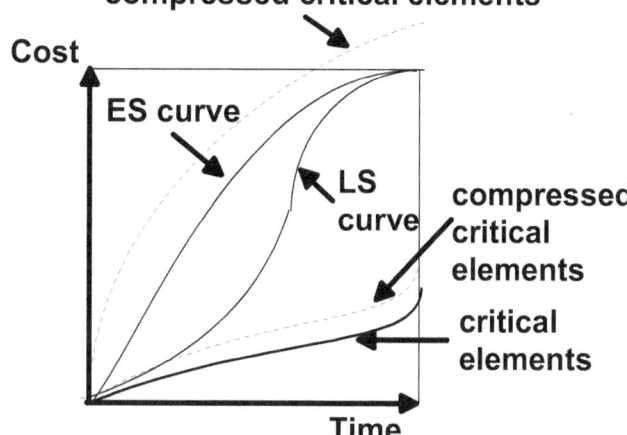

Figure 10.8.
ES and LS cost curves and effect of compressing critical elements.

Then this result affects the cost curve for the project, as shown in Figure 10.8 where the higher costs for the compressed critical elements raise the project cost curve (to the dashed result).

This is shown for the earliest start curve for the sake of clarity. In practice, however, we would generally prefer to use the LS curve and then make any adjustments by compressing critical elements of this. This is because the LS curve delays payments associated with non-critical elements as much as possible, thereby reducing interest charges for the project.

Conclusion

Whilst crashing of critical elements is generally attempted only in extreme circumstances, some compression of the critical path, however, may reduce total project costs as a result of reduced overhead costs and the like.

It is also important, however, to use LS times for non-critical elements as this will generally reduce interest charges for the project.

It is then possible to combine these two measures to reduce project cost significantly.

Note, however, that the effect shown in Figure 10.8 can be included in a cost curve for each element and this modification is discussed in Section. 10.5.

10. CRITICAL PATH METHOD

10.4. PERT

PERT is a simple modification of CPM in which three time estimates are provided for each element, these being:

1. An optimistic time (*a*) which is the best result that could be achieved in, say, 10 attempts.

2. A median or most likely time (*m*) which is the time most likely to be obtained in a number of attempts.

3. A pessimistic time (*b*) which is the worst result that could be achieved in, say, 10 attempts.

Then the expected time for each element is calculated as

$$t_e = (a + 4m + b)/6 \tag{10.2}$$

and this is equivalent to assuming a parabolic frequency distribution.

Then according to the *central limit theorem* of statistics the distribution of the total time *T* for *n* sequential tasks is approximately normal (that is, random and symmetrical) with a mean equal to the sum of the individual means and a variance equal to the sum of the individual variances as $n \to \infty$ regardless of the distribution of the individual tasks.

Then the probability of completing the job in a time *T* is given by the Normal probability

$$P(\{T - T_e\}/\sigma > 0) \tag{10.3}$$

where
$$T_e = \Sigma \, t_e \quad \text{and} \quad \sigma^2 = n \Sigma \, \sigma_i^2 \tag{10.4}$$
and
$$\sigma_i = (b - a)/6 \tag{10.5}$$

for the standard deviation of the individual elements.

Then analysis proceeds as with CPM using a forward pass but now this gives an earliest time, a latest time and a scheduled or chosen time for each node and we can attach a probability to this scheduled time. Following with a backward pass expected, latest and scheduled times of completion are obtained for each element and probabilities are attached to the scheduled times.

In practice simplified PERT (or CPM as we have described it) is usually used but some attempt to provide probabilities of elements completing on schedule is useful in making management decisions.

10. Critical Path Method

It should also be noted, however, that PERT makes no attempt at optimizing anything. It simply forms a schedule in which three (rather than two) times are attached to each element, attaching a probability to the likely actual completion time for an element.

It is nevertheless worthwhile to use formulas such as those of Equations 10.3 - 10.5 to estimate the variance for typical elements and thus for the entire project without actually including this data in the CPM analysis.

Conclusion

The simple estimates of probability required for the PERT method are well worth making, even if they are not used in the CPM analysis. Then, summing variances along the critical path, for example, the variance for the whole project is easily estimated.

10.5. Optimization of the critical path

A useful modification of CPM is obtained when each element is given a cost versus time curve. Then the steepest descent method can be used to obtain an optimum solution for the resulting critical path problem.

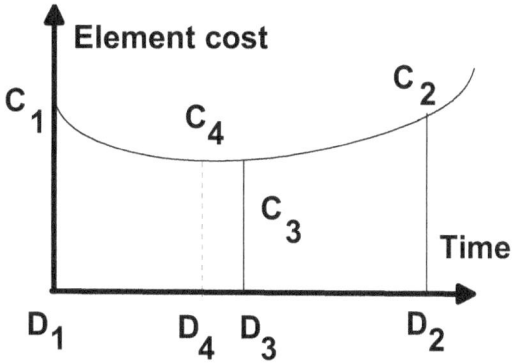

Figure 10.9.
Element cost function.

Figure 10.9 shows the quadratic cost function assumed by Mohr for elements of a CPM network. Here three durations D_1, D_2 and D_3 are specified along with their associated costs, $D_3 = (D_1 + D_2)$ being the median time.

Substituting $s = 2x - 1$ in Equations 3.59 the quadratic interpolation for the cost is:

$$C = C_1(1 - 3x + 2x^2) + 4C_3 x(1 - x) + C_2(2x^2 - x) \tag{10.6}$$

and the minimum cost is given by

$$dC/dx = 0 = C_1(-3x + 4x) + 4C_3(1 - 2x) + C_2(4x - 1) \tag{10.7}$$

giving the dimensionless coordinate at which the minimum cost is obtained as

$$x^* = (3C_1 - 4C_3 + C_2)/(4C_1 - 2C_3 + C_2) \tag{10.8}$$

so that

$$D_4 = D_1 + x^*(D_2 - D_1) \tag{10.9}$$

and C_4 is given by substituting x^* into Equation 10.6.

Providing the three point data for each element D_4 and C_4 are calculated for each element and the forward and backward passes carried out using these values. The total project cost is calculated as

$$P = \Sigma\, C_i + F\, T_{proj} \tag{10.10}$$

by summing the element costs and adding a term for the fixed costs shown in Figure 10.7. This is the product of a fixed cost per unit time (F) and the total project time (T_{proj}) which is the time for the last node of the network.

Then, applying the steepest descent method to each critical element, its duration is increased by an amount δD, giving a perturbed value

$$D^* = D_4 + \delta D \tag{10.11}$$

Then using the quadratic interpolation of Equation 10.6 with

$$x = (D^* - D_1)/(D_2 - D_1) \tag{10.12}$$

the corresponding element costs C^* are calculated.

Collecting the results for all critical elements gives a gradient vector

$$\{g\} = \{(C^* - C_4 + F\delta D)/\delta D\} \tag{10.13}$$

Then trial step lengths S are used to search in this direction for the optimum solution and the optimum durations for the critical elements are calculated as

$$\{D^*\} = \{D\} - S_{opt}\{g\} \tag{10.14}$$

where S_{opt} is the step length which gives the minimum total project cost, the trial values of which are calculated as

$$P^* = P + \Sigma_{cr}(C^* - C_4 + \delta D\, F) \tag{10.15}$$

Finally the critical path analysis is repeated and, if the critical path is unchanged the procedure is complete. If not, the steepest descent procedure is repeated to determine a new optimum solution for this new critical path.

The potential savings resulting from this procedure are not large, in part because minimum element costs D_4 are used at the outset and this is where the main savings lie. In the case of small networks that represent the operations in the mass production of some item, however, these savings would be substantial over time.

Conclusion

The quadratic cost function approach illustrated in Figure 10.9 is of potential value in providing small savings in networks representing mass production processes. In addition Equations 10.6- 10.9 are useful as a means of providing improved data for standard CPM analyses.

10.6. Simple CPM program

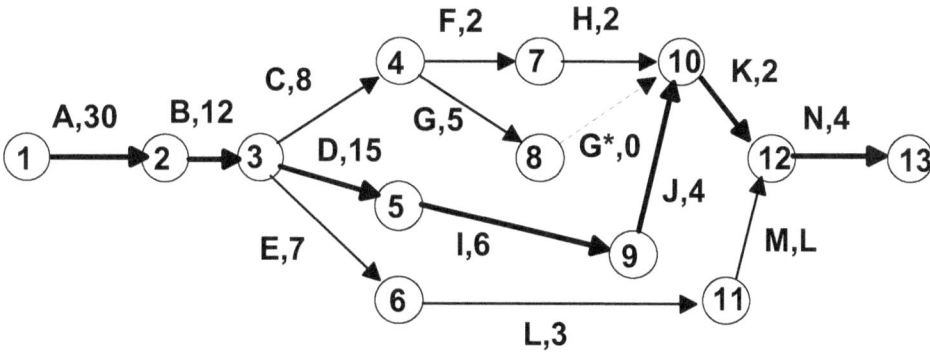

Figure 10.10. Critical path network.

The listing for a simple program follows. Note that the precedence matrix is P(,), the coding being very transparent. The data is for the problem shown in Figure 10.10, the first line being the number of nodes and elements. The remaining lines each give the pair of node numbers, the duration, a unit cost and a wastage or tolerance figure giving the possible fractional cost overrun. Note the dummy element G* (with zero duration) to enforce a precedence.

Output gives the ES, EF, LS and LF times for each element (they are input in 'alphabetical' order and output in the same order) and these will correspond to the critical path shown in Figure 10.10.

10. Critical Path Method

```
5 REM CRITICAL PATH METHOD PROGRAM
6 RESTORE 500
10 DIM N(20, 2), D(20), C(20), W(20), T(20), P(3, 20)
20 DIM S1(20), F1(20), S2(20), F2(20)
30 A$ = "        ": READ Z, E: REM INPUT NO. NODES AND ELEMENTS
40 FOR I = 1 TO 3: FOR J = 1 TO 10
50 P(I, J) = 0: NEXT: NEXT: REM INTITIALIZE PRECEDENCE MATRIX
60 FOR I = 1 TO E
70 READ N(I, 1), N(I, 2), D(I): REM ,C(I),W(I);Rem I/P ELE DATA - N.B> ELEMENTS
80 NEXT: REM MUST BE IN NUMERICAL ORDER
90 Q = 0: Q2 = 0: REM INITIALIZE TOTAL PROJECT COSTS
100 FOR K = 1 TO Z: T(K) = 0: NEXT: REM INITIALIZE LF TIMES FOR NODES
110 FOR K = 1 TO E: J = N(K, 2): I = 1
120 FOR M = 1 TO 3: IF P(M, J) = 0 THEN GOTO 140
130 I = I + 1: NEXT M: REM COLLECT PRECEEDING ELEMENT
140 P(I, J) = K: NEXT K: REM NUMBERS FOR EACH NODE
150 FOR K = 1 TO E: REM COMMENCE FORWARD PASS **********
160 I = N(K, 1): J = N(K, 2): S1(K) = T(I): REM S1(K)=ES TIME FOR ELEMENT
170 F1(K) = T(I) + D(K): REM F1(K)=EF TIME FOR ELEMENT
180 IF F1(K) > T(J) THEN T(J) = F1(K)
REM INCREASE NODE LF TIME IF MUST
190 Q = Q + D(K) * C(K): Q2 = Q2 + D(K) * C(K) * W(K)
200 NEXT: REM END FORWARD PASS       **********
210 PRINT "JOBTIME = ", T(Z): PRINT "JOBCOST = ", Q:
PRINT "PESSIMISTIC COST VARN = ", Q2
220 FOR I = 1 TO E: F2(I) = 1000: NEXT: REM INTITIALIZE LF TIMES
230 FOR K = 1 TO E: REM COMMENCE BACKWARD PASS %%%%%%%%%
240 R = E - K + 1: I = N(R, 1): J = N(R, 2)
REM BACKWARDS THRU  ELEMENTS
250 IF J = Z THEN F2(R) = T(Z): REM LF TIME FOR LAST ELEMENT
260 S2(R) = F2(R) - D(R): REM LS = LF - DURATION
270 FOR M = 1 TO 3: S = P(M, I): IF S = 0 THEN GOTO 290
280 IF F2(S) > S2(R) THEN F2(S) = S2(R): REM LF OF PREC ELES = LS OF THIS ELE
290 NEXT
300 IF S1(R) = S2(R) THEN F = F + D(R) * W(R)
REM Increase proj delay estimate
310 NEXT: REM END BACKWARD PASS      %%%%%%%%%
320 PRINT "PESSIMISTIC JOB DELAY = ", F
PRINT A$, "ES", A$, "EF", A$, "LS", A$, "LF"
330 FOR K = 1 TO E
PRINT USING "##########"; S1(K);F1(K); S2(K); F2(K):NEXT
340 END
```

```
400 DATA 6,7                    : REM DATA FOR PROBLEM OF FIG 10.13
410 DATA 1,2,7,10,0.1
420 DATA 2,5,5,10,0.1
430 DATA 2,5,11,10,0.1
440 DATA 1,6,7,10,0.1
450 DATA 2,3,6,10,0.1
460 DATA 3,5,2,10,0.1
470 DATA 5,6,6,10,0.1
500 DATA 13,15
510 DATA 1,2,30, 2,3,12, 3,4,8, 3,5,15, 3,6,7
520 DATA 4,7,2, 4,8,5, 8,10,0, 7,10,2, 5,9,6, 9,10,4, 10,12,2
530 DATA 6,11,3, 11,12,1, 12,13,4
```

The output will be (program does not print element 'tags', as noted OP being in same order as IP, but could easily be modified to do so).

Element	A	B	C	D	E	F	G	G*	H	I	J	K	L	M	N
ES	0	30	42	42	42	50	50	55	52	57	63	67	49	52	69
EF	30	42	50	57	49	52	55	55	54	63	67	69	52	53	73
LS	0	30	54	42	58	63	62	67	65	57	63	67	65	68	69
LF	30	42	62	57	65	65	67	67	67	63	67	69	68	69	73

Then we see that critical elements do indeed have ES = LS and EF = LF and the dummy element has ES = EF and LS = LF. Of course, printout of the floats could easily be added when zero float quickly indentifies a critical element.

Conclusion

This short program is useful for small exercises and it is extended in Section 10.8 to optimize a network whose elements have quadratic time functions.

10. CRITICAL PATH METHOD

10.7. CPM Program with quadratic elements

The following program deals with elements with quadratic cost functions and uses steepest descent to optimize the solution, as described in Section 10.5. The data is for the problem of Figure 10.4 and is shown in Table 10.2

Table 10.2. Data for CP optimization program

Element	Nodes	D_1	D_2	c_1	c_2	c_3
1	1,2	7	14	10	6	20/3
2	2,5	5	10	10	6	20/3
3	2,5	11	11	10	10	10
4	1,6	7	14	10	6	20/3
5	2,3	6	12	10	6	20/3
6	3,5	2	4	10	6	20/3
7	5,6	6	12	10	6	20/3

The minimum durations D_1 correspond to the original data in Figure 10.4 for which the project cost result is P = 440 and the project time is 24. Including the fixed cost F of Equation 10.10 (= FC in program, read in line 50) with value = 1, this increases P by 24 (i.e., to 464). Note that $F = 1$ seems a small value but is not totally unrealistic, adding about 5% to the total project cost and larger values simply crash the project to a minimum time solution.

To obtain the data of the last two columns of Table 10.2 REM is removed from the two lines following statement 90 as the data appended to the program is for a further test problem with these two data columns modified.

To cost data is unit costs for the minimum, median and maximum durations, so that the total costs are

$$C_1 = c_1 D_1, \quad C_2 = c_2 D_2, \quad C_3 = c D_3$$

Then the program calculates D_4 and C_4 using Equations 10.6 - 10.9.

```
10 REM CRITICAL PATH METHOD PROGRAM
20 TOL = .1: REM Accuracy limit on times
30 DIM N(10, 3), D(10, 4), C(10, 4), T(10), P(3, 10), G(10)
40 DIM S1(10), F1(10), S2(10), F2(10): REM ES,EF,LS,LF times
50 A$ = "     ": READ NN, NE, FC
60 FOR I = 1 TO 3: FOR J = 1 TO 10
70 P(I, J) = 0: NEXT: NEXT: REM Initialize precedence matrix
80 FOR I = 1 TO NE
90 READ N(I, 1), N(I, 2), D(I, 1), D(I, 2), C(I, 1), C(I, 2), C(I, 3)
REM IF I <> 3 THEN C(I, 3) = 20 / 3: Rem S = -2.1 with these two lines
REM IF I <> 3 THEN C(I, 2) = 6
100 NEXT: REM Elements must be in numerical order
```

```
110 PC = 0: REM Initialize total project cost
120 FOR K = 1 TO NN: T(K) = 0: NEXT: REM Initialize LF times for nodes
130 FOR K = 1 TO NE: J = N(K, 2): I = 1
140 FOR M = 1 TO 3: IF P(M, J) = 0 THEN GOTO 160
150 I = I + 1: NEXT M: REM Collect preceding element
160 P(I, J) = K: NEXT K: REM Numbers for each node
170 FOR I = 1 TO NE
180 C1 = D(I, 1) * C(I, 1): C2 = D(I, 2) * C(I, 2): REM Min & Max total costs
190 D(I, 3) = (D(I, 1) + D(I, 2)) / 2: REM Median duration
210 C3 = C(I, 3) * D(I, 3): REM Median total cost
220 C(I, 1) = C1: C(I, 2) = C2: C(I, 3) = C3
230 DT = 3 * C1 - 4 * C3 + C2
240 DEN = 4 * (C1 - 2 * C3 + C2)
250 IF DEN = 0 THEN DT = 0
255 IF DEN = 0 THEN 270
260 DT = DT / DEN
270 REM Duration for min cost (EQN 10.8)
275 D(I, 4) = D(I, 1) + DT * (D(I, 2) - D(I, 1))
280 IF D(I, 1) = D(I, 2) THEN DT = 0
300 REM Next line gives min cost for element (EQN 10.6)
310 C(I, 4) = C1*(1 - 3*DT + 2*DT*DT) + 4* C3 *DT*(1 - DT) + C2*(2*DT*DT - DT)
320 NEXT I
330 PC = 0
340 FOR I = 1 TO NE: N(I, 3) = 0: NEXT
350 FOR I = 1 TO NN: T(I) = 0: NEXT
360 FOR I = 1 TO NE: S1(I) = 0: F1(I) = 0: S2(I) = 0: F2(I) = 0: NEXT
370 FOR K = 1 TO NE: REM Start forward pass
380 I = N(K, 1): J = N(K, 2): S1(K) = T(I): REM S1(K)=ES TIME FOR ELEMENT
390 F1(K) = T(I) + D(K, 4): REM F1(K)=EF TIME FOR ELEMENT
400 IF F1(K) > T(J) THEN T(J) = F1(K): REM Increase LF time if must
410 PC = PC + C(K, 4)
420 NEXT: REM End forward pass          **********
430 PC = PC + FC * T(NN)
440 PRINT "JOBTIME = ", T(NN); : PRINT " JOBCOST = ", PC
450 FOR I = 1 TO NE: F2(I) = 1000: NEXT: REM Initialize LF times
460 FOR K = 1 TO NE: REM Start backward pass %%%%%%%%
470 R = NE - K + 1: I = N(R, 1): J = N(R, 2): REM Move backwards thru eles
480 IF J = NN THEN F2(R) = T(NN): REM LF time for last element
490 S2(R) = F2(R) - D(R, 4): REM LS = LF - Duration
500 FOR M = 1 TO 3: S = P(M, I): IF S = 0 THEN GOTO 520
510 IF F2(S) > S2(R) THEN F2(S) = S2(R): REM LF of prec eles = LS of this ele
520 NEXT
530 IF ABS(F2(R) - F1(R)) < TOL THEN N(R, 3) = 1
540 NEXT K: REM End backward pass
550 PRINT "Critical flags: "; : FOR I = 1 TO NE: PRINT N(I, 3); : NEXT
555 PRINT "   Element times follow:"
560 FOR K = 1 TO NE: PRINT S1(K), F1(K), S2(K), F2(K): NEXT
570 TC = -1: REM Element duration increment
```

10. CRITICAL PATH METHOD

```
580 FOR I = 1 TO NE: REM Commence gradient calc. (CRIT. ELES ONLY)
590 IF N(I, 3) = 0 THEN 680
600 ET = D(I, 4) + TC
610 IF ET < D(I, 1) THEN ET = D(I, 1)
620 IF ET > D(I, 2) THEN ET = D(I, 2)
630 IF D(I, 1) = D(I, 2) THEN DT = 0: IF D(I, 1) = D(I, 2) THEN 660
640 DT = (ET - D(I, 1)) / (D(I, 2) - D(I, 1))
650 REM Next line is new element cost (Eqn 10.6)
660 EC = C(I, 1)*(1 -3*DT+2*DT*DT) + 4*C(I, 3)*DT*(1 -DT) + C(I, 2)*(2*DT*DT -DT)
670 G(I) = (EC - C(I, 4) + FC * TC) / 1
680 NEXT I
690 REM: Next line inputs trial search step length (CNTRL C TO STOP)
700 INPUT SN: IF SN <> 0 THEN S = SN: IF SN = 99 THEN END
710 PC2 = PC
720 FOR I = 1 TO NE
730 IF N(I, 3) = 0 THEN 850
740 ET = D(I, 4) - S * G(I): REM New element time
750 IF ET < D(I, 1) THEN ET = D(I, 1)
760 IF ET > D(I, 2) THEN ET = D(I, 2)
770 IF D(I, 1) = D(I, 2) THEN DT = 0: IF D(I, 1) = D(I, 2) THEN 800
780 DT = (ET - D(I, 1)) / (D(I, 2) - D(I, 1))
790 REM Next line gives new element cost (Eqn 10.6)
800 EC = C(I, 1)*(1-3*DT+2*DT*DT) + 4*C(I, 3)*DT*(1- DT) + C(I, 2)*(2*DT*DT - DT)
810 TC = ET - D(I, 4)
820 PC2 = PC2 + EC - C(I, 4) + TC * FC: REM Adjust project cost
830 IF SN = 0 THEN D(I, 4) = ET: REM Store ele duration if search ended
840 IF SN = 0 THEN C(I, 4) = EC: REM Store ele cost if search ended
850 NEXT I
860 PRINT PC2
870 IF SN = 0 THEN 330: REM Return to CPA if search ended
880 GOTO 700: REM Continue search

890 DATA 6,7,1           : REM Data for test problem
900 DATA 1,2,7,14,10,8,7
910 DATA 2,5,5,10,10,8,7
920 DATA 2,5,11,11,10,10,10
930 DATA 1,6,7,14,10,8,7
940 DATA 2,3,6,12,10,8,7
950 DATA 3,5,2,4,10,8,7
960 DATA 5,6,6,12,10,8,7
```

Running the program, the project time is 27.25 and the total cost is P = 459 with the initial minimum element costs and their associated durations (given by Equations 10.6 - 10.9).

After printing this initial solution the program prompts for a *search length* S (with ?) and careful trial with a succession of incremented values is needed to locate a turning point.

10. Critical Path Method

Note that when a TP is located (P increases) conclude the search with the most successful previous search length to leave the model at that point. In this case the TP is found with search length = -2.1, giving P = 458.1895 with project time 25.65.

To try a further search, now use a zero search length. The program then calculates a new gradient vector (by the usual perturbation, applied only to the critical elements) and again gradually increasing search lengths are tried. In this case no reduction in P occurs with a very small S so this is the usual cue to end, which is done by entering S = 99.

Note that a negative search length was used here because in line 570 a negative perturbation (of -1) was used to calculate the gradients for steepest descent search.

Our tiny example problem is relatively 'rigid' in terms of P and project time, but the project schedule is significantly altered. Not surprisingly the CP is not altered but project time was significantly reduced from 27.5 to 25.65 with a cost of about 458. This is little less than the minimum time value of 464, but a great deal less than the maximum time value of 543.

As a further test, with the REMs left in place in the two statements after line 90 the full data in the DATA lines is used, changing the entries in the last two columns in Table 10.2 to 8 and 7, with the exception of element 3. Now the initial solution with the minimum element durations is project time and cost = 26.6 and 453.4.

Now using search S = 0.54 the optimum solution is project time and cost = 26.0 and 453.1. Again the savings from the initial solution with optimum element times are small, but the saving compared to the maximum project time cost are considerable.

If element 3 has max time double min time, like the rest, along with the same unit costs, however, search does result in greater savings. Thus, if it has max time = 22 and unit costs as for the other elements in Table 10.2, the initial project time and cost with optimum element times are = 30 and 459 and with search with S = -2.1 the optimum solution = 27.1 and 457.5.

Conclusion

The Critical Path Method, of which PERT is a variant, is an essential tool for project and production scheduling and control. In designing efficient project schedules, however, some understanding of the Flowline Method is very useful, the reason for brief discussion of it here.

With the use of quadratic cost-time interpolations for each element it is possible to determine an optimum schedule which minimizes total project cost as the simple program given here demonstrates.

In this program the element median costs are calculated from the values at the limiting times but in general they should be included in the input data as independent estimates and the reader should try this as an exercise.

10.8. References

Ackoff RL, Sasieni MW, *Fundamentals of Operations Research*, Wiley, NY, 1968.

Enrick NL, *Management Operations Research*, Holt Rinhart & Winston, NY, 1965.

Hillier FS, Lieberman GJ, *Introduction to Operations Research*, 3rd end, Holden-Day, Oakland CA, 1980.

_____, A *Programmed Introduction to PERT*, ITT/Federal Electric Corp., Wiley, NY, 1963.

Mohr WE, Bawden AE, *Network Analysis Reference Manual*, 6th edn, EPAC P/L, Melbourne, 1974.

Mohr WE, *Flowline Reference Manual*, EPAC P/L, Melbourne, 1977.

Mohr WE, *Project Management and Control*, 3rd edn, Dept. of Architecture and Building, Univ. of Melbourne, 1981.

Mohr GA, Optimization of critical path models using finite elements, *Trans Instn Civil Engineers, Australia,* vol. CE35(2), p 123-126, 1994.

Neter, J, Wasserman, W, Whitmore, GA, *Applied Statistics*, Allyn and Bacon, Boston MS, 1978.

Powers MJ, Adams DR, Milles, HD, *Computer Information Systems Development: Analysis and Design*, South-Western, Cincinnati OH, 1984.

Schmenner RW, *Production/Operations Management: Concepts and Situations*, 4th edn, McMillan, NY, 1990.

Smith KM, *Critical Path Planning*: A Practical Guide, MacDonald, London, 1971.

Wild R, *Mass Production Management*, Wiley, London, 1972.

Chapter 11

PRODUCTION/OPERATIONS MANAGEMENT

A number of methods of production/operations management are discussed, beginning with the *Line of Balance* (LOB) and *flow line* methods. Then assembly lines and *Group Technology* for efficient batch production are discussed.

Next dynamic programming, shortest route and minimal spanning tree problems are discussed, giving further examples of network problems, a principal focus of the text.

Finally inventory management, simulation and production assessment and control are discussed.

11.1. Line of balance systems

Line-of-balance systems are especially useful for certain manufacturing situations where emphasis is based on *assembly* of a product from components. The lines of production of the various components are drawn backwards from the LOB to schedule the operations on these.

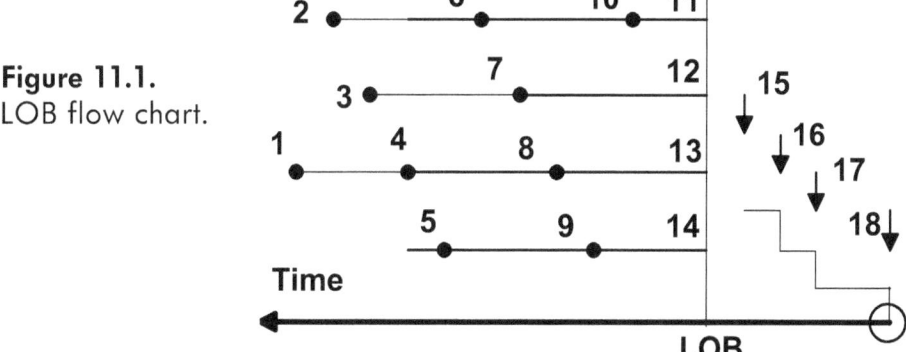

Figure 11.1. LOB flow chart.

Figure 11.1 shows a simple example of a LOB flow chart, time originating at the extreme right hand side. Then flow lines for four components are drawn back from the LOB, the nodes in these corresponding to completion of some stage of their manufacture.

11. Production/Operations Management

Then to the right of the LOB the assembly stages are scheduled, as shown, completion occurring when $t = 0$.

The LOB approach corresponds to parallel production in the flow line method whilst as in CPM float can easily be introduced into LOB flow charts.

Figure 11.2.
LOB production schedule.

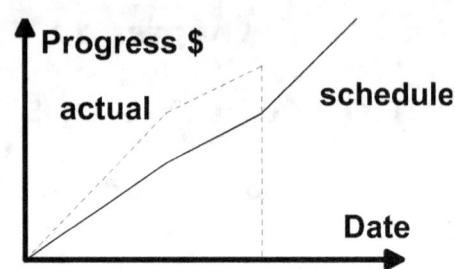

Then, as shown in Figure 11.2, progress can be checked at any point on the LOB calendar and checked against the schedule (here the dollar value of progress of work on each flow line is summed).

Conclusion

LOB flow charts are a very simple means of scheduling and are particularly appropriate where emphasis is on assembly of a product. This situation corresponds to that of parallel production in flow line analysis (except that the lines will have different starting points).

11.2. The flow line method

In the following section we describe the flow line method of production scheduling. For this a project or part thereof is broken into sections which are carried out at similar rates. This approach is usually applied to mass production lines but it is especially useful in the case of multistorey building projects or construction of 'project' homes, for example. The method is easily understood by considering three contrasting production systems which are discussed in this section.

Parallel production

Figure 11.3.
Parallel production.

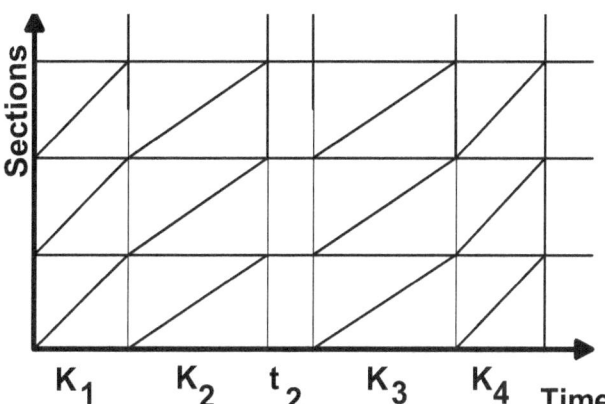

Figure 11.3 illustrates production in which all 'sub-projects' or *sections*, for example a number of houses, are built at the same time.

For parallel production the total project time is given by

$$T_p = \Sigma (K_i + t_i) \tag{11.1}$$

where K_i is called the *production module* for steps i and t_i are waiting times (for delivery, holidays etc.). In the case where all step rates are the same the total production time when there are m steps and no waiting times is

$$T_p = K m \tag{11.2}$$

This approach gives the shortest total time but requires maximum usage of resources and its only logical use is for one-off situations, not for ongoing business.

Sequence production

Figure 11.4.
Sequence production.

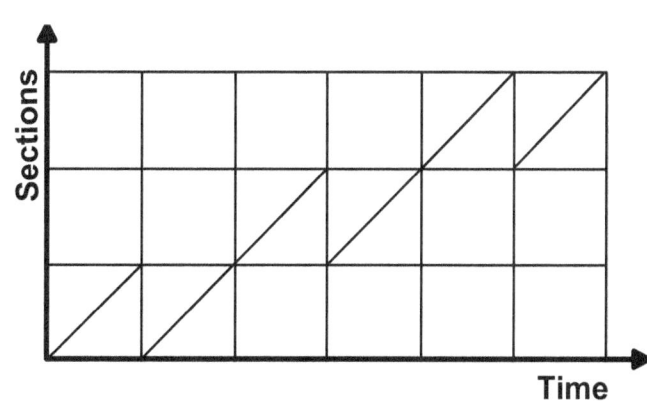

Figure 11.4 illustrates sequence production in which each sub-project or section is completed before starting the next.

11. Production/Operations Management

This gives the total project time as:

$$T_s = n \Sigma (K_i + t_i) \tag{11.3}$$

when there are n sections or sub-projects. Then when the modules for the steps in these are equal and there are no waiting times the total time is given by:

$$T_s = K\,m\,n \tag{11.4}$$

where we have $m = 2$ and $n = 3$ in the example of Figure 11.4.

This approach results in the longest total time and delaying one section does not affect others. This again represents an extreme situation in relation to the flow line approach and both Figures 11.3 and 11.4 are of little practical value except as an introduction to the flow line production model.

Flow line production

Figure 11.5 shows an example of flow line production where, for example, line A might be excavation for footings, B for pouring footings, C for brickwork and D for roof framing in the case of house construction.

Then for flow line production the total production time is given by

$$T_f = K(m + n - 1) \tag{11.5}$$

where the production modules or rates are equal, as must be the case to prevent lines interfering (unless there are gaps between the lines and still only a temporary difference in the 'general' rate is permitted as flow lines cannot cross).

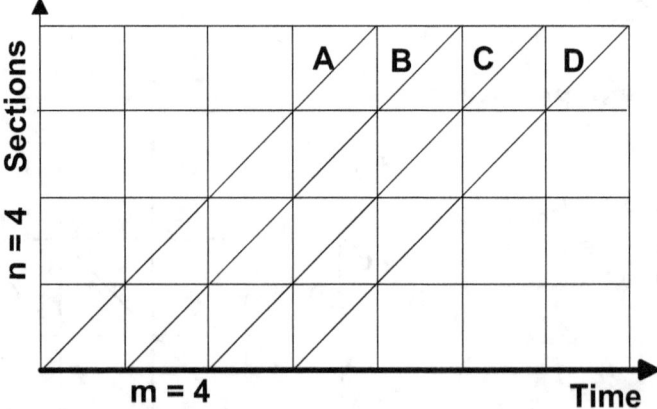

Figure 11.5.
Flow line production.

Then in Figure 11.5 the time until all lines are in operation is given by

$$K(m - 1) \tag{11.6}$$

and this is called the *running in time* and is equal to the *running out time*, that is the time for cessation of production after the first line finishes.

11. Production/Operations Management

Hence the *time of full production* can be calculated as

$$K(m + n - 1) - 2K(m - 1) = T_{full} = K(n - m + 1) \qquad (11.7)$$

and in practice it is desirable to maximize the ratio

$$T_{full}/T_f = K(n - m + 1)/K(n + m - 1) \qquad (11.8)$$

so that the larger the number of sections the more efficient the process, for example in mass production where $n \gg m$.

Conclusion

The flow line method is an important tool for production scheduling and can also be used elsewhere when a number of similar project are undertaken or when a project can be broken into sections of similar nature, as in construction of a multistorey building, for example. Then, as flow line method emphasizes, the work on these sections should be overlapped as much as possible to maximize the efficiency of operations.

Finally, flow-line diagrams provide many interesting exercises when some lines are sped up or slowed down, adjusting others to prevent overlapping. The changes in results of the form of Equation 11.7 then clearly indicate the effect of such changes, generally emphasizing that the ideal form of Equation 11.5 with $n \gg m$ should be the objective.

11.3. Assembly lines

Having discussed the flow line method of production scheduling, observing that this can be applied to any situation where a number of lines of similar nature have to be produced, we now discuss assembly lines and some of the specific details of these that must be considered in designing and operating mass production systems.

Assembly line balancing

Figure 11.6 shows a mixed-model assembly or flow line with $N = 3$ stations. Here two products are assembled using components fed to the stations as well as *buffer stocks* of components.

When the line uses or is modeled on the principle of using a belt or other mechanical conveyor the gap time for component inputs T_F is called the *feed time* and the time components are available for access at a station is called the *tolerance time*.

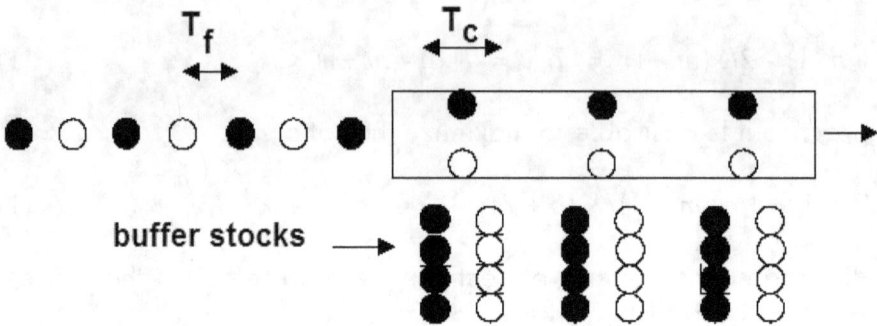

Figure 11.6. Mixed model line with three stations

In such a line the *cycle time* is given by

$$T_C = T_S + T_L \tag{11.9}$$

where T_S is the *service time* and T_L is the lost time (non productive work and idle time).

Ideally *rigid pacing* in which T_C is assumed constant can be attained but in practice *pacing with margin* is used and this requires buffer stocks.

Now in balancing the line we seek to minimize the sum of the idle times at the stations (the *balancing loss*), that is we minimize

$$L = \sum_{i-1}^{N} T_L = \sum_{i-1}^{N}(T_C - T_S) \tag{11.10}$$

where

$$T_S = \Sigma\, T_E \tag{11.11}$$

is the sum of the *work element* times at a station.

Statistical variations

In designing balanced lines, estimates of cycle times should not be unreasonably small as ultimately this may result in greater losses in efficiency than those desired in making 'tight' estimates.

One solution is to take the variance of the work element times into account, giving the standard deviation of the service time as

$$S_S = \sqrt{(\Sigma\, \sigma_E^2)} \tag{11.12}$$

and in balancing the line we then seek to minimize

$$\sum_{i=1}^{N} (T_C - T_S - zS_S) \tag{11.13}$$

where z is an appropriate value of the variate for the normal distribution, for example 1.96 at the 97.5% level (that is work at a station would be completed within the cycle time provided 97.5% of the number of occasions).

Double lines

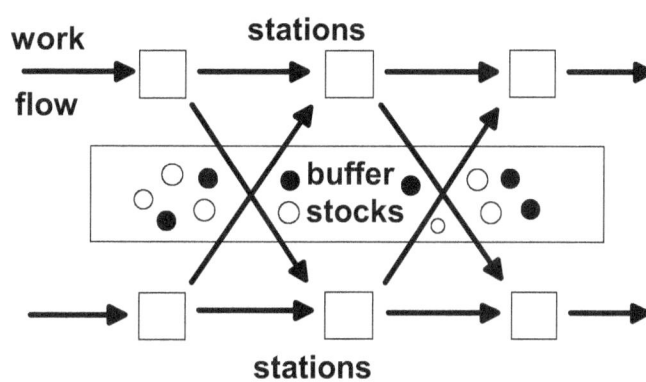

Figure 11.7.
A double line.

Figure 11.7 illustrates a double line. These are, when practical, more efficient than single lines because stations other than the first two are fed by two stations, reducing the likelihood of starving or blocking of stations. Rotary lines are an example of another such variation.

Mixed model lines

Figure 11.8 shows the layout of a more complex form of mixed-model line where three products move between the stations:

Product A: stations 3, 5, 8, 10, 13 or 3, 6, 9, 11, 14

Product B: stations 1, 4, 7, 10, 12

Product C: stations 2, 5, 8, 10, 13

11. Production/Operations Management

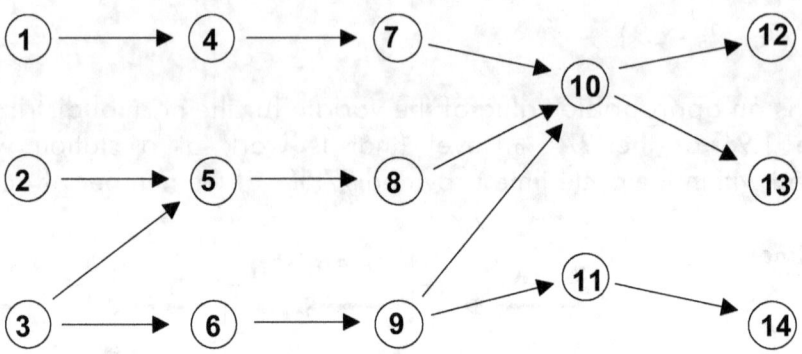

Figure 11.8. Mixed model line.

Here products share only some processes and balancing workloads at the different stations, the product flows and minimizing time losses requires careful tabulation of the number of operations required at each station, its service time (which may vary for the different products) and hence the total work time required at each station. Then iteration using a simple computer program is the only way of practically modeling the problem with a view to maximizing its efficiency.

Line efficiency
In practice a 5% balancing loss is a good result and cycle times (or tolerance times in the case of belt lines) should be set close to the mean unpaced service times (which may require measurement). Then feed times should be set within a margin from the cycle times, depending upon such factors as the availability of buffer stocks and the variance in the service time.

Conclusion
The flow line method of production scheduling is based on an overview of the different stages of production, each being classified merely by a name (of the activity) and a number (its module).

Assembly line balancing then takes an 'inside' look at the processes involved in production and resulting improvements in efficiency will reduce the K value applicable in flow line analysis.

Many of the systems considered here, however, are more concerned with mass production in a factory situation only. Then when production takes the form shown in Figure 11.8, for example, the group technology approach described in Section 11.5 is also useful.

11. Production/Operations Management

11.4. Group Technology

Group technology is an approach more suited to such applications as engineering manufacture where grouping components into families by identifying common manufacturing requirements is more important than an assembly line approach. In this approach some of the key considerations are:

1. Group technology is directed at *batch production* and more emphasis is placed on dealing with *components.*

2. Components are grouped into families in which they have similar manufacturing requirements to other family members.

3. Machines or production units are grouped into *production cells* which deal with *component families.*

4. These production cells are the approximate equivalent of a flow line in assembly line models and the component families are comparable to the sections or 'sub-projects' in Section 11.3.

Component families

For each component a *component-process-routing (CPR)* program can be established. Then where grouping of components into families is not obvious comparison of their CPR programs to determine whether they visit similar sequences of production cells may help in component grouping.

Sometimes a component's CPR program may be 'all over the place' and this may be indicative of a need to rearrange the factory layout.

Design problems

In designing an efficient production system component quantities and production cell capacities must be balanced approximately and some manipulation of component families and grouping of facilities may be needed to achieve a reasonable balance.

In some cases physical layout corresponding to the product flow may require rearrangement to improve overall efficiency.

11. PRODUCTION/OPERATIONS MANAGEMENT

Process sequencing

Using the CPR program data a *travel chart* such as that shown in Table 11.1 can be constructed for the component flows for a period of time.

Table 11.1. Travel chart.

r/c	Opn	\multicolumn{8}{c}{Operation}	r

r/c	Opn	1	2	3	4	5	6	7	8	r
5	1		20	10	5	5	10			50
1.6	2	5		10	10	5			10	40
1	3				5	5	15			25
1.2	4	5		5		5	10			25
0.5	5				→	To	5	5		10
0.8	6			5	→ From			15	15	35
0.6	7						5		10	15
0.14	8							5		5
	c	10	25	25	20	20	45	25	35	

Then for flow line assembly Table 11.1 should yield an upper triangular matrix. To improve the sequencing we sum the row and column entries, as shown, and then calculate the ratio of these sums on the left side of Table 11.1.

Then operations with high values of this ratio should be placed earlier in the sequence and operations with low values placed later. Such rearrangement will maximize in-sequence movement and minimize 'backtracking.'

Then, observing the extreme left column of Table 11.1 the required order of operations is:

Operation sequence: 1, 2, 4, 3, 6, 7, 5, 8

and the travel chart provides a convenient means of improving the sequencing. Note, however, that the criterion for this must be the ratio of the row and column totals and not the individual totals.

In addition, a limitation of the travel chart is that it cannot take into account the possibility of 'U-lines', for example, where shortcuts alter the situation considerably.

11. Production/Operations Management

11.5. Dynamic programming

Dynamic programming is a process of *recursive optimization* in which steps toward the optimum solution are taken using information from previous steps, typically for time dependent problems.

The general procedure used in dynamic programming is:

1. Divide the problem into stages, a process referred to as *decomposition*.

2. At each state decisions are made based on an optimization objective. This objective is called the *recursion equation*.

3. The results are combined to yield a solution, a process referred to as *composition*. Sometimes the 'summation' of decisions made at each stage may be said to form a *policy*.

A common example is the critical path method (CPM) where when the schedule is revised at various stages in the calendar for the project. The overall process is then referred to as PERT, or Program Evaluation and Review Technique, noting that in 'full PERT' statistical time estimates are given for the elements of the project.

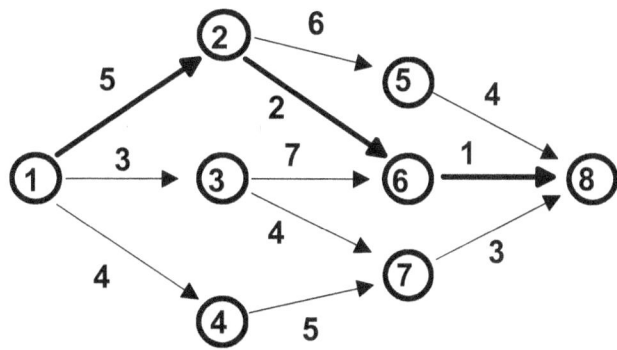

Figure 11.9.
Shortest route problem

Figure 11.9 shows the shortest route or 'stagecoach problem.
Here the nodes are towns and the distances between them are shown on the arrows between nodes. We seek to determine the shortest route systematically and this can be done using a tabular dynamic programming approach

Table 11.2 shows dynamic programming of the problem broken into three stages at which distance totals to each node are compared.

11. Production/Operations Management

Table 11.2. Dynamic programming solution for Figure 11.9.

Stage	Travel to node	Travel from node			Decision	ΣDistance
		1				
I	2*	5			1	5
	3	3			1	3
	4	4			1	4
II		2	3	4		
	5	5+6			2	11
	6*	5+2	3+7		2*	7
	7		3+4	4+5	3	7
		5	6	7		
III	8	11+4	7+1	7+3	6*	8 (min)

Then the distances to nodes 2, 3 and 4 in stage I are carried through as data for stage II. Here choices are made of the shortest cumulative distances to nodes 6 and 7 and the cumulative distances (the shortest values having been chosen) are carried through to stage III. Here node 6 is found to have given the shortest cumulative distance to node 8 (a distance = 8 units).

This completes the *forward pass*.

Now we carry out a *backward pass* in Table 11.2, moving through the points marked with an asterisk (*). Thus from stage III we note that it was node 6 which gave use the shortest distance and move back to the row for this at stage II. There we note that node 2 gave the shortest distance to node 6 and we move back to the row for node 2 at stage I.

Finally, we have found the nodes giving the shortest distance to be 1, 2, 6 and 8.

This particular problem is similar to the critical path problem except that we seek the shortest route rather than the longest time. Indeed, as we shall now show it is easily solved by a computer program using a similar approach to that used to program CPM.

The tabular approach of Table 11.2, however, can, with a little ingenuity be applied to almost any type of capital budgeting, inventory or like problem. In the former case alternative projects would correspond to nodes, their net present values (NPVs) then correspond to the stages (of the capital program) and their individual costs correspond to the route times between nodes. Then we use a tabular approach like that of Table 11.2 to determine the cheapest program (to gain a certain total NPV).

11. Production/Operations Management

Program for the shortest route problem

The following BASIC program for the shortest route problem is similar to the CPM program of Sec. 10.7, reading in the number of nodes (Z) and the number of links between them (E) at line 20. Then the node number pairs and distances for each of these links or elements are read in line 30.

The data included in lines 180 - 200 is for the problem of Figure 11.9 and the output (from line 160) will simply be the node numbers of the shortest route in reverse order (excluding node 1), that is 8, 6 and 2.

```
5 REM Program for Shortest Route Problem
10 DIM N(20, 20), D(20), T(20), P(20, 3), B(20)
20 READ Z, E: PRINT "Shortest route is:"
30 FOR I = 1 TO E: READ N(I, 1), N(I, 2), D(I): NEXT
40 FOR I = 1 TO E: FOR J = 1 TO 3: P(I, J) = 0: NEXT: NEXT
50 FOR K = 1 TO E: J = N(K, 2): I = 1
60 FOR M = 1 TO 3: IF P(J, M) = 0 THEN 70
I = I + 1: NEXT
70 P(J, M) = K: NEXT
80 FOR I = 1 TO Z: B(I) = 0: T(I) = 100: NEXT: T(1) = 0
90 FOR K = 1 TO E: I = N(K, 1): J = N(K, 2): T2 = T(I) + D(K)
100 IF T2 < T(J) THEN T(J) = T2
105 NEXT
110 FOR K = Z TO 1 STEP -1: F = 100
120 FOR M = 1 TO 3: IF P(K, M) = 0 THEN 150
130 L = P(K, M): N1 = N(L, 1): N2 = N(L, 2): T2 = T(N1) + D(L)
140 IF T2 < F THEN B(N2) = N1: F = T2
150 NEXT: NEXT: K = Z
160 PRINT K: K = B(K): IF K = 1 THEN END
170 GOTO 160
180 DATA 8,11
190 DATA 1,2,5, 1,3,3, 1,4,4, 2,5,6, 2,6,2
200 DATA 3,6,7, 3,7,4, 4,7,5, 5,8,4, 6,8,1, 7,8,3
```

As in CPM, a *precedence matrix* is formed in lines 50 to 70 and this stores the element numbers leading to each node. Then a *forward pass* is used in lines 80 to 105 to find the earliest finish/shortest distance for the nodes.

Then a *backward pass* is carried out in lines 110 to 150. Here the precedence matrix is used to store the node which gives the shortest distance to each node in array B( ).

Then, finally, in line 160 the shortest route is output. Such programs, of course, are a more attractive approach to dynamic programming problems than tables such as Table 11.2 which, except for the simplest of problems, quickly become rather cumbersome.

11. PRODUCTION/OPERATIONS MANAGEMENT

Conclusion

Dynamic programming in practice may simply mean procedures of regular review and adjustment of project and other schedules. Sometimes, however, very useful tabular methods of solution can be devised for capital budgeting problems.

For problems like the shortest route problem, on the other hand, simple programs such as that given here solve the problem readily.

11.6. Other network problems

We have already encountered network problems such as shortest route problems. In the present section we discuss two further network problems which may be of interest.

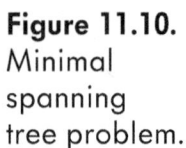
Figure 11.10. Minimal spanning tree problem.

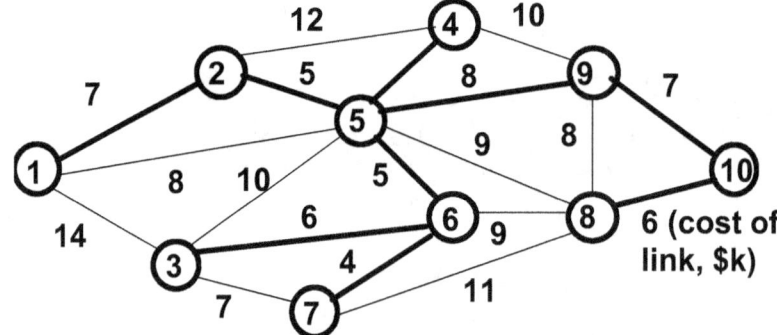

6 (cost of link, $k)

Figure 11.10 shows a minimal spanning tree problem where we seek to minimize the total cost of the links between the nodes (or the total cost associated with these connections) without leaving any node 'hanging' without a link to another (an example of such a situation might be a water supply or irrigation system).

A procedure for solving this problem is as follows:

1. Select *any* node and connect it to the closest node, breaking any links that are crossed in the process.

2. Connect any unconnected nodes to the nearest node, breaking any links that are crossed in the process.

3. Repeat the process until all nodes are connected.

Repeating this process and beginning at node 1 in Table 11.3 we obtain the results shown in Table 11.3.

11. PRODUCTION/OPERATIONS MANAGEMENT

Table 11.3. Steps taken for the problem of Figure 11.10

Step	Nodes connected	Cost ($k)	Σ Cost
1	1-2	7	7
2	2-5	5	12
3	5-6	5	17
4	6-7	4	21
5	6-3	6	27
6	5-9	6	33
7	5-4	7	40
8	9-10	7	47
9	10-8	6	53

Then the steps used in Table 11.3 give the minimal spanning tree shown in Figure 11.10 (the heavier lines). The reader can easily verify that this result does indeed give the minimal total cost of linkage of the points.

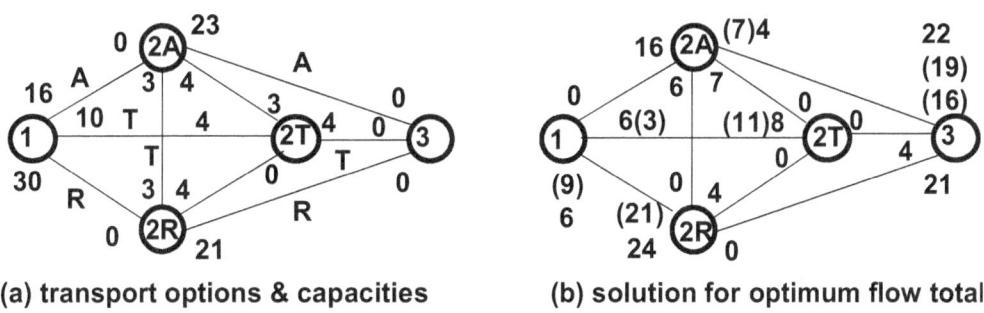

(a) transport options & capacities   (b) solution for optimum flow total

Figure 11.11. Maximum flow problem.

Figure 11.11 shows a maximal flow problem. Here we wish to deliver the maximum amount of mail from node 1 (the source or origin) to node 3 (a sink) by a combination of air, truck and rail transport and the links using these are marked A, T and R in Figure 11.11(a).

Nodes 2A, 2T and 2R are air, truck and rail terminals and the capacities for flow *away* from each node are shown in Figure 11.11 for each link, having different values at each end.

11. PRODUCTION/OPERATIONS MANAGEMENT

Then the problem is solved using the following procedure (known as the Fulkerson-Ford algorithm):

1. Find any path from origin to sink with positive flow capacities (C) on each link. If no such path exists we have the optimum solution.

2. Find the maximum positive capacity C* for this path and increase the flow along the path by this amount.

3. Compensate for this flow increase by:
    (a) Subtracting C* from all outgoing flows along this path.
    (b) Adding C* to all in going flows along this path.

Then following this procedure for the problem of Figure 11.11(a) the steps involved are:

Step	Path	Flow Change
1	1-2A-3	16
2	1-2R-3	21
3	1-2T-3	4
4	1-2T-2A-3	3
5	1-2R-2A-2	3

and the maximum total flow obtained is 47 (units/time).

Once again a remarkably simple procedure is involved as is typical of network problems, though these are often of crucial importance in business science.

Conclusion

We have now encountered an interesting variety of network problems, whilst CPM/PERT is dealt with in PP (Project Planning) and the distribution problem is given the 'works' in FM (Finite Methods).

11. Production/Operations Management

11.7. Inventory models

Inventory models, like queuing models, may be deterministic or *stochastic*. In addition, they may have some of the following features:

1. A *lead time* t_L is specified for ordering and this is the time taken to receive goods after ordering.
2. Inventory systems may be fixed-order or variable-order quantity systems.
3. Inventory systems may use a continuous inventory record or use a periodic review system giving a discontinuous inventory record.
4. The system may be single or multi-tier, involving different 'levels' of storage.
5. The system may hold single or multiple items.
6. If stockouts are allowed there may be provision for *backordering,* that is, orders are taken and filled at a later data to avoid loss of sales.
7. The system may have a continuous time horizon (as in the classical deterministic/analytical models) of a finite or discrete horizon in time.
8. Costs of purchase or production of items may be fixed or variable.
9. Ordering, shortage and other secondary costs may be taken into account (shortages involving an opportunity cost).

EOQ model

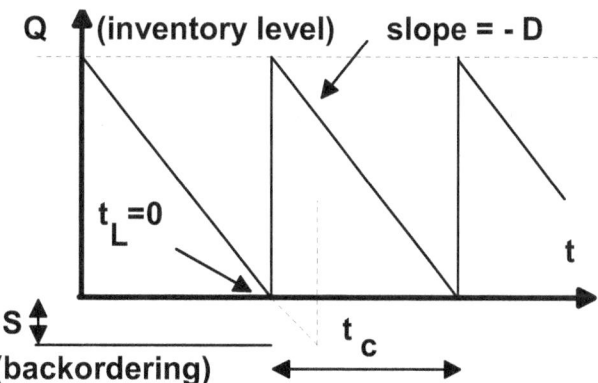

Figure 11.12. Inventory diagram.

Figure 11.12 illustrates the economic order quantity (EOQ) inventory model for a vendor. This deterministic model has a single level of stock of a single item with fixed cost, zero lead time and a continuous time horizon.

This uses a regular inventory cycle time t_c as shown in Figure 11.12.

The slope of the falling stock level = $-D$ where D is the demand per unit time, as shown.

11. Production/Operations Management

If we let the ordering or setup cost = C_0 and the holding or carrying cost = C_h the total cost per unit time is as shown in Figure 11.13.

Here the total cost is given by the function

$$C(Q) = f_1(Q) + f_2(Q) = (D/Q)C_0 + (Q/2)C_h \qquad (11.14)$$

where the holding cost is assumed directly proportional to the quantity held and the ordering cost is taken as inversely proportional to this quantity.

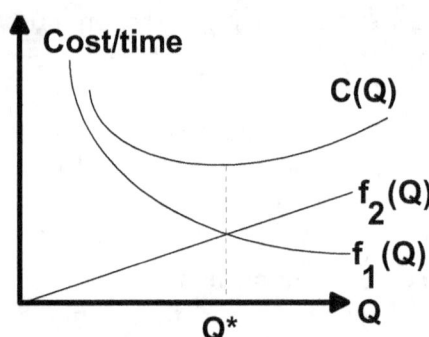

Figure 11.13. Minimum cost stock level Q^*.

Then, as shown in Figure 11.13, there is a quantity Q^* for which the total cost is a minimum. By differentiating Equation 11.14 with respect to Q this is obtained as

$$Q^* = \sqrt{(2DC_0/C_h)} \qquad (11.15)$$

and the corresponding inventory cycle time is $t_c^* = Q^*/D$.

Other inventory models

Many other inventory models can, of course, be devised, some of these including:

1. EOQ with lead time. For these the lead time demand is calculated as

$$R = t_L D - \text{Int}(t_L/t_c^*)Q^* \quad \text{where Int( ) = integer result/value} \qquad (11.16)$$

the second term on the RHS allowing for the situation $t_L > t_c^*$ when stocks are replenished by earlier orders. Then orders must be placed when stocks drop to the 'reserve' amount R.

2. EOQ with backordering. For these we include a cost of shortage C_s per unit time (of shortage). Then the EOQ is given by

$$Q^* = \sqrt{\{(2DC_0/C_h)[(C_h + C_s)/C_s]\}} \qquad (11.17)$$

and the maximum permitted shortage quantity is given by

$$S^* = \sqrt{[2C_0DC_h/(C_hC_s + C_s^2)]} \qquad (11.18)$$

11. PRODUCTION/OPERATIONS MANAGEMENT

3. EOQ with lost sales and models with deterministic periodic review. For these the EOQ is still that given by Equation 11.15.

4. Production inventory models. For these the EOQ approach can be used but is really not designed for the production situation. For this dynamic programming or the MRP approach discussed below are more helpful.

5. EOQ with discounts. When discounts for large orders are available a term DP where P = purchase cost, is added to Equation 11.14. Then Q^* is calculated with P as both the normal and discount value and decisions made on the basis of these results.

6. Stochastic demand can be dealt with approximately by using a mean value of the demand D when again Equation 11.15 gives the EOQ.

Material requirements planning (MRP)

This approach is useful in complex production situations and involves the following steps:

(a) A master production schedule is made.

(b) This is *exploded* to give schedules for the 'ingredients' of the 'recipe' with which the total product is made up. Sometimes a *bill of materials* is used for this purpose.

(c) These individual material schedules are used to determine the gross material requirements.

(d) Comparing these results with the existing inventories the net materials requirements are determined.

Establishing and maintaining such records requires a considerable effort sometimes but the resulting databases ultimately result in economies of operation in the long run.

Periodic maintenance scheduling

Maintenance scheduling can be considered a special case of the inventory problem. Then if we write a cost function for maintenance as

$$C(M) = (D/M)C_b + (M/2)C_p \qquad (11.19)$$

where M is the quantity of maintenance activity, C_b is the cost of breakdown and C_p is the cost per unit time of periodic maintenance, we obtain the same form of result as in Figure 11.13.

Then an economic maintenance quantity (units per year, for example) and associated cycle time can be established as for inventory in Equation 11.15.

Conclusion

The classical EOQ inventory model is both simple and useful and applies, sometimes with slight modification, to a wide range of inventory problems and also to such problems as maintenance scheduling.

In complex production situations such models as the EOQ model may be applied to a range of components and computer data bases are frequently used to cope with inventories.

11.8. Simulation

In the following section we briefly discuss (mathematical) simulation, paying particular attention to *stochastic simulation* using the well known *Monte Carlo method.* In this random numbers are used to generate data for a particular distribution so that its parameters can be estimated or to generate a random distribution.

Example:

The observed distribution of replacement times for cars in a car pool are shown in Table 11.4.

Then the right hand column of Table 11.4 shows the cumulative frequency range associated with each replacement time and this interval is used to 'capture' random numbers (1 - 100), each capture simulating a car requiring replacement at the corresponding time.

Table 11.4. Car replacement data.

Replacement time (months)	Frequency %	Random number range
12	4	1-4
16	7	5-11
20	13	12-24
24	17	25-41
28	27	42-68
32	11	69-79
36	7	80-86
40	6	87-92
44	5	93-97
48	2	98-100

11. PRODUCTION/OPERATIONS MANAGEMENT

Then using random numbers the simulation is summarized in Table 11.5. Here we wish to determine the number of replacement cars for a pool of ten cars that will be needed in a period of 12 years. The table shows the random numbers used for trial 1 of the simulation, using only the first two digits of these numbers.

Table 11.5. Car pool replacement simulation.

Car	Random number Trial:	Months to replacement						
		1	2	3	4	5	6	7
A	96(268)	44	20	24	16	28	36	
B	03(550)	12	16	24	32	32	24	20
C	22(188)	20	44	16	28	28		
D	63(759)	28	36	28	28	28		
E	55(006)	28	20	28	24	28		
F	81(972)	36	28	28	28	44		
G	06(344)	16	24	24	32	28	32	
H	92(363)	40	20	44	16	28		
I	96(083)	44	40	24	44			
J	92(993)	44	36	28	20	24		

Then trials are ceased for each car (or row) of the table when the next entry would cause that total number of months for that car to exceed 144 (or 12 years). Then finally the total number of cars needed is 53.

Note that in practice such a simulation should be repeated several times to obtain an averaged result.

Other applications

The Monte Carlo process may be applied to queuing problems.

For example, the times could be gap times between customer arrivals and/or the service times.

Once again, however, note that such simulation exercises need to be repeated a number of times to gain an accurate picture of the problem under study.

11.9. Queueing theory

Deterministric queueing models

As an example let $1/s = 4$ (service time), $1/a = 2$ (gap time) and $K = 2$ (system capacity) and assume that arrivals who cannot find a place in the queue *baulk* the system. Then the problem can be represented as shown in Figure 11.14.

The diagram completely describes the problem and shows, for example, that the first baulk occurs at time $t = 8$.

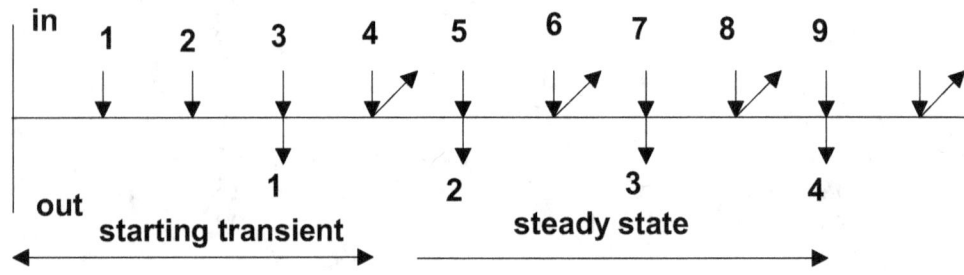

Figure 11.14. Deterministic queueing model.

Poisson distribution

The Poisson distribution is much used in queueing theory and is also useful in studying accident rates, numbers of defects in manufactured articles, variations in traffic flow etc. It gives the probability of *r* events occurring in an interval as

$$p(r) = \lambda^r e^{-\lambda}/r! \qquad (11.20)$$

where λ is the average number of events for that interval, that is, λ is the mean of distribution and it is also the variance.

11. Production/Operations Management

As an example consider a telephone exchange with 8 lines which averages 6 calls per minute. What is the probability that a caller can't connect within one minute? This is the probability of 9 or more calls in the one minute. Using Equation 11.20 with $\lambda = 6$ this is

$$\sum_{r=9}^{\infty} 6^r e^{-6}/r! = 1 - \sum_{r=0}^{8} 6^r e^{-6}/r! \qquad (11.21)$$

and we calculate the probabilities to be summed using

$$p(0) = e^{-6} = 0.0025, \quad p(r+1) = \lambda p(r)/(r+1) \qquad (11.22)$$

giving the table:

r	$\lambda/(r+1)$	p(r)
0	6	0.0025
1	3	0.015
2	2	0.045
3	1.5	0.09
4	1.2	0.135
5	1	0.162
6	6/7	0.162
7	0.75	0.1389
8		0.1042
		$\Sigma = 0.8546$

giving the answer

$p(\geq 9) = 1 - 0.8546 = 0.1454$ (to 4 d.p.)

Markov models: M/M/c/K case

Here M indicates a Markov or random model using a Poisson distribution for both the arrival gap times and the service times. There are c channels and the system capacity is once again finite and equal to K.

Then using the same process as in the telephone exchange example the probability of n customers being in the system is given by

$$p_n = r^n p_0/n! \qquad 0 \leq n < c \qquad (11.23a)$$

$$= r^n p_0/c^{n-c} c! \qquad c \leq n \leq K \text{ where } r = a/s \qquad (11.23b)$$

11. PRODUCTION/OPERATIONS MANAGEMENT

Substituting these results in the 'boundary condition' $\sum_{n=0}^{K} p_n = 1$ we obtain:

$$p_0 = [(r^c/c!)\{1 - z^{K-c+1}\}/(1 - z)\} + \sum_{n=0}^{c-1} r^n/n!]^{-1}$$

where $z = a/cs$ and the { } term is replaced by $\{K - c + 1\}$ if $z = 1$, is the probability of zero customers in the system

Similarly it can also be shown that the expected length of the queue is

$$L_q = \{p_0(cz)^c z\}/\{c!(1-z)^2\}[1 - z^{K-c+1} - (1-z)(K-c+1) z^{K-c}] \quad (11.24)$$

and the expected number of customers in the system (in the queue) is

$$L = L_q + c - p_0 \sum_{n=0}^{c-1}(c-n)(zc)^n/n! \quad (11.25)$$

The expected waiting time in the system is given by

$$W = L/a', \text{ where } a' = a(1 - p_K) \quad (11.26)$$

where a' is the 'effective' arrival rate, and the expected waiting time in the queue is simply

$$W_q = W - 1/s \quad (\text{or } L_q/a') \quad (11.27)$$

Example

Consider a car inspection centre with three bays ($c = 3$) for one car and space for only four further cars to queue, so that $K = 7$. Assume Poisson distributed arrivals at an average of one per minute ($a = 1$) and that the service time is also Poisson distributed with an average of 6 minutes ($s = 1/6$) so that we have $r = a/s = 6$ and $z = a/cs = 2$.

Than applying Equations 11.23 - 11.27 we obtain

$$p_0 = [(6^3/3!)\{1 - 2^5)/(1 - 2)\} + \sum_{0}^{2} 6^n/n!]^{-1} = 1/1141 = 0.00088$$

$$L_q = (p_0 6^3 \times 2)/3!(-1)^2[1 - 2^5 + 5 \times 2^4] = 3528 p_0 = 3.09$$

$$L = 3.09 + 3 - p_0 \sum_{0}^{2}(3-n)6^n/n! = 6.06$$

$$W = L/a(1 - p_7) = L/(1 - p_0 6^7 3^4 3!) = 12.3 \text{ mins}$$

$$W_q = W - 1/s = 12.3 - 6 = 6.3 \text{ mins}$$

and from these details it can be decided whether to alter the system.

11. PRODUCTION/OPERATIONS MANAGEMENT

Simulation

Queues can also be modelled by simulation simply by using the RND( ) function and a few lines of code. The following program simulates a queue with arrival time gap average = L = 1 and server time average = S = 2.5. Here in RND(ns) ns < 0 always gives same number (use for program test), ns = 0 gives last number (for demonstration purposes) and ns > 0 gives next random number generated and this is used for program applications.

```
5 REM Queue Simulation Program
a$ = CHR$(219) + CHR$(219) + CHR$(219) + CHR$(219) + CHR$(219)
RANDOMIZE TIMER: ns = 1: REM TIMER gives seed & ns selects same/last/new
REM same #, ns < 0; next #, ns > 0; last # ns = 0
10 L = 2: t1 = 0: t2 = 0: r = 0
20 s = 5: q = 0: g1 = 0: G2 = 0
30 FOR t = 1 TO 20
40 IF g1 > 0 THEN 60
50 r = 100 * RND(ns): r = INT(r) / 100: g1 = L * r: t1 = t1 + g1: X = RND(ns)
60 IF t < t1 THEN 65
q = q + 1: g1 = 0
65 IF G2 > 0 THEN 80
70 r = 100 * RND(ns): r = INT(r) / 100: G2 = s * r: t2 = t2 + G2: X = RND(ns)
80 IF t < t2 THEN 85
q = q - 1: G2 = 0
85 IF q < 0 THEN q = 0
90 FOR k = 1 TO q: PRINT a$; : NEXT: PRINT " "
95 NEXT t
96 PRINT t, q
100 END
```

The queue is plotted for 20 time increments and extension of this approach to two or more queues is straightforward and typically a limited queue length is allowed but arrivals baulking the first queue try the second queue before baulking the system.

Figure 11.15 shows the output from such a program (in Visual Basic) for two queues.

11. Production/Operations Management

Figure 11.15. Program output for simulation of two queues.

Here, arrival time gap = 1.25 and service time = 1.5 for both queues. When the second queue is shorter arrivals join this and when either queue is longer than 5 average service time is reduced to 1.

As shown in Figure 11.15, at the end of 200 time intervals both queue lengths are two and 164 services have been completed.

11.10. Project Control and Assessment

In the following section we discuss observations of production processes with a view to quality control, data being recorded on *control charts*. Brief mention is then made of the results that are typically obtained from *time and motion* or *method studies*.

Control charts

Control charts are a very simple means of monitoring production variations and are widely used. These take the appearance shown in Figure 11.16 where daily observations of the mean of sample variables relating to a product are plotted and compared with the required mean value for the product.

Figure 11.16. Control chart.

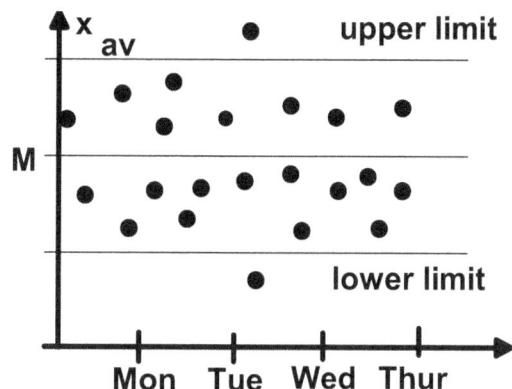

Consider for example the case of a pharmaceutical company manufacturing aspirin tablets with a mean weight of M = 0.441 and variance V = 0.008 and suppose that small samples of 5 tablets are taken to measure the mean weight x_{av}. Then the expected mean and standard deviation are:

$E(x_{av}) = M = 0.441$ (11.28)

$V(x_{av}) = V/\sqrt{n} = 0.008/\sqrt{5} = 0.00358 = S$ (11.29)

Then assuming that a deviation from the mean of 3S is allowable the upper and lower limits for the control chart are:

Upper limit = $M + 3S = 0.452$ (11.30a)

Lower limit = $M - 3S = 0.430$ (11.30b)

Then the observer notes any measurement falling outside these limits, recording the time (and date) and any reasons that might be thought responsible for it (if any). Later, therefore, trends in the deviant result might help locate the source of the problem or at least suggest what remedial action should be taken.

Assuming a Normal Distribution, the limits +/- 3S should be satisfied 99.4% of the time (hence the reason for taking note if they are not). These limits are fairly 'wide', however, and limits +/- 2S are also commonly used (95.4% for normal distribution).

In addition it is also of interest to plot the frequency distribution of the sample data to get an idea of its variance and any skew, for example.

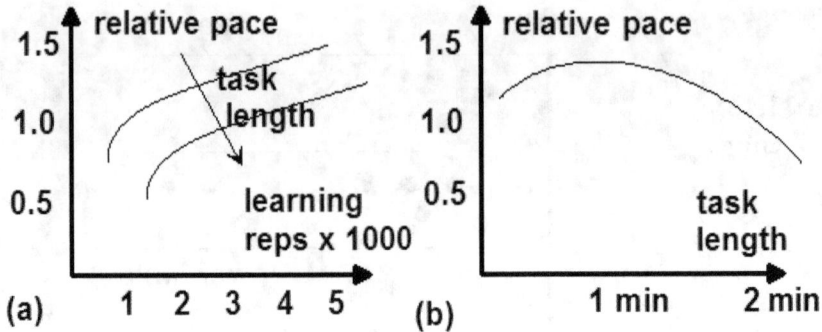

Fig. 11.17. Pace/standard vs learning reps & task length.

Figure 11.17 shows examples of the many results obtained from analysis of task performance. Case (a) shows that pace relative to a standard pace is asymptotic to a value somewhat above the standard value after a large number of learning repetitions. The learning curve is then found to be a little lower as the length of the task increases

Then case (b) shows that the relative pace achieved ultimately peaks at task lengths of around one minute.

Other factors that might contribute to the results of such studies include:
1. The complexity of the task.
2. The similarity of the task to known tasks (i.e. its familiarity).
3. The level of skill required by the task.
4. Operator attitude, motivation etc.
5. Operator turnover (i.e. replacement through retirement etc.).

Many other factors can be involved on the human side, such as group empathy, managerial style.

Conclusion

Control charts and the like are an important aid to production control. These may also be used for behavioural studies wherein, of course, some production problems will lie.

11. Production/Operations Management

11.11. References

Ackoff RL, Sasieni MW, *Fundamentals of Operations Research*, Wiley, NY, 1968.

Enrick, NL, *Management Operations Research*, Holt Rinehart & Winston, NY, 1965.

Hillier FS, Lieberman GJ, *Introduction to Operations Research*, 3rd end, Holden-Day, Oakland CA, 1980.

_____, A *Programmed Introduction to PERT*, ITT/Federal Electric Corp., Wiley, NY, 1963.

Mohr WE, *Flowline Reference Manual*, EPAC P/L, Melbourne, 1977.

Mohr WE, *Project Management and Control*, 3rd edn, Dept. of Architecture and Building, Univ. of Melbourne, 1981.

Mohr GA, Optimization of critical path models using finite elements, *Trans Instn Civil Engineers, Australia,* vol. CE35(2), p 123, 1994.

Neter, J, Wasserman, W, Whitmore, GA, *Applied Statistics*, Allyn and Bacon, Boston MS, 1978.

Powers MJ, Adams DR, Milles, HD, *Computer Information Systems Development: Analysis and Design*, South-Western, Cincinnati OH, 1984.

Schmenner RW, *Production/Operations Management: Concepts and Situations*, 4th edn, McMillan, NY, 1990.

Smith KM, *Critical Path Planning: A Practical Guide*, MacDonald, London, 1971.

Wild R, *Mass Production Management*, Wiley, London, 1972.

11. Production/Operations Management

Chapter 12

NUMERICAL METHODS FOR ECONOMETRICS

Input-Output Analysis (IOA), a very widely used matrix method of modeling the fluctuations in flows of goods and services between groups of companies, sectors of a national economy, or between nations, is briefly discussed and useful techniques for applying constraints to IOA models introduced.

Time stepping of macroeconomic models is then briefly discussed as such time stepping can be applied to many numerical models in management science.

Finally coupling of separate IOA models, regarding each as an *element* of a larger system, is discusses and a program given to demonstrate this process.

12.1. Input-output analysis

Input-output analysis is one of the most important applications of numerical methods. At a microeconomic level it applies to the $ inputs of goods and labour services to a company from other companies and to the $ outputs of goods and services from that company to other companies. At a macroeconomic level these inputs and outputs are between sectors of the economy, at the international level being the trade between nations.

Input-output analysis was developed by Wassily Leontief at Harvard in 1931 and his study of the US economy with it gained a Nobel Prize and later Laurence Klein applied IOA to the world economy, also receiving a Nobel Prize.

At a basic level input-output analysis analyses the interdependence of various industries. Consider, for example, three companies X, Y and Z that sell/buy products/materials to/from each other, the value of these transactions over some regular period being shown in Table 12.1.

12. Numerical Methods for Econometrics

Table 12.1. Input-output analysis data

	Purchases				Total
	X	Y	Z	External	Output ($)
Sales					
X	-	60	40	100	200
Y	40	-	100	260	400
Z	50	100	-	50	200
Labour	110	240	60	-	410
Total input	200	400	200	410	1,210

This table also includes labour costs for the period, as well as *external* sales (other than to the other two companies). Then company Y, for example, sells $40 of goods to X and $100 to Z, the remaining $260 of its total output ($400) being sold externally.

To produce this output Y purchases $60 in goods from X and $100 from Z, also spending $240 on labour costs.

Then from Table 12.1 we can easily calculate *input coefficients* by dividing the three X,Y,Z columns by their totals, giving the results shown in Table 12.2.

Table 12.2. Input coefficients

	X	Y	Z
X	-	0.15	0.2
Y	0.2	-	0.5
Z	0.25	0.25	-
Labour	0.55	0.6	0.3

For company Y, for example, Table 12.2 shows that for each $1 of output produced 15 cents is spent on purchases from X, 25 cents on purchases from Z and 60 cents is spent on labour costs.

Then using the coefficients of Table 12.2 we can write the outputs x,y,z for companies X, Y, Z as

$$x = 0.15y + 0.20z + 100 \qquad (12.1a)$$
$$y = 0.20x + 0.50z + 260 \qquad (12.1b)$$
$$z = 0.25x + 0.25y + 50 \qquad (12.1c)$$

Now suppose we wish to determine the effect of increasing the external sales of X to $120 (from $100).

To do this we change the last number in Equation 12.1a and rearrange the equations to give:

$$M\{x\} = \begin{bmatrix} 1 & -0.15 & -0.20 \\ -0.20 & 1 & -0.50 \\ -0.25 & -0.25 & 1 \end{bmatrix} \begin{Bmatrix} x \\ y \\ x \end{Bmatrix} = \begin{Bmatrix} 120 \\ 260 \\ 50 \end{Bmatrix} = \{q\}$$

(12.2)

and solving these equations using the program given in Section 3.5 we obtain:

$$x = \$223, \quad y = \$408, \quad z = \$208$$

From these results we are then, for example, able to calculate the increased labour costs resulting for each company as:

X: 223 x 0.55 = 122.7   (increase of $12.7)
Y: 408 x 0.60 = 244.8   (increase of $4.8)
Z: 208 x 0.30 = 62.4   (increase of $2.4)

Here a 'flow through' effect to other companies is immediately apparent (a more superficial approach would predict the increase in labour cost for X as increase in external output (20) multiplied by 0.55 = $11 and affects on other companies would be neglected).

12.2. Optimizing IOA problems

The foregoing problem can be optimized by choosing the unconstrained objective function

$$f_u = x_1 + x_2 + x_3 \tag{12.3}$$

subject to the constraints

$$x_i \geq 0 \tag{12.4}$$

$$(x_i - x_{av}) = 0 \tag{12.5}$$

which allow only positive x_i and we seek to make them equal (to an average value) and are applied using the penalty augmented objective function

$$f = f_u + \beta \Sigma (x_i - x_{av})^2 + \beta \Sigma x_i^2 \mid x_i < 0 \tag{12.6}$$

12. NUMERICAL METHODS FOR ECONOMETRICS

Using the off-diagonal input coefficients as design variables a 'gradient matrix' for minimization by steepest descent is given by

$$[G_{ij}] = [\delta f / \delta M_{ij}] \quad i \neq j \qquad (12.7)$$

where $\delta M_{ij} = M_{ij}/10$ is used as a perturbation.

Then trial searches of length S are conducted with the trial M matrix given by

$$M'_{ij} = M_{ij} - SG_{ij} \quad i \neq j \qquad (12.8)$$

to find a minimum in f, disallowing off diagonal values of M_{ij} greater than -0.05.

With only $\beta = 1$ successive searches are:

$S = 0.0000043, \ f = 8290, \ f_u = 1106$
$S = 0.0000024, \ f = 7110, \ f_u = 1114$
$S = 0.0000071, \ \ f = 6375, \ f_u = 1034$
$S = 0.0000074, \ f = 914, \ f_u = 864$
$S = 0.0000032, \ f = 902, \ f_u = 866$
$S = 0.00000054, \ f = 900, \ f_u = 868$

finally yielding the solution:

$$x_1 = 289.7, \ x_2 = 293.2, \ x_3 = 285.3 \qquad (12.9)$$

with

$$M = \begin{bmatrix} 1 & -0.5087 & -0.0718 \\ -0.05 & 1 & -0.0657 \\ -0.2776 & -0.5282 & 1 \end{bmatrix} \qquad (12.10)$$

and with $\beta = 10$ the solution cannot be significantly improved.

If, on the other hand, only the first two of the latter searches with $\beta = 1$ are carried out, then a further two searches with $\beta = 10, 100$ and 1000, a similar solution is obtained, that is $x_1 = 295.8$, $x_2 = 297.7$ and $x_3 = 290.8$.

The solution, though approximate, is much closer to satisfying Equation 12.5 than the initial solution of Equations 12.1, that is $x_1 = 200$, $x_2 = 400$, $x_3 = 200$, and the method used here shows some promise.

12.3. Applying constraints to matrix problems

Equation 12.11 is a hypothetical input-output analysis problem with the constraint $x_1 = 0.3x_3$ imposed using the *Lagrange multiplier* method.

$$\begin{bmatrix} 1 & -0.2 & -0.1 & -0.05 & 1 \\ -0.3 & 1 & -0.2 & -0.1 & 0 \\ -0.4 & -0.3 & 1 & -0.2 & -0.3 \\ -0.5 & -0.3 & -0.4 & 1 & 0 \\ 1 & 0 & -0.3 & 0 & 0.000001 \end{bmatrix} \begin{Bmatrix} x_1 \\ x_2 \\ x_3 \\ x_4 \\ \lambda \end{Bmatrix} = \begin{Bmatrix} 1 \\ 7 \\ 12 \\ 17 \\ 0 \end{Bmatrix} \qquad (12.11)$$

The inclusion of the extra row and column corresponding to the Lagrange multiplier λ presents no difficulty and Mohr's *small slack variable* $1/\beta$, $\beta = 10^6$, is included on the diagonal so that pivoting is not required by the solution routine (normally a zero appears in this position).

Without this constraint the solution is $\{x\} = \{10, 20, 30, 40\}$, but with it we obtain (to 3 d.p.)

$$\{x\} = \{8.839, 19.448, 29.462, 39.039, 0.949\} \qquad (12.12)$$

and this satisfies the constraint to 5 d.p., i.e., it is satisfied to the accuracy imposed by β (note that β should be 2-3 d.p. less than the precision of the computation).

Now, however, the original equations are only satisfied approximately (we have in effect altered them), for example substituting the values of Equation 12.12 into the first we obtain

$$x_1 - 0.2x_2 - 0.1x_3 - 0.05x_4 = 0.051 \qquad (12.13)$$

not = 1 as required, so that the value of λ must be included as well to obtain the correct result. The degree of approximation, and in turn the severity of the constraints, is then indicated by the magnitude of the Lagrange multiplier(s).

Such problems can be written in the general form

$$\begin{bmatrix} S & G^T \\ G & -I_m/\beta \end{bmatrix} \begin{Bmatrix} x \\ \lambda \end{Bmatrix} = \begin{Bmatrix} q \\ q_c \end{Bmatrix} \qquad (12.14)$$

where G is a matrix of m constraint equations and I_m is a unit matrix of order m.

12. NUMERICAL METHODS FOR ECONOMETRICS

Using the second row of Equation 12.14 we can write

$$\{\lambda\} = \beta G\{x\} - \beta\{q_c\} \tag{12.15}$$

and substituting this result into the first row of Equation 12.14 gives

$$[S + \beta G^T G]\{x\} = \{q\} + \beta G^T\{q_c\} \tag{12.16}$$

and this λ–β *transformation* was discovered by Mohr.

Now β acts as a *penalty factor* (so that the small slack variables might be described as inverse penalty factors). These are the preferred means of imposing such constraints because the original matrix is not increased in size, instead being augmented by the *penalty matrix* $\beta\, G^T G$.

This penalty method is easy to program, in the present example reading in a constraint row 1, 0, -0.3, 0, 0, where note that the last entry is the RHS or 'load' value (corresponding to q_c in Equation 12.14).

Using the penalty method (again with $\beta = 10^6$) the solution of Equation 12.12 is again obtained but there is no Lagrangian multiplier value to remind us of the degree of approximation (in relation to the unconstrained original equations). But if we calculate

$$\beta\,(x_1 - 0.3x_3) = 0.949 \text{ (not zero)} \tag{12.17}$$

we see that that an implicit Lagrange multiplier value is revealed (the same as that obtained in Equation 12.12).

As noted above, RHS values for the constraints must be given (as indeed is the case for Lagrange multiplier constraints) and, for example, constraints such as $x_1 = x_3 + 10$ are easily imposed, the solution to our example then being (this replacing the original constraint)

$$\{x\} = \{31.326,\ 25.549,\ 21.326,\ 48.858\} \tag{12.18}$$

Note that such constraints as the latter can be added to any matrix solution routine such as that given earlier by adding:

$$\beta \begin{bmatrix} 1 & 0 & -1 & 0 \\ 0 & 0 & 0 & 0 \\ -1 & 0 & 1 & 0 \\ 0 & 0 & 0 & 0 \end{bmatrix} = 10\beta \begin{Bmatrix} 1 \\ 0 \\ -1 \\ 0 \end{Bmatrix} \tag{12.19}$$

to the reduced/problem (without row/column 5) problem of Equation 12.11, giving the same result as Equation 12.18 (given the same β).

Then note that in the special case where we want to suppress a variable to zero (the most common *boundary condition* in physical problems) we simply add a large (penalty) factor to the diagonal location in the coefficient matrix corresponding to that variable (i.e. in position (3,3) if it is the third variable).

Finally a third way of enforcing matrix constraints is *basis transformation* (the 'basis' in any problem being the set of variables used to model it). If for example we wish to enforce the constraint $x_2 = x_4$ in our example problem we use the transformation:

$$\{x'\} = \begin{Bmatrix} x'_1 \\ x'_2 \\ x'_3 \\ x'_4 \end{Bmatrix} = \begin{bmatrix} 1 & 0 & 0 & 0 \\ 0 & 1 & 0 & -1 \\ 0 & 0 & 1 & 0 \\ 0 & 0 & 0 & 1 \end{bmatrix} \begin{Bmatrix} x_1 \\ x_2 \\ x_3 \\ x_4 \end{Bmatrix} = T\{x\} \quad (12.20)$$

to transform the problem variables, using the *congruent transformation*

$$T^T S T\{x\} = \{q\} \quad (12.21)$$

to transform the coefficient matrix to that for the new variables.

Basis transformation is much used by Mohr's *method of nested interpolations* for *finite element* formulation to transform a *global* set of element variables to a more convenient *local* set corresponding to a known (convenient) interpolation.

The following program can be used to demonstrate all three constraint methods described above:

```
5 REM Example of Lagrange Multiplier & Penalty constraints
10 DIM C(20, 20), V(20), G(10, 20), F(20): a$ = "####": B$ = "#######.###"
20 DIM T(20, 20), S(20, 20): B = 100000
30 RESTORE 420
40 READ NV, NC, NS, IB
50 FOR I = 1 TO NV: FOR J = 1 TO NV
60 READ C(I, J): NEXT: NEXT
70 FOR I = 1 TO NV: READ V(I): NEXT
80 FOR I = 1 TO NC: FOR J = 1 TO NV
90 READ G(I, J): NEXT: READ F(I): NEXT
100 IF IB = 0 THEN 160
110 FOR I = 1 TO NV: FOR J = 1 TO NV: READ T(I, J)
120 S(I, J) = C(I, J): NEXT: NEXT
130 FOR I = 1 TO NV: FOR J = 1 TO NV: C(I, J) = 0
140 FOR K = 1 TO NV: C(I, J) = C(I, J) + S(I, K) * T(K, J)
150 NEXT: NEXT: NEXT
```

12. NUMERICAL METHODS FOR ECONOMETRICS

```
160 FOR I = 1 TO NV: FOR K = 1 TO NC
170 V(I) = V(I) + B * G(K, I) * F(K): NEXT: NEXT
180 FOR I = 1 TO NV: FOR J = 1 TO NV
190 FOR K = 1 TO NC
200 C(I, J) = C(I, J) + G(K, I) * G(K, J) * B: NEXT K
210 NEXT J: NEXT I
220 FOR K = 1 TO NS
230 READ N, SP
240 FOR I = 1 TO NV
250 C(N, I) = 0: V(I) = V(I) - SP * C(I, N)
260 C(I, N) = 0: NEXT I
270 V(N) = SP: C(N, N) = 1: NEXT
280 FOR I = 1 TO NV: X = C(I, I): V(I) = V(I) / X
300 FOR J = I + 1 TO NV: C(I, J) = C(I, J) / X: NEXT
320 FOR K = 1 TO NV
330 IF K = I THEN GOTO 370
340 X = C(K, I): V(K) = V(K) - X * V(I)
350 FOR J = I + 1 TO NV
360 C(K, J) = C(K, J) - X * C(I, J): NEXT J
370 NEXT K
380 NEXT I
390 PRINT "Node    Value"
400 FOR I = 1 TO NV
410 PRINT USING a$; I; : PRINT USING B$; V(I): NEXT
420 DATA 5,1,0,1
430 DATA 1,-.2,-.1,-.05,1
440 DATA -.3,100000,-.2,-.1,0
450 DATA -.4,-.3,1,-.2,-1
460 DATA -.5,-.3,-.4,1,0
470 DATA 1,0,-1,0,.000001        : REM L CONSTRAINT X1 = X3
480 DATA 1,7,12,17,0
490 DATA 1,-1,0,0,0,0            : REM PENALTY CONSTRAINT X1 = X2
500 DATA 1,0,0,0,0               : REM BASIS TRANS. MATRIX For X2 = X4
510 DATA 0,1,0,-1,0
520 DATA 0,0,1,0,0
530 DATA 0,0,0,1,0
540 DATA 0,0,0,0,1
```

The data is for the problem of Equation 12.11 and line 420 = 5 equations, 1 penalty constraint, no *specified (boundary)* values for the variables (if any these would be the last data lines, being read in line 230). The solution routine is Gauss-Mohr reduction, that is, the GJR routine of Section 3.4 modified for *direct solution* to operate only to the right of pivot and on the right side (i.e. the inverse matrix is not formed).

12. Numerical Methods for Econometrics

As noted above the penalty method is preferable to and equivalent to the Lagrange multiplier method (first proved by Mohr), whilst the basis transformation method is generally used for *transforming*, not constraining, variables.

Indeed trying to use all three methods at once and using the 'BT' method does not give the same results as for the other two methods because, in Equation 12.20, for example, it does not effectively *eliminate* variables from the solution (as the other methods do) but 'rescales' them'. At this point only some attention to the penalty method is recommended, and particularly the 'big number on the diagonal' method of suppressing variables to zero.

12.4. Time stepping macroeconomic models

Klein modeled the performance of the US economy in the years 1921 - 1941 using three *structural equations* (in $B US):

$$C = 16.8 + 0.02P + 0.23P_L + 0.8(W + S) \tag{12.22}$$

$$I = 17.8 + 0.23P + 0.55P_L - 0.15K_L \tag{12.23}$$

$$W = 1.6 + 0.42X + 0.16X_L + 0.131|t - 1931| \tag{12.24}$$

where $|t - 1931|$ is a heavy side step function (i..e. $= 0$ of $t < 1931$ and $= 1$ if $t \geq 1931$), adding three *definitive equations*

$$X = C + I + G \tag{12.25}$$

$$P = X - W - T \tag{12.26}$$

$$K = K_L + I \tag{12.27}$$

where now C = consumption, I = total investment, W, S are the private/public sector wages, X is the private sector production, P are the profits (non wage income), K = stocks (capital goods at end of year), T = business taxes, G = government spending, and subscript L denotes value for the previous year.

We can make the model more 'self contained' by assuming

$$S = 0.8G \quad \text{and} \quad T = 0.2(W + P) \tag{12.28}$$

and including these in Klein's equations.

12. NUMERICAL METHODS FOR ECONOMETRICS

Then the equations can be rearranged and written in the matrix form

$$A\{V\} = \begin{bmatrix} 1 & 0 & -0.8 & 0 & -0.02 & 0 \\ 0 & 1 & 0 & 0 & -0.23 & 0 \\ 0 & 0 & 1 & -0.42 & 0 & 0 \\ -1 & -1 & 0 & 1 & 0 & 0 \\ 0 & 0 & 1.2 & -1 & 1.2 & 0 \\ 0 & -1 & 0 & 0 & 0 & 1 \end{bmatrix} \begin{Bmatrix} C \\ I \\ W \\ X \\ P \\ K \end{Bmatrix} = \begin{Bmatrix} Q_1 \\ Q_2 \\ Q_3 \\ G \\ 0 \\ K_L \end{Bmatrix} \quad (12.29)$$

where $Q_1 = 16.8 + 0.23 P_L + 0.8 S$ (and $S = 0.8 G$)

$Q_2 = 17.8 + 0.55 P_L - 0.15 K_L$

$Q_3 = 1.6 + 0.16 X_L + 0.13 | t - t_0 |$

Now they can be coded and *time stepping* used with the simple routine given in Section 3.4 used to solve for the variables $\{V\}$ after each of a succession of one year steps.

```
5 DIM A(6, 6), q(6), R(6), v(6), S(6), F(6), PR(100, 2), FR(6)
10 FOR j = 1 TO 6: S(j) = 0: F(j) = 1: L(j) = 0: NEXT j: SCREEN 1: COLOR 4, 1
15 F(6) = 2: REM S(2)=100:S(3)=100:S(5)=100
20 n = 6: z = 0: D = 0: K1 = 100: X1 = 100: P1 = 10: W1 = 25
25 FOR I = 1 TO n: FOR j = 1 TO n: READ A(I, j): NEXT j: NEXT I: GOSUB 100
30 T = .2: G = .3: z = z + 1: IF z > 30 GOTO 85
32 REM IF z >= 10 OR z = 11 THEN G = .5 AND T = .5
33 REM ? "IP - if 99 then end":input g,t:if g=99 goto 85
35 R(2) = 17.8 + .55 * P1 - .15 * K1: R(3) = 1.6 + .16 * X1 + .13 * D: R(6) = K1
40 R(5) = -T * (W1 + P1): R(4) = G* R(5)
S = .8 * R(4): R(1) = 16.8 + .23 * P1 + .8 * S
45 FOR I = 1 TO n: q(I) = 0: FOR K = 1 TO n
50 q(I) = q(I) + A(I, K) * R(K): NEXT K: NEXT I
55 FOR j = 1 TO n: v(j) = (2 * q(j) + S(j)) / F(j)
60 A = 10 * (z - 2): B = 150 - L(j)
65 X = 10 * (z - 1): y = 150 - v(j): LINE (A, B)-(X, y): v = INT(y / 8.5) + 2
66 IF z < 30 GOTO 68
67 LOCATE v, 38: PRINT j
68 NEXT j
70 P1 = q(5): X1 = q(4): K1 = q(6): W1 = q(3)
75 FOR j = 1 TO n: L(j) = v(j): NEXT j: IF z > 10 THEN D = D + 1
80 PR(z, 1) = P1: PR(z, 2) = K1
82 GOTO 30
```

```
85 FOR I = 1 TO n: FR(I) = q(I): NEXT I
PRINT "PP = ", q(4), "Profit = ", q(5)
86 DRAW "bm0,150 m300,150 bm0,0 m0,200"
LOCATE 21, 2: PRINT "1=C 2=I 3 = WP 4 = priv. prod 5 = profit 6 = stocks"
90 END
100 FOR I = 1 TO n: X = A(I, I): A(I, I) = 1
105 FOR j = 1 TO n: A(I, j) = A(I, j) / X: NEXT j
110 FOR K = 1 TO n: IF K = I GOTO 120
112 X = A(K, I): A(K, I) = 0
115 FOR j = 1 TO n: A(K, j) = A(K, j) - X * A(I, j): NEXT j
120 NEXT K: NEXT I
125 RETURN
130 DATA 1,0,-.8,0,-.02,0
135 DATA 0,1,0,0,-.23,0
140 DATA 0,0,1,-.42,0,0
145 DATA -1,-1,0,1,0,0
150 DATA 0,0,1,-1,1,0
155 DATA 0,-1,0,0,0,1
```

Here the initial values of *P* etc. are set in line 20 and the values chosen in Equations 12.28 are set in line 30. Originally we have $T = 0.2$ and $G = 0.3$ (in line 30) and at the conclusion of the 20 one year steps the values of private production and profit are output (before line 86), the results being 33.49 and 4.45 respectively.

If the REM is removed from line 32 then values $T = 0.5$ and $G = 0.5$ apply at and after year 10, and the final values output for private production and profit are then 39.32 and 5.93. Thus by increasing taxes, and thence government spending, we have increased private production and profits substantially, a good example of Keynesian economic principles.

Figure 12.1 shows typical output from a Visual Basic version of this program with changes in *T* and *G* only occurring at years 10 and 11, giving the expected disturbance in activity.

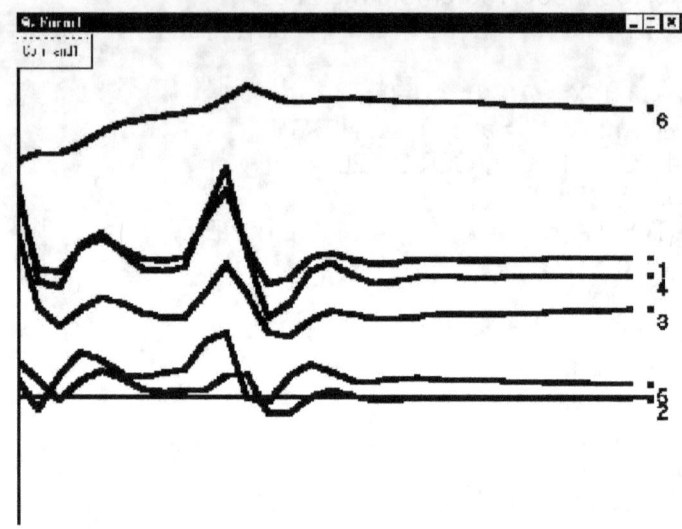

Figure 12.1. Output from time stepping program.

12.5. Finite element IOA models

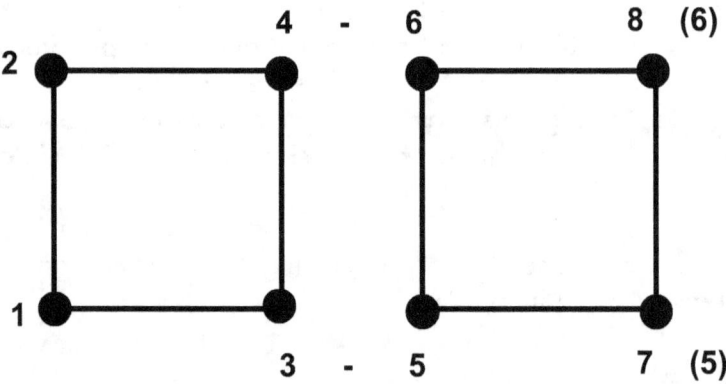

Figure 12.2. Two element system for IOA.

Here we see two 'elements' with four 'nodes'. For the first element Equation 12.11 without its Lagrange multiplier constraint applies. For the second Equation 12.11 in symmetric form, with the below diagonal entries made equal to those above, is used.

12. Numerical Methods for Econometrics

The following listing is of a program which uses Gauss reduction to solve both symmetric and unsymmetric banded matrix problems.

Line 30 sets number of nodes per element (NCN) and the length of the band width to the left of the pivot (NM), that is *exclusive* half band width NBW, where half band width = (max. node no. difference in any element) X NDF, here with NDF = 1. For symmetric problems set NM = 0 and for unsymmetric problems set NM $\geq$ 1 (its value is calculated in line 40).

Line 50 reads the nodal loads and following data lines give the node numbers for each element followed by its IOA matrix.

```
10 REM Band Solution Routine For I/O Analysis
20 DIM EM(6, 6), S(80, 41), R(41), Q(80), NN(10, 6)
30 RESTORE 500: NCN = 4: nm = 1
40 READ NP, NE, NBW: IF nm > 0 THEN nm = NBW
50 FOR I = 1 TO NP: READ Q(I): NEXT: REM Read loads
60 FOR N = 1 TO NE
70 FOR J = 1 TO NCN: READ NN(N, J): NEXT: REM Read element data
80 FOR I = 1 TO NCN: FOR J = 1 TO NCN
90 READ EM(I, J): NEXT: NEXT
100 FOR I = 1 TO NCN: NR = NN(N, I)
110 FOR J = 1 TO NCN: NC = NN(N, J)
120 NCB = NC - NR + nm + 1: IF NR > NC AND nm = 0 THEN 140
130 S(NR, NCB) = S(NR, NCB) + EM(I, J)
140 NEXT: NEXT
150 NEXT N
160 FOR L = 1 TO NP: REM ##### start reduction loop
170 NDIF = NP - L + 1: IF NDIF > NBW THEN LIM = NBW + 1
180 LIM = LIM - 1
190 XK = 1 / S(L, nm + 1): Q(L) = Q(L) * XK
200 FOR J = 1 TO LIM: IA = L + J: JA = nm + 1 - J: IF nm = 0 THEN IA = L
IF nm = 0 THEN JA = J + 1
210 IF JA < 1 THEN 220
R(J) = S(IA, JA): REM Collect row multipliers
220 NEXT
230 FOR J = 2 TO LIM + 1: S(L, J + nm) = S(L, J + nm) * XK: NEXT
REM Row/pivot
240 FOR I = 1 TO LIM: NR = L + I: NR = L + I
250 IF R(I) = 0 THEN 290
LC = nm - I + 2: IF nm = 0 THEN LC = 1
NC = LC + LIM
260 FOR J = LC TO NC: JP = J + I
270 S(NR, J) = S(NR, J) - S(L, JP) * R(I): NEXT: REM Row subtraction
280 Q(NR) = Q(NR) - R(I) * Q(L)
290 NEXT I
300 NEXT L: REM ##### end reduction loop
```

12. NUMERICAL METHODS FOR ECONOMETRICS

```
310 FOR L = NP TO 1 STEP -1
320 IF LIM < NBW THEN LIM = LIM + 1
330 FOR J = 1 TO LIM: JA = J + 1 + nm
340 Q(L) = Q(L) - S(L, JA) * Q(L + J): NEXT: NEXT: REM Back substitution
350 FOR I = 1 TO NP: PRINT I, Q(I): NEXT
360 END
500 DATA 8,2,3
510 DATA 1,7,12,17,1,7,12,17
520 DATA 1,2,3,4
530 DATA 1,-.2,-.1,-.05
540 DATA -.3,1,-.2,-.1
550 DATA -.4,-.3,1,-.2
560 DATA -.5,-.3,-.4,1
570 DATA 5,6,7,8
580 DATA 1,-.2,-.1,-.05
590 DATA -.2,1,-.2,-.1
600 DATA -.1,-.2,1,-.2
610 DATA -.05,-.1,-.2,1
800 DATA 6,1,5
803 DATA 1,7,13,24,12,17
805 DATA 1,2,3,4,5,6
810 DATA 1,-.2,-.1,-.05,0,0
820 DATA -.3,1,-.2,-.1,0,0
830 DATA -.4,-.3,2,-.4,-.1,-.05
840 DATA -.5,-.3,-.6,2,-.2,-.1
850 DATA 0,0,-.1,-.2,1,-.2
860 DATA 0,0,-.05,-.1,-.2,1
```

The data appended in lines 500 - 610 to the program is for problem of Figure 12.2 with the two elements separate and Table 12.3 shows the results for this as case (a). In case (b) NM = 0 is specified (in line 30) and the element matrices are assumed symmetric (and treated accordingly) so that the solutions are the same four numbers.

In case (c) the node pairs 3,5 and 4,6 are merged and nodes 7,8 become 5,6, so that the node number set for element 2 is 3,4,5,6 and NBW = 3 still. Combining the 'loads' at the merged nodes we have $q_3 = 12$ and $q_4 = 24$. The data for this case is given with the program listing in Appendix B (note that there NBW is the *inclusive* value, that is greater by 1 than in the program above).

The results are, of course, quite different but note that with overlapping elements two diagonal entries will be two, not one as usual.

Table 12.3. Solutions for system of Figure 12.2.

Node	(a)	(b)	(c)	(d)
1	10.00	7.12	6.90	25.51
2	20.00	14.76	14.90	45.47
3	30.00	20.24	16.85	93.24
4	40.00	22.88	24.63	121.74
5	7.12	7.12	23.62	54.62
6	14.76	14.76	25.03	44.76
7	20.24	20.24	-	
8	22.88	22.88	-	

Altering these to one, the result in case (d), now very different indeed, and it appears that case (c), in fact, is the appropriate solution for the overlapping element case.

This was confirmed by applying the constraints $x_3 = x_5$, $x_4 = x_6$ to the 8 node problem (case (a)) using penalty factors when exactly the same results as case (c) are obtained. Here $\beta > 10^4$ and 14 d.p. computation was used. With 8 d.p. computation and $\beta = 10^5$ the results are similar but less so with $\beta = 10^6$, illustrating that we require β about 3 'places' less than the precision of computation.

It is also confirmed by using the data in lines 800+ above, where the two element matrices have been summed manually, when NCN = 6 must be set at the start of the program. Again the results of case (c) in Table 12.3 are obtained.

Conclusion

IOA problems such as that of Section 12.1 can be modeled as distribution problems. The steepest descent and FRD procedures used in Chapters 7, 8 and 9 can then be applied to such models, yielding identical optimum solutions in the small problems studied so far.

Though IOA is a matrix problem, however, assumption of simple linear two freedom elements like those for distribution requires the assumption of arbitrary cost parameters to be associated with the links between companies and their exports.

What is quite practical, is optimization of IOA models, as shown in Section 12.2, and use of the penalty technique of Section 12.3 to link nodes of otherwise unconnected IOA models, perhaps of different countries.

This can also be done as a 'finite' element exercise as shown in Figure 12.2. In Appendix B a more sophisticated program is given for large banded matrices which reduces the equations in blocks and writes these blocks to a temporary file, reading them back in reverse order during back substitution.

12.6. References

Cunningham, BM, Loren, AN, Bazeley JD, *Accounting: Information for Business Decisions*, Dryden Press, Orlando FL, 2000.

Caves RE, Frankel JA, Jones RW, *World Trade and Payments, An Introduction*, Scott Foresman/Little Brown, Glenview IL, 1990.

Hogarth R, Makridakis S, Forecasting and planning: an evaluation, *Management Science* 87 (1981) 115-138.

Klein LR, The World Economy - a Global Model, *Perspectives in Computing*, 2 (1982) 4-17.

Leontief WW, *The Structure of the American Economy*, 1919-1939, 2nd edn. OUP, Fair Lawn NJ, 1951.

Mohr GA, Finite element analysis of viscous fluid flow, *Computers & Fluids*, 12 (1984) 217-233.

Mohr GA, Caffin DA, Penalty factors, Lagrange multipliers and basis transformation in the finite element method, *Trans Inst. Engineers Australia* CE27 (1985) 174-180.

Mohr GA, Numerical procedures for input-output analysis, *Applied Mathematics & Computation* 101 (1999) 89-98.

Mohr GA, Time Stepping of Macroeconomic Models. *Applied Mathematics & Computation*, 101 (1999) 273-278.

Mohr GA, *Economics: A Basic Introduction,* Amazon-Kindle (2019).

Theil H, Boot JCG, Kloek T, *Operations Research and Quantitative Economics*, McGraw-Hill, NY, 1965.

Waud, RN, *Microeconomics*, 3rd edn, Harper & Row, New York, NY 1986.

Vernon, J. *Macoeconomics*. Dryden Press, Hinsdale IL, 1980.

Wonnacott P, Wonnacott R, *Economics*, McGraw-Hill, New York 1979.v

Chapter 13

TWO DIMENSIONAL FINITE ELEMENTS

The finite element method grew out of the use of matrix analysis of skeletal structures in the mid 1940s, originally aircraft frames, using 'lumping' of stiffnesses for two dimensional panels to approximate them as 'equivalent' spar elements. The term 'Finite' was coined for this 'discrete element method' in the 1960s after the first two dimensional finite elements were developed in the mid 1950s.

In this chapter we consider two dimensional elements for *potential field* problems and these can be used to provide a *continuum* model of traffic flows between particularly prominent sources and destinations of traffic in a large city, for example. In such models the two dimensional elements might be used to simulate a 'background' flow in minor streets and the line elements of Chapter 8 could be added to represent flows in major routes, including terms to model diffusion from these into the 2D elements.

13.1. Two dimensional finite elements

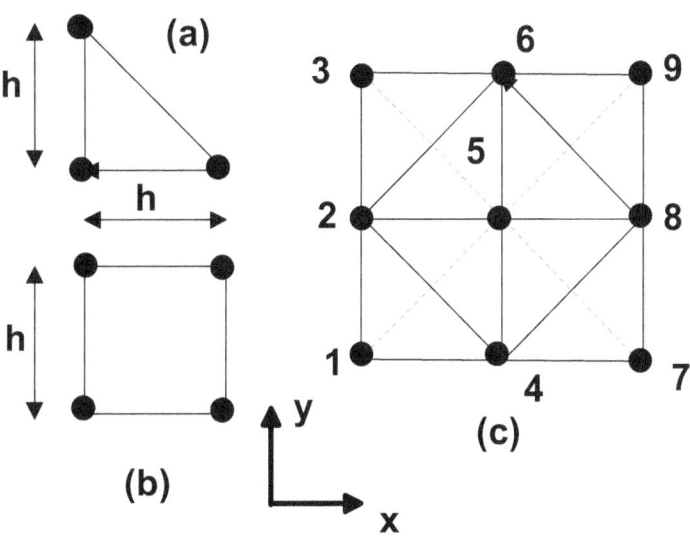

Figure 13.1. Illustration of use of triangular and rectangular elements.

13. Two Dimensional Finite Elements

Using right angled isosceles triangular elements of the form shown in Figure 13.1(a) the appropriate finite element matrix when the governing DE is Laplace's equation ($\nabla^2 \phi = 0$) is given by

$$(t/2h)\begin{bmatrix} 2 & -1 & -1 \\ -1 & 1 & 0 \\ -1 & 0 & 1 \end{bmatrix}\begin{Bmatrix} \phi_1 \\ \phi_4 \\ \phi_2 \end{Bmatrix} = \begin{Bmatrix} q_1 \\ q_2 \\ q_2 \end{Bmatrix} \qquad (13.1)$$

where $\{q\}$ are the nodal loads or fluxes, $\{\phi\}$ are the nodal potentials for the bottom left hand corner element in Figure 13.1(c), and t is the (uniform) transverse thickness. The element matrices are deployed in the system matrix according to its node numbers in the same fashion as for line elements in earlier chapters.

For a square element of with one freedom (such as a *potential* function) at each corner the element matrix takes the form

$$k = (t/12h)\begin{bmatrix} 8 & -2 & -4 & -2 \\ -2 & 8 & -2 & -4 \\ -4 & -2 & 8 & -2 \\ -2 & -4 & -2 & 8 \end{bmatrix} \qquad (13.2)$$

Figure 13.2.
2D flow problem.

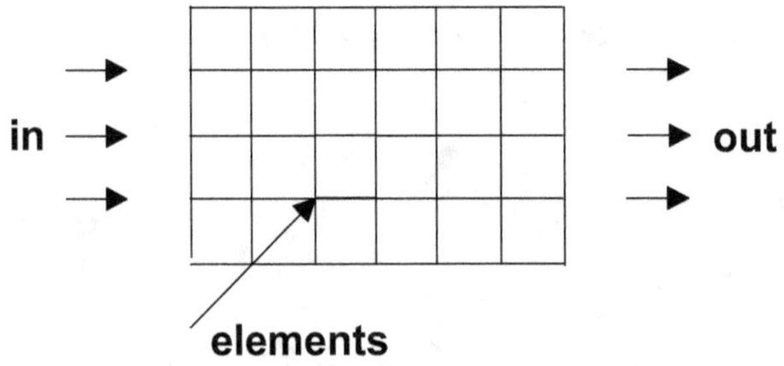

Such simple matrices can be used to model pretty well any problem of physical science, for example that of *rectilinear flow* (e.g. of fluid, traffic) in a two dimensional field, as illustrated in Figure 13.2.

Here there are input and output fluxes, as shown, and the problem might be one in which the *permeabilities* differ in the x and y directions.

A useful finite element for *potential flow* is formulated in Section 13.3 and a program for it given in the following section.

13. Two Dimensional Finite Elements

13.2. Potential flow

Two dimensional potential flow is governed by the partial differential equation (*Laplace's equation*),

$$\nabla^2 \phi = \partial^2 \phi/\partial x^2 + \partial^2 \phi/\partial y^2 = 0 \quad \phi = \phi(x, y) \tag{13.3}$$

where ϕ is a two dimensional potential function and $\nabla^2(\ )$ is called the *Laplacian function* or *operator*.

The equations for a finite element are formed using the following procedure:

1. In each element an interpolation function of the nodal values is formed:

$$\phi = \{f\}^\tau \{\phi\} \tag{13.4}$$

2. This interpolation is substituted into the governing PDE, giving, if this is Equation 13.3,

$$\int [\{f_{xx}\}^t + \{f_{yy})^t] \{\phi\} \, dV = R \, (\simeq 0) \tag{13.5}$$

where f_{xx} and f_{yy} are the second partial derivatives of the interpolation functions and the PDE is approximately satisfied (leaving a small *residual* R) over the volume V of the element.

3. Then the *method of weighted residuals (MWR)* is used, multiplying the residuals for each element by a weighting factor. In the *Galerkin method* the interpolation functions themselves are used as weights so that we obtain

$$\iint \{f\} [\{f_{xx}\}^t + \{f_{yy}\}^t] \, dxdy \, \{\phi\} \simeq 0 \tag{13.6}$$

4. Applying *integration by parts* to this result (writing $f = \{f\}$ to simplify the resulting expressions) we obtain

$$\iint \{f\}[\{f_{xx}\}^t dxdy = \int f f_x^t \, dy \mid - \iint f_x f_x^t \, dxdy \tag{13.7}$$

$$\iint \{f\}[\{f_{yy}\}^t dxdy = \int f f_y^t \, dy \mid - \iint f_y f_y^t \, dxdy \tag{13.8}$$

where the first terms on the right sides are boundary forcing terms for the problem.

13. TWO DIMENSIONAL FINITE ELEMENTS

Then combining Equations 13.7 and 13.8 we obtain element equations of the form

$$k \{\phi\} = \{ q \} \tag{13.9}$$

5. These element equations are summed to give system equations of the form

$$K \{\phi\} = \{ Q \} \tag{13.10}$$

and, first setting the boundary conditions or known values of ϕ, these equations are solved to determine the unknown ϕ values at the nodes.

We have already worked through this procedure for a line element in Section 4.1 and in the following section it is used to formulate a very useful 2D element.

Note that using the *Galerkin method,* and thence using the interpolation functions as a multiplying weighting factor, yields element matrices involving 'squaring' terms on the RHSs of Equations 13.7 and 13.8. This gives the solutions a maximal 'least squares' type of accuracy so that the weighting by {f} is the natural and most accurate option in FEM.

13.3. The quadratic triangle element

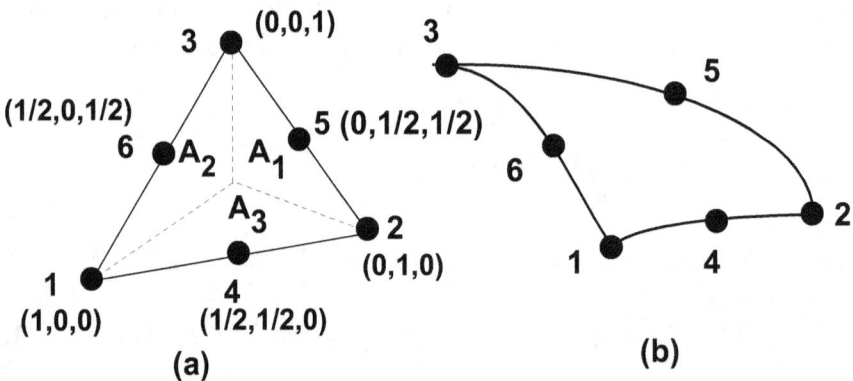

Figure 13.3. (a) Quadratic triangle element showing area coordinates of nodes; (b) mapped isoparametrically.

Figure 13.3 shows one of the most useful finite elements, a triangular element with six nodes, three of these at the mid points of the sides.

Using a process called *isoparametric mapping* the element can have the curved sides shown in Figure 13.3(b), making it particularly useful.

Area coordinates

For triangular elements it is useful to define *area coordinates* for any point in the element using the ratios of the areas shown in Figure 13.3(a) to the total area A of the element. After a little algebraic manipulation it can be shown that the area coordinates L_1, L_2, L_3 are given by

$$L_1 = A_1/A = (a - y_{32}x + x_{32}y)/2A \tag{13.11a}$$

$$L_2 = A_2/A = (a - y_{13}x + x_{13}y)/2A \tag{13.11b}$$

$$L_3 = A_3/A = (a - y_{21}x + x_{21}y)/2A \tag{13.11c}$$

where $a = 2A/3$ and $2A = x_{21}y_{32} - x_{32}y_{21}$ with

$$x_{32} = x_3 - x_2, \quad x_{13} = x_1 - x_3, \quad x_{21} = x_2 - x_1$$

$$y_{32} = y_3 - y_2, \quad y_{13} = y_1 - y_3, \quad y_{21} = y_2 - y_1$$

and the reader can verify that Equations 13,11 give the nodal coordinates shown in Figure 13.3a. From the nature of the definition of the area coordinates the identity

$$L_1 + L_2 + L_3 = 1 \tag{13.12}$$

also follows and note that the coordinates of the centroid are $L_1 = L_2 = L_3 = 1/3$.

Interpolation

To develop an interpolation for the element we begin by writing an interpolation polynomial in terms of a vector of modes $\{M\}$ and modal amplitudes $\{c\}$

$$\phi = \{c\}^t\{M\} = c_1 L_1^2 + c_2 L_2^2 + c_3 L_3^2 + c_4 L_1 L_2 + c_5 L_2 L_3 + c_6 L_3 L_1 \tag{13.13}$$

13. Two Dimensional Finite Elements

and substituting the areal coordinates of the nodes we obtain

$$\{\phi\} = \begin{Bmatrix} \phi_1 \\ \phi_2 \\ \phi_3 \\ \phi_4 \\ \phi_5 \\ \phi_6 \end{Bmatrix} = \begin{bmatrix} 1 & 0 & 0 & 0 & 0 & 0 \\ 0 & 1 & 0 & 0 & 0 & 0 \\ 0 & 0 & 1 & 0 & 0 & 0 \\ 1/2 & 1/2 & 0 & 1/2 & 0 & 0 \\ 0 & 1/2 & 1/2 & 0 & 1/2 & 0 \\ 1/2 & 0 & 1/2 & 0 & 0 & 1/2 \end{bmatrix} \begin{Bmatrix} c_1 \\ c_2 \\ c_3 \\ c_4 \\ c_5 \\ c_6 \end{Bmatrix} = C\{c\} \quad (13.14)$$

Inverting the matrix C (alternatively Equations 13.14 are easily solved by elimination) the interpolation functions $\{f\}$ for the interpolation

$$\phi = \{f\}^t\{\phi\} \quad (13.15)$$

are given by

$$\{f\}^t = \{M\}^t C^{-1} = \{M\}^t \begin{bmatrix} 1 & 0 & 0 & 0 & 0 & 0 \\ 0 & 1 & 0 & 0 & 0 & 0 \\ 0 & 0 & 1 & 0 & 0 & 0 \\ -1 & -1 & 0 & 4 & 0 & 0 \\ 0 & -1 & -1 & 0 & 4 & 0 \\ -1 & 0 & -1 & 0 & 0 & 4 \end{bmatrix} \quad (13.16)$$

yielding the results

$$f_1 = L_1^2 - L_1 L_2 - L_3 L_1 = L_1(2L_1 - 1)$$
$$f_2 = L_2(2L_2 - 1), \quad f_3 = L_3(2L_2 - 1) \quad (13.17)$$
$$f_4 = 4L_1 L_2, \quad f_5 = 4L_2 L_3, \quad F_6 = 4L_3 L_1$$

using the identity of Equation 13.12 to simplify the results for f_1, f_2 and f_3. These area coordinate functions are much simpler than the Cartesian formulas obtained by substituting Equations 13.11 into Equations 13.17.

13. TWO DIMENSIONAL FINITE ELEMENTS

Isoparametric mapping

Using the area coordinate interpolation functions we can now calculate the derivatives using the interpolation matrix

$$S = \begin{Bmatrix} \partial(\ )/\partial L_1 \\ \partial(\ )/\partial L_2 \end{Bmatrix} = \begin{bmatrix} 4L_1-1 & 0 & 4L_1+4L_2-3 & 4L_2 & -4L_2 & 4-8L_1-4L_2 \\ 0 & 4L_2-1 & 4L_1+4L_2-3 & 4L_1 & 4-4L_1-8L_2 & -4L_1 \end{bmatrix}$$

(13.18)

using the identity of Equation 13.12 to eliminate L_3.

Then the Cartesian derivatives are related to these local derivatives by

$$\begin{Bmatrix} \partial\phi/\partial L_1 \\ \partial\phi/\partial L_2 \end{Bmatrix} = \begin{bmatrix} \partial x/\partial L_1 & \partial y/\partial L_1 \\ \partial x/\partial L_2 & \partial y/\partial L_1 \end{bmatrix} \begin{Bmatrix} \partial\phi/\partial x \\ \partial\phi/\partial y \end{Bmatrix} \qquad (13.19)$$

and the connecting matrix is the *Jacobian matrix J*. This can be calculated numerically at each integration point (using numerical integration to form the element equations) using the matrix of Equation 13.18:

$$J = S[\{x\}\ \{y\}] \qquad (13.20)$$

so that the interpolation for the Cartesian derivatives is given by

$$\begin{Bmatrix} \partial\phi/\partial x \\ \partial\phi/\partial y \end{Bmatrix} = J^{-1} S\{\phi\} = T\{\phi\} \qquad (13.21)$$

and this process is easily coded in the program of Section 13.5. Now the reason for eliminating L_3 in Equation 13.18 is clear, namely in order to obtain an invertible 2 X 2 Jacobian matrix.

Numerical integration

The appropriate numerical integration when first derivatives of the interpolation functions are used to form the element equations is simply at the three midside nodes. This exactly integrates terms of the form $\int L_1^2$, as required, so that we calculate contributions to the element matrix which take the form:

$$\iint \{f_x\}\{f_x\}^t dx dy \qquad (13.22)$$

as

$$\sum_{i=1}^{3} T_1 T_1^t \; |J|_{abs} \, \omega_i/2 \qquad \omega_i = 1/3 \qquad (13.23)$$

where T_1 denotes row 1 of the matrix T obtained in Equation 13.21 and $|J|_{abs}$ gives approximately twice the element area as Equation 13.19 suggests.

Then to calculate finite element matrices for the quadratic triangle element an integration loop is required by Equation 13.23 and in this loop Equation 13.18 is coded literally and this result used to calculate the Jacobian matrix using Equation 13.20. The matrix T is formed numerically using Equation 13.21 and the result used in Equation 13.23 to calculate the terms required for the element matrices by equations like Equations 13.7 and 13.8 derived in the following section.

Conclusion

Using areal coordinates the interpolation functions for the quadratic triangle are much simplified. Then use of the numerically calculated Jacobian matrix at each integration point allows the element to have curved (quadratic) sides, greatly simplifying element formulation as well.

13.4. FEM Analysis of potential flow

In the following section we develop the equations required to form mathematical models of potential flow problems. Using the results of Section 13.3 we are then able to formulate finite elements to analyze potential flow problems.

Potential flow

In potential flow the flow pattern is represented by *orthogonal* sets of curves (that is, intersecting at right angles) for the values of a *potential function* ϕ and a *stream function* ψ. In terms of these functions the velocities of flow are given by

$$u = -\partial\phi/\partial x, \; v = -\partial\phi/\partial y \qquad (13.24)$$

$$u = \partial\psi/\partial y, \; v = -\partial\psi/\partial x \qquad (13.25)$$

and the contours of the stream function are the *streamlines* of flow whilst the orgthogonal contours of the potential function are those of the *potential* of the flow.

We will use the potential function approach as it is more appropriate for our present purposes (e.g. we have already defined a 'potential' in FEM distribution models).

13. Two Dimensional Finite Elements

Equations 13.24 already satisfy the *irrotationality condition*

$$\omega_z = (\partial v/\partial x - \partial u/\partial y)\hat{k} = 0 \qquad (13.26)$$

where ω_z = is the vorticity, being a vector with the direction of $\hat{k}$, the unit vector perpendicular to the plane.

We must also satisfy the *continuity condition*

$$\partial u/\partial x + \partial v/\partial y = 0 \qquad (13.27)$$

this ensuring conservation of matter as it states that for a control volume *dxdy* 'flow in = flow out'.

Then substituting Equations 13.24 into Equation 13.27 we obtain the governing equation for the problem

$$\nabla^2 \phi = \partial^2 \phi/\partial^2 x^2 + \partial^2 \phi/\partial y^2 = 0 \qquad (13.28)$$

namely Laplace's equation.

Finite element interpolation

Substituting the interpolation $\phi = \{f\}^t\{\phi\}$ into Equation 13.28 we obtain

$$\int\int \{f\}[\{f_{xx}\}^t + \{f_{yy}\}^t]\, dxdy\, \{\phi\} = \{0\} \qquad (13.29)$$

using Galerkin weighting with the interpolation functions and integrating over the element volume (assuming the element has constant thickness = 1).

Then applying integration by parts to both terms on the left of Equation 13.29 the results of Equations 13.7 and 13.8 are obtained so that the element equations are given by

$$k\{\phi\} = \{q\} \qquad (13.30)$$

where

$$k = \int[\{f_x\}\{f_x\}^t + \{f_y\}\{f_y\}^t]dxdy \qquad (13.31)$$

$$\{q\} = \int\{f\}\{f_x\}^t\{\phi\}dy + \int\{f\}\{f_y\}^t\{\phi\}dx \qquad (13.32)$$

The forcing terms of Equation 13.32 can be simplified by transforming to the normal and tangential axes at the boundary shown in Figure 13.4.

13. Two Dimensional Finite Elements

Denoting the angle of the normal to the boundary from the x axis as α the direction cosines at the boundary are

$$c_x = \cos\alpha \quad \text{and} \quad c_y = \sin\alpha$$

we can write, assuming all *direction cosines* positive (an artifice used by Mohr to ensure that $\int ds$ around the boundary yields a positive result)

$$dx/dn = c_x, \quad dy/dn = c_y \qquad (13.33a)$$

$$dx/ds = c_y, \quad dy/ds = c_x \qquad (13.33b)$$

Using Equations 13.33b in Equation 13.32 we obtain

$$\{q\} = \int \{f\}[c_x\phi_x + c_y\phi_y]ds$$
$$= -\int \{f\}[c_x u + c_y v]ds \qquad (13.34a)$$

including the definitions of Equations 13.24 to obtain the final result.

Then, for example, for a side of an element parallel to the y axis we have $\alpha = 0$, $c_x = 1$, $c_y = 0$ and the flux loads on it are given by

$$\{q\} = \int \{f\} u\, dy = \int \{f\}\{f\}^t \{u\}\, dy = (\int \{f\}\, dy)\{u\} \qquad (13.34b)$$

Then the element matrices are obtained by using Equations 13.31 and 13.23 to evaluate Equation 13.31 by numerical integration and a short program which does this is given in Section 13.5.

Rectilinear flow

Figure 13.4 shows an element mesh of quadratic triangular elements for the rectilinear flow problem. To force the flow the loads shown are specified at inlet and $\phi = 0$ is set as a datum at outlet.

Here the *consistent* (with a quadratic interpolation) loads corresponding to a uniformly distributed load q normal to the side of an element are $qh/6$, $4qh/6$, $qh/6$ if h is the length of this side. This follows from Equation 13.34b and thus integrating the 1D quadratic Lagrangian interpolation given in Section 3.8 between the limits $s = -1$ and $s = 1$, noting that the element length here = 2.

13. Two Dimensional Finite Elements

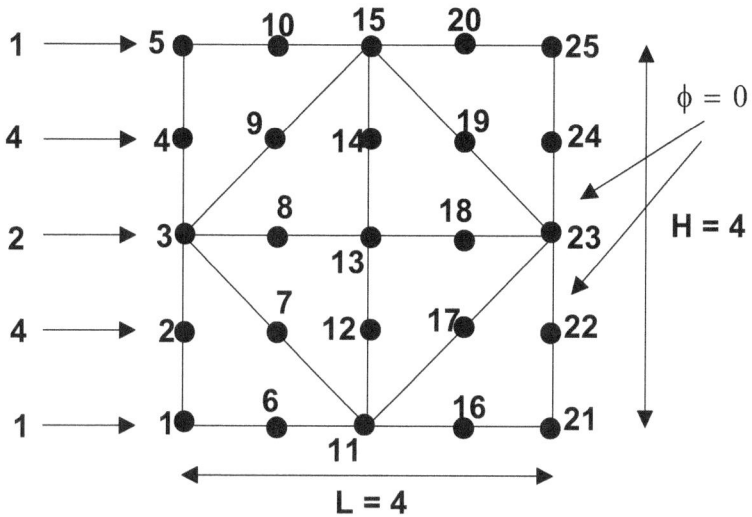

Figure 13.4. Rectilinear flow.

For this simple problem the exact solutions are

$$\phi_{in} = QL/H, \quad u = -\phi_{in}/L$$

where $Q = \Sigma\, q_\phi$ at inlet.

A program for such potential flow problems is given in the following section. This uses the quadratic triangle element described earlier and for best results the *consistent loads* shown must be used.

The problem is simple but with the use of FEM irregular domains, sources and sinks etc. can be dealt with simply by the addition of a line or two of data and a program for this purpose is given in Section 13.5.

13.5. Program for potential flow

The following program is for potential flow problems and uses the quadratic triangle element described earlier. It automatically generates the mesh (with the diagonals 'one-way' as in the bottom left quadrant in Fig. 13.4) for a rectangular domain, given the dimensions of this. After obtaining the solution for the nodal potentials these are used to calculate the velocities (= the gradients of the potentials) at the nodes, then calculating average nodal velocities = sum of velocities calculated in the N elements impinging at the node (the *nodal valency*) divided by N.

13. Two Dimensional Finite Elements

Data is read as

Line 1: # nodes = NP, # elements = NE, # b.c. nodes = NB, half band width = BW = max value of (max node # - min node # + 1) for an element.

With specification of a band width, reduction of the system matrix sweeps to the right of the pivot only the the extent of the band width. This decreases computation considerably in larger problems.

Line 2: # grid lines in X direction = NX, # grid lines in Y direction, domain size in X direction = XLIM, domain size in Y direction = YLIM

NB lines: number of set values for potential function

Loads: nodal loads - terminate with a 0,0 line.

The program output is the nodal potentials, then a ? prompt from an input statement. Input any number and the final output of the boundary node reactions and the average nodal horizontal and vertical velocities will be given.

The first data set is the mesh for a source and sink problem (+/- 10 at two interior points).

```
5  REM Potential Flow Program
10 UDL = 0: REM RESTORE 900
15 DIM CORD(90, 2), EM(6, 6), S(90, 90), Q(90), XY(6, 2), NOP(40, 6), SI(90, 90)
20 DIM CI(6, 2), DL(2, 6), TJ(2, 2), T(2, 6), IB(90), EV(6), NCN(90), U(90), V(90)
25 REM ***** Integration at midside nodes
30 CI(1, 1) = 1: CI(1, 2) = 0: CI(2, 1) = 0: CI(2, 2) = 1: CI(3, 1) = 0: CI(3, 2) = 0
35 CI(4, 1) = .5: CI(4, 2) = .5: CI(5, 1) = 0: CI(5, 2) = .5: CI(6, 1) = .5: CI(6, 2) = 0
40 READ NP, NE, NB, BW
45 READ NX, NY, XLIM, YLIM
50 NEX = NX - 1: NEY = NY - 1: DX = XLIM / NEX: DY = YLIM / NEY
55 FOR I = 1 TO NX: FOR J = 1 TO NY: NN = NY * (I - 1) + J
60 CORD(NN, 1) = DX * (I - 1): CORD(NN, 2) = DY * (J - 1): NEXT: NEXT
65 NEX = (NX - 1) / 2: NEY = (NY - 1) / 2
70 FOR I = 1 TO NEX: FOR J = 1 TO NEY
75 NI = (I - 1) * 2 * NY + (J - 1) * 2 + 1: NJ = NI + 2 * NY
80 NS = NEY * (I - 1) + J: NN = 2 * NS - 1
85 NOP(NN, 1) = NI: NOP(NN, 2) = NJ: NOP(NN, 3) = NI + 2
90 NOP(NN, 4) = NI + NY: NOP(NN, 5) = NOP(NN, 4) + 1: NOP(NN, 6) = NI + 1
95 NN = 2 * NS
100 NOP(NN, 1) = NI + 2: NOP(NN, 2) = NJ: NOP(NN, 3) = NJ + 2
105 NOP(NN, 4) = NOP(NN - 1, 5): NOP(NN, 5) = NJ + 1: NOP(NN, 6) = NOP(NN - 1, 4) +2
110 NEXT: NEXT
```

13. Two Dimensional Finite Elements

```
112 REM READ Node numbers
FOR J=  TO 6: READ NOP(NN, J): NEXT: IF NN=0 THEN 115
113 REM GOTO 112: REM These two lines to make mesh '2-way'
115 FOR L = 1 TO NE: REM ####### LOOP ON ELEMENTS
120 FOR I = 1 TO 6: K = NOP(L, I)
125 XY(I, 1) = CORD(K, 1): XY(I, 2) = CORD(K, 2)
130 FOR J = 1 TO 6: EM(I, J) = 0: NEXT: NEXT
135 FOR IP = 4 TO 6
140 F1 = 4 * CI(IP, 1): F2 = 4 * CI(IP, 2)
145 GOSUB 510
150 F = ABS(DJ) / 6
155 FOR K = 1 TO 3: NK = NOP(L, K + 3): Q(NK) = Q(NK) + F * UDL / 3: NEXT
160 FOR I = 1 TO 6: FOR J = 1 TO 6
165 EM(I, J) = EM(I, J) + F * (T(1, I) * T(1, J) + T(2, I) * T(2, J)): REM EQN 12.31
170 NEXT: NEXT
175 NEXT IP: REM END NUMERICAL INTEGRATION LOOP ********************
180 FOR I = 1 TO 6: NR = NOP(L, I)
185 FOR J = 1 TO 6: NC = NOP(L, J)
190 S(NR, NC) = S(NR, NC) + EM(I, J): NEXT: NEXT: REM ADD k TO SYSTEM M
195 NEXT L: REM END LOOP ON ELEMENTS #########################
200 FOR I = 1 TO NP: FOR J = 1 TO NP
205 SI(I, J) = S(I, J): NEXT: NEXT
210 FOR L = 1 TO NB: REM LOOP BOUNDARY CONDITION NODES
215 READ N, F: IB(N) = 1: Q(N) = F
220 FOR I = 1 TO NP
225 IF IB(I) = 1 THEN 235
230 Q(I) = Q(I) - F * S(I, N)
235 NEXT I
240 Q(N) = F: NEXT L
270 READ NQ, F
275 IF NQ = 0 THEN 290
280 IF IB(NQ) = 1 THEN 270
285 Q(NQ) = Q(NQ) + F: GOTO 270
290 REM 245 - 265 FOR = B.C.s & 270 - 285 FOR LOADS
295 FOR I = 1 TO NP
300 IF IB(I) = 1 THEN 360
305 X = S(I, I): Q(I) = Q(I) / X: REM X=PIVOT
310 J2 = I + BW: IF J2 > NP THEN J2 = NP
315 FOR J = I + 1 TO J2
320 S(I, J) = S(I, J) / X: NEXT J: REM ROW/PIVOT
325 FOR K = 1 TO J2: IF K = I THEN GOTO 355
330 IF IB(K) = 1 THEN 355
335 X = S(K, I): IF X = 0 THEN 355
340 Q(K) = Q(K) - X * Q(I)
345 FOR J = I + 1 TO J2
```

13. Two Dimensional Finite Elements

```
350 S(K, J) = S(K, J) - X * S(I, J): NEXT J: REM ROW SUBTRACTION OPERATION
355 NEXT K
360 NEXT I
365 PRINT : PRINT "Nodal Stream Function Values"
370 FOR I = 1 TO NP
375 PRINT USING "#####"; I; : PRINT USING "#######.#####"; Q(I);
380 NEXT
383 INPUT "I/P a # to continue O/P", ZZ
385 PRINT "Boundary Flows"
390 FOR I = 1 TO NP
395 IF IB(I) <> 1 THEN 420
400 F = 0: FOR K = 1 TO NP
405 F = F + S(I, K) * Q(K)
410 NEXT
415 PRINT USING "#####"; I; : PRINT USING "#######.#####"; F
420 NEXT I
425 REM
430 FOR I = 1 TO NP: NCN(I) = 0: U(I) = 0: V(I) = 0: NEXT
435 FOR I = 1 TO NE: FOR J = 1 TO 6
440 NN = NOP(I, J): NCN(NN) = NCN(NN) + 1: NEXT: NEXT
445 FOR EN = 1 TO NE
450 FOR I = 1 TO 6: K = NOP(EN, I)
455 XY(I, 1) = CORD(K, 1): XY(I, 2) = CORD(K, 2): EV(I) = Q(K): NEXT
460 FOR NL = 1 TO 6: N = NOP(EN, NL)
465 F1 = 4 * CI(NL, 1): F2 = 4 * CI(NL, 2): GOSUB 510
470 FOR J = 1 TO 6
475 U(N) = U(N) - T(1, J) * EV(J) / NCN(N)
480 V(N) = V(N) - T(2, J) * EV(J) / NCN(N): NEXT
485 NEXT NL: NEXT EN
490 PRINT "Nodal average velocities u,v"
495 FOR I = 1 TO NP
500 PRINT USING "#####"; I; : PRINT USING "#####.###"; U(I); V(I); : NEXT
505 END
510 DL(1, 1) = F1 - 1: DL(1, 2) = 0: DL(1, 3) = F1 + F2 - 3
515 DL(1, 4) = F2: DL(1, 5) = -F2: DL(1, 6) = 4 - 2 * F1 - F2: REM Derivs interp
520 DL(2, 1) = 0: DL(2, 2) = F2 - 1: DL(2, 3) = F1 + F2 - 3
525 DL(2, 4) = F1: DL(2, 5) = 4 - F1 - 2 * F2: DL(2, 6) = -F1
530 FOR I = 1 TO 2: FOR J = 1 TO 2: TJ(I, J) = 0: FOR K = 1 TO 6
535 TJ(I, J) = TJ(I, J) + DL(I, K) * XY(K, J): NEXT: NEXT: NEXT: REM Det(J)
540 DJ = TJ(1, 1) * TJ(2, 2) - TJ(1, 2) * TJ(2, 1): DD = TJ(1, 1)
545 TJ(1, 1) = TJ(2, 2) / DJ: TJ(2, 2) = DD / DJ: REM INVERT JACOBIAN
550 TJ(1, 2) = -TJ(1, 2) / DJ: TJ(2, 1) = -TJ(2, 1) / DJ
555 FOR I = 1 TO 2: FOR J = 1 TO 6: T(I, J) = 0: FOR K = 1 TO 2
560 T(I, J) = T(I, J) + TJ(I, K) * DL(K, J): NEXT: NEXT: NEXT: REM EQN 13.21
565 RETURN
```

13. Two Dimensional Finite Elements

```
600 DATA 15,4,2,7
610 DATA 5,3,4,2
620 DATA 6,10
630 DATA 12,-10
640 DATA 0,0

900 DATA 25,8,1,11
910 DATA 5,5,4,4
911 DATA 3,3,13,15,8,14,9, 4,3,15,5,9,10,4
912 DATA 5,11,21,23,16,22,17, 6,11,23,13,17,18,12, 0,0,0,0,0,0,0
915 DATA 25,0
920 DATA 2,110
930 DATA 3,160
940 DATA 4,150
950 DATA 22,-140
960 DATA 23,-200
970 DATA 24,-80
980 DATA 0,0
```

The second data set is for the distribution problem of Figure 7.1 posed as a two dimensional problem and is invoked by removing the REM before the RESTORE 900 statement at the start of the program. In this node number sets are read in for 4 of the 8 elements to form a 'two-way' (diagonals) mesh, and to allow this remove the REM in lines 112 and 113.

Using this data set the flow rates obtained are those of Table 13.1 and these reflect fairly well the supplies and demands of the original network problem of Figure 7.1.

Table 13.1.

y	x =0	x = 2	x = 4
0	56.3	84.6	30
1	98.5	85.1	69.5
2	149	105	158.4
3	79.6	87.4	97.4
4	41.3	87.9	52.5

The resemblance would be even greater, of course, if we added *line elements*, giving these much greater 'conductance' than the 2- D (continuum) elements which would then serve to model the 'background flow' (e.g. minor streets in a road traffic problem).

Indeed if we attempted to optimize the 2-D model (with a fine mesh without line elements) it would tend to reduce to one of line elements, as in the usual network models of distribution.

13. Two Dimensional Finite Elements

As a more traditional example, the same data set can be used to solve the potential flow problem of Figure 13.4 if it is modified to:

```
900 DATA 25,8,5,11
910 DATA 5,5,4,4
911 DATA 3,3,13,15,8,14,9, 4,3,15,5,9,10,4
912 DATA 5,11,21,23,16,22,17, 6,11,23,13,17,18,12, 0,0,0,0,0,0,0
915 DATA 21,0, 22,0, 23,0, 24,0, 25,0
920 DATA 1,1
930 DATA 2,4
940 DATA 3,2
950 DATA 4,4
960 DATA 5,1
970 DATA 0,0
```

The solution will be potentials = 12 at inlet, decreasing in steps of 3 to zero at the RHS. The nodal average velocities will be 3 horizontally and zero vertically, corresponding to the exact solution given in Section 13.4.

13.6. Inclusion of line elements

Figure 13.5 shows a source and sink problem modeled using Mohr's Patch Method, a hybrid finite difference/FEM method. As shown, there are two line or link elements and these have conductances = 10/12, compared to values of 4/12 for half a grid division width for the continuum.

The result for $\phi(I=1, J=5)$ is 6.36 whereas with no links it was 4.98. This indicates a flow between grid points (3,5) and (1,5) of approximately

$$\delta\phi(k + \delta k)/k = (10 - 6.4)(10 + 4)/4 \simeq 12 \qquad (13.35)$$

whereas without the links the flow is

$$\delta\phi k/k = \delta\phi = 10 - 4.98 \simeq 5 \qquad (13.36)$$

so that the links have indeed increased the flow, as expected. In the structural context we would be speaking of increased stiffness absorbing more load and reducing deformations.

13. Two Dimensional Finite Elements

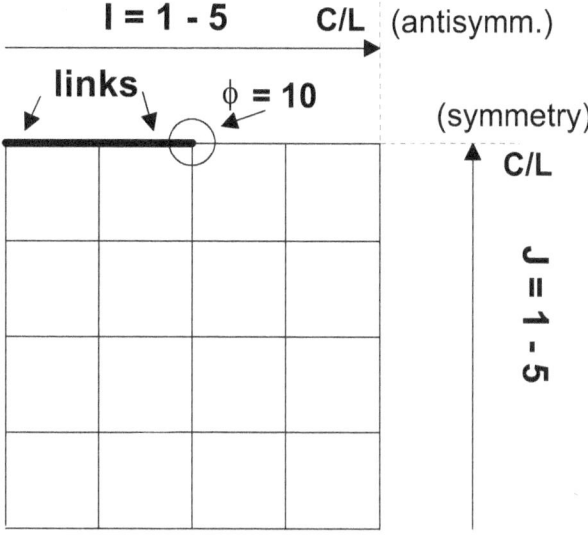

Figure 13.5. Problem including line elements.

Inclusion of such line elements requires just a few lines of coding to read in their node numbers and conductances and deploy these in the same way as for the simple two freedom DC network elements of Chapter 4.

13.7. Infinite boundary modeling

Figure 13.6 shows a quadrant of a circular domain (of radius 4) with a point source at its centre modeled using (a) 6 node isoparametric elements, and (b) cubic Hermitian elements with nine freedoms.

Then to simulate an infinite domain no boundary conditions other than ϕ = 1000 at the centre are imposed but 'stiffnesses' equal to the angle (in radians) subtended by each node's 'share' of the boundary added to the pivot for each boundary node's ϕ freedom before the final solution of the problem.

In Figure 13.6(a), for example, the added values (in degrees) are 11.25 for the two nodes at x = 0 and y = 0 and 22.5 at the other three nodes of the circular boundary.

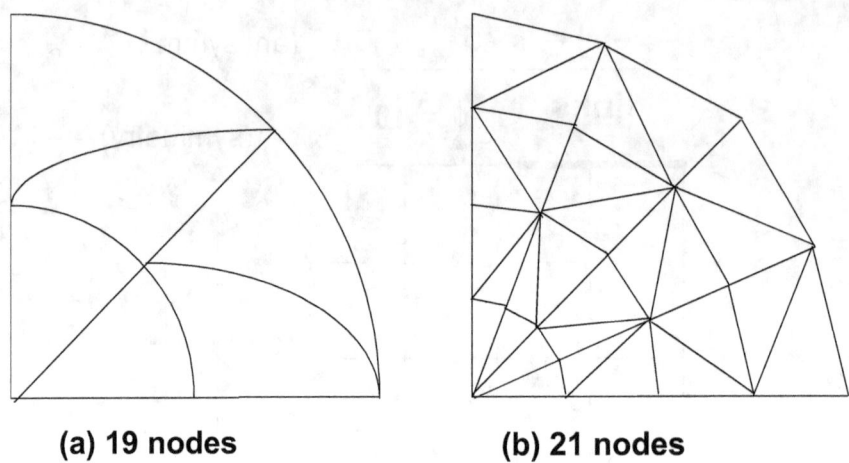

(a) 19 nodes **(b) 21 nodes**

Figure 13.6.
Meshes for a quadrant of an infinite domain with point source at centre.

Table 13.2 shows the results obtained. The expected results are obtained by fitting the appropriate decay function which is

$$\phi = -(1/2\pi)\phi_0 \ln(r) + C \tag{13.37}$$

and this is that much used in the boundary element method.

Table 13.2. Results for the problem of Figure 13.6

Case	$r = 1$	$r = 2$	$r = 3$	$r = 4$
6 node FE (1a)	525	367	276	210
6 node FE (1b)	520	365	275	209
Cubic FE (2a)	620	447	341	261
Cubic FE (2b)	520	374	284	218
Expected (3)	520	410	345	299
Expected (4)	480	370	305	259

Then in case (3) (results row 5) the constant C is calculated by substituting $\phi = 520$ at $r = 1$ in Equation 13.37 and using the result to calculate ϕ for the other radii. Then for case (4) $\phi = 370$ and $r = 2$ is used to obtain row 6.

13. Two Dimensional Finite Elements

Cases (1a) and (2a) are the FEM results with only 'elastic' boundary conditions. Here a 'natural' decay rate occurs in the meshes used but in general the desired rate of decay should be modeled by choosing an appropriate C value and setting a corresponding ϕ value as a boundary condition at an inner radius.

This is done for cases (1b) and (2b), setting $\phi = 520$ for the nodes at $r = 1$. Agreement of the two FEM results is now good and agreement with the expected (logarithmic) decay results is reasonable with such coarse meshes and such a rapid decay rate.

Finally, note that from Equation 13.37 it follows that $\partial\phi/\partial r = -\phi_0/2\pi r$ and this can be set as a boundary condition in Figure 13.6 (at $r = 4$) but this gives little change in the results of Table 13.2.

13.8. Conclusions

Two dimensional finite elements can be combined with the simple line elements discussed in previous chapters to form quite sophisticated models of traffic flow and other networks.

It would have been easier to use elements such as those given by Equations 13.1 or 13.2, but these can only be used to model rectangular domains.

Linear triangular elements of arbitrary shape are little more complex, however, but these too would have limited application and the mathematics of the potential flow problems itself still cannot be avoided.

Given that we have had to deal with partial derivatives etc., therefore, it was worthwhile introducing the quadratic triangle with isoparametric mapping to allow modeling of curved boundaries with relatively few elements. Such mapping requires numerical integration to form the element matrix but, in order to obtain more general finite elements that is the norm in any case.

13.9. References

Agryris JH, Dunne PC, The finite element method applied to fluid mechanics, pp 159-197 in *Computational Methods and Problems in Aeronautical Fluid Dynamics* (Proc. Conf. at Univ. Manchester, 1974), Academic, London, 1976.

Connor JJ, Brebbia CA, *Finite Element Techniques for Fluid Flow*, Newnes-Butterworths, London, 1976.

Chung TJ, *Finite Element Analysis in Fluid Dynamics*, McGraw-Hill, NY, 1978.

Irons BM, Ahmad S, *Techniques of Finite Elements*, Ellis Horwood, Chichester, 1980.

Meek JL, *Matrix Structural Analysis*, McGraw-Hill Kogakusha, Tokyo, 1971.

Mohr GA, Power AS, Elastic boundary conditions for finite elements of infinite and semi-infinite media, *Proc. Instn Civil Engineers* (UK), part 2, 68 (1978) 675-684.

Mohr GA, A contact stiffness matrix for finite element problems involving external elastic restraint, *Computers & Structures* 12 (1980) 189-191.

Mohr GA, Finite element analysis of viscous fluid flow, *Computers & Fluids*, 12 (1984) 217-233.

Mohr GA, Milner HR, *A Microcomputer Introduction to the Finite Element Method*, Pitman, Melbourne, 1986; Heinemann, London, 1987.

Mohr GA, *Finite Elements for Solids, Fluids, and Optimization*, OUP, Oxford, 1992.

Mohr, GA, Numerical procedures for input-output analysis, *Applied Mathematics & Computation*, vol. 101, p 98, 1999.

Mohr, GA, The finite patch method: a nodal equation method based on FEM, *Advances in Engineering Software* 32 (2001) 327-335.

Mohr GA, Optimization and finite element modeling of input-output analysis problems. *Int. J. Arts & Sciences* 2 (2002) 23-29.

Mohr GA, Power AS. Natural cubic element formulation and infinite domain modeling for potential type problems. *Australian & NZ J Applied Mathematics*, vol. 44 (2003), pp 133-143.

Chapter 14

CONCLUSIONS

14.1. Key applications of the present work

Novel applications of the work of the present text might include:

➢ Use of FEM to model distribution networks.

➢ Use of FEM to model traffic flow networks.

➢ Application of steepest descent to these models to optimize them.

➢ Application of flow ratio design to these models to obtain approximate optimum solutions.

➢ Inclusion of time interpolations in scheduling networks and thence optimization of them.

➢ Optimization and inclusion of penalty constraints and other modifications in input-output analysis.

➢ Modeling of traffic flows with 2D elements for the background flow and 1D elements for the major routes, including sources, sinks, infinite boundaries and other refinements.

In addition, many of the numerical methods discussed might find application in many areas of management science, for example

➢ The iterative, search and predictor-corrector methods.

➢ The matrix inversion and solution methods.

➢ Interpolation and numerical integration methods.

➢ The LP programs for MIN and MAX.

➢ The direct LP program for distribution.

➢ The steepest descent method.

➢ The CPM and shortest route programs.

➢ Time stepping of macroeconomic models.

14. CONCLUSIONS

To take a couple of simple examples:

(a) The idea of perturbing a system to determine *gradients*, as in the steepest descent method might be applied to any large accounting system, treating it as a black box and simply altering one variable at a time to determine the *sensitivity* of the system to them.

(b) The idea of iterating a system according to some *optimality criterion*, as in the FRD method, might be applied to any numerical model or business system.

14.2. Future research of the present work

There is much scope for further research and extension of the present work. Consider again, for example, the input-output analysis problem of Table 14.1.

Table 14.1. Input-output analysis problem

	Purchases				Total
	X	Y	Z	External	Output ($)
Sales					
X	-	60	40	100	200
Y	40	-	100	260	400
Z	50	100	-	50	200
Labour	110	240	60	-	410
Total input	200	400	200	410	1,210

Figure 14.1 shows a crude FEM model. Here one way links with 'unit costs' c_{ij} are used, the element matrices being

$$k_{ij} = (1/c_{ij})\begin{bmatrix} 1 & -1 \\ -1 & 1 \end{bmatrix} \tag{14.1}$$

and route costs of 10 are assigned to routes 14, 25, 36, 27 and costs of 5 to the routes between nodes 1, 2, 3.

Applying the flows (in $)

$$q_1 = 200,\ q_2 = 400,\ q_3 = 200,\ q_4 = -100,\ q_5 = -260,\ q_6 = -50 \tag{14.2}$$

to the nodes, with the boundary condition $p_7 = 0$, the route flows shown in Table 13.2 are obtained.

14. Conclusions

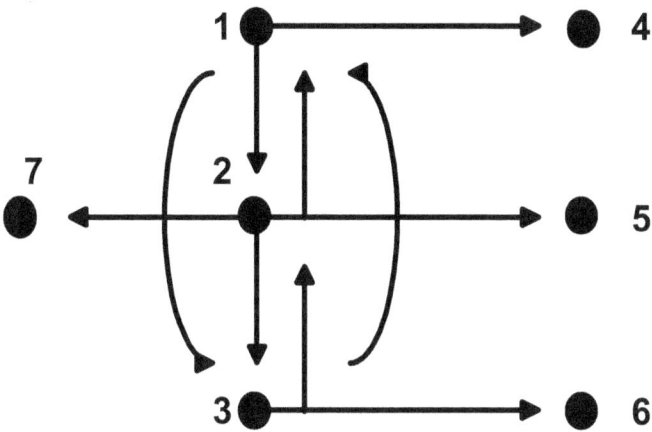

Figure 14.1. FEM model of an input-output analysis problem.

Table 14.2. Initial and optimum route flows for FE IOA model.

Route	Initial flows	Optimum flows
14	100	100
25	260	260
36	50	50
27	390	390
12	59.375	100
13	-9.375	0
21	-59.375	0
23	-68.75	0
31	9.375	0
32	68.75	150

Applying steepest descent to this model with the objective function $\Sigma f = c_{ij} q_{ij}$, the initial value of f of 9333 is reduced to 9250 after only two searches, when the optimum solution shown Table 14.2 is obtained.

14. CONCLUSIONS

The corresponding input-output matrix is

$$M = \begin{bmatrix} 1 & -0.5 & 0 \\ 0 & 1 & 0 \\ 0 & -0.75 & 0 \end{bmatrix} \quad (14.3)$$

This is a similar result that obtained in Section 12.2 by applying steepest descent to the original input-output matrix with the off-diagonal entries as variables, seeking to minimize the total output and constraining the flows to equal their average value.

The same result of Table 14.2 is obtained using the FRD method with 'median' flow = 25 and upper and lower cost limits of 10^6 and 1.

The model of Figure 14.1 is crude, for example because route 27 acts like a 'sink' to take the internal flow and routes 4, 5 and 6 take the export flows without providing an opportunity for these to vary.

In fact input-output analysis is essentially an accounting exercise, one not readily adaptable to modeling as a network.

Perhaps, however, with the IOA problem posed as an equivalent distribution problem, it might be possible to model it more sensibly.

Nevertheless there is some success in the latter work, for example that FRD again yields the same results as steepest descent is encouraging.

Higher order elements for network problems

Cubic elements with freedoms v and its derivative $\phi = d(v)/d(x)$ at each end have the interpolation derived in Section 3.9,

$$v = f_1 v_1 + L f_2 \phi_2 + f_3 v_2 + L f_4 \phi_4 = f_1 v_1 + f_2 \phi_1^* + f_3 v_3 + f_4 \phi_2^*$$

where $f_1 = (1 - 3s^2 + 2s^3)$, $f_2 = (s - 2s^2 + s^3)$, $f_3 = (3s^2 - 2s^3)$, $f_4 = (s^3 - s^2)$

$$(14.4)$$

Differentiating this

$$\phi = dv/dx = (1/L)(dv/ds) = (1/L)(d\{f\}^t/ds)\{v, \phi\}$$

$$= (6s^2 - 6s)v_1/L + (1 - 4s + 3s^2)\phi_1 + (6s - 6s^2)v_2/L + (3s^2 - 2s)\phi_2$$

$$(14.5)$$

14. Conclusions

Then in problems where this first derivative gives the required *flux* quantity, the element matrix is given by Equation 4.4,

$$A\kappa \int \{f_x\}\{f_x\}^t \, dx \, \{T\} = A\kappa \{f\} \, \partial T/\partial x \mid \qquad (14.6)$$

Substituting the interpolation of Equation 14.5 on the LHS in Equation 14.6 the element matrix is obtained as

$$(A\kappa/L) \begin{bmatrix} 1,2 & 0.1L & -1.2 & 0.1L \\ 0.1L & 4L^2/30 & -0.1L & -L^2/30 \\ -1.2 & -0.1L & 1.2 & -0.1L \\ 0.1L & -L^2/30 & -0.1L & 4L^2/30 \end{bmatrix} \qquad (14.7)$$

This matrix is deployed in the usual way to form system matrices. Then in traffic flow problems, for example, the setting one of the first derivative freedoms to zero would correspond to setting flow at that node to zero.

14.3. Conclusion

There is clearly scope for improvement of the techniques discussed, for example we might seek to optimize the FEM distribution models by selecting elements to omit using rules similar to those used to select pivots in Linear Programming, perhaps choosing the element with maximum cost subject to constraints such as omission not being allowed where it is the only element remaining at a node.

FEM, FRD and many of the other methods and techniques considered here have wide potential application, as has been well demonstrated.

The idea in FRD of reducing the cost/resistance of routes with higher than average flows is clearly a generally applicable one.

That the optimum solutions so obtained have all route costs equal (to the lower cost limit) is also worth note. In practice we might have to set different lower limits for each route, but, corresponding to Michelle's classical 'constant strain' criterion for optimal structural frames, the most efficient system would have them all the same, as intuition will suggest.

Note too that this constancy criterion is much used in *benefit-cost analysis* to prioritize activities in a program, choosing to undertake those with higher r/c values first.

14. Conclusions

References

Michelle AGM, The limits of economy in frame structures, *Phil. Mag.* 8 (1904) 589-597.

Mohr GA, *The Finite Element Method for Solids, Fluids, and Optimization,* OUP Oxford (1992).

Mohr GA, Numerical procedures for input-output analysis, *Applied Mathematics & Computation* 101 (1999) 89-98.

Mohr GA, Optimization and finite element modeling of input-output analysis problems, *Int. J. Arts & Sciences* 2 (2002) 23-29.

Mohr GA, Flow ratio design of primal and dual network models of distribution, *Australian and New Zealand Institute of Applied Mathematics Journal*, vol. 45 (2004), 573 - 583.

Mohr GA, *The Doomsday Calculation, The End of the Human Race,* Xlibris, Sydney (2012).

Mohr GA, *The Pretentious Persuaders, A Brief History & Science of Mass Persuasion,* 2nd ed., Horizon Publishing Group, Sydney (2013).

Mohr GA, *Elementary Thinking for the 21st Century,* Xlibris, Sydney (2014).

Mohr GA, Fear E, Sinclair R, *World War 3: When & How Will It End?,* Inspiring Publishers, Canberra (2015).

Mohr GA, Fear E, *The Brainwashed: From Consumer Zombies to Islamism and Jihad,* Inspiring Publishers, Canberra (2016).

Mohr GA, Sinclair R, Fear R, *Human Intelligence, Learning & behavior,* Inspiring Publishers, Canberra (2017).

Mohr GA, *The Scientific MBA,* 5th ed., Balboa Press, Bloomington IN (2017).

Mohr GA, *Elementary Thinking for Modern Management,* Amazon-Kindle (2018).

Mohr GA, Mohr RS, Mohr PE, *The Psychology of Hope,* Balboa Press, Bloomington IN (2018).

Mohr GA, *The Psychology of Life: A practical introduction to psychology,* Amazon-Kindle (2018).

Mohr GA, *Mohr's Law of Hierarchies, and many other Mohr's Laws,* Amazon-Kindle (2018).

Mohr GA, Mohr PE, Mohr RS, *Brainwashed Zombies: Religious, Political & Consumer Persuasion,* Amazon-Kindle (2018).

Mohr GA, Mohr RS, Mohr PE, *Human Psychology, Learning and Intelligence,* Amazon-Kindle (2018).

Mohr GA, Mohr PE, Mohr RS, *The Population Explosion,* Amazon-Kindle (2018c).

Mohr GA, *The Bullying Epidemic: The Psychology, Incidence & Prevention,* Amazon-Kindle (2019).

Mohr GA, *New Ideas for The 21st Century,* Amazon-Kindle (2019).

Mohr GA, *Economics: A Basic Introduction,* Amazon-Kindle (2019).

Mohr GA, Mohr PE, Mohr RS, *DIY Psychology & Psychotherapy: A Practical Introduction,* Amazon-Kindle (2019).

Mohr GA, Mohr PE, Mohr RS, *Real Democracy: Not Westminster-style brawling, oligarchical capitalism & corruption*, Amazon-Kindle (2019).

14. Conclusions

Appendix A

INTRODUCTION TO BASIC

A.1. A brief history of BASIC

BASIC was developed by Kemeny and Kurtz at Dartmouth College (New Hampshire) in the early 1960s and was much used on minicomputers (which typically had 16 terminals, each being allowed 16 kb of RAM, the amount required by the then versions of BASIC) in the 1970s.

In 1975 the first microcomputer was sold, a clumsy box + switches affair with storage of only 256 bytes. In the same year Tiny BASIC, consisting of just 20 pages of code, was written and many versions of this quickly appeared and, also in 1975, Gates and Allen launched Microsoft Corporation with their version, this being marketed with the Altair microcomputer.

A flood of microcomputers with as little as 16 kb of RAM then appeared, the Apple, the Commodore 64, the Spectravideo, the HP85 and many others, all having their own version of BASIC.

In the early 1980s IBM quit their near monopoly of the electric ('golfball') typewriter market, switching to production of *PCs* with about a MB of RAM. Now there was a flood of PCs: Apple, IBM, ICL, NEC, Olivetti etc., as well as many IBM 'clones.'

On the IBM BASICJ, BASICA and GW ('Gee Whiz') BASIC appeared. All used about 64 kb of RAM and the latter is quite powerful. With the advent of a MB of RAM or more Chris Cochran and American Planning Corp's MegaBasic appeared to make full use of it.

From Microsoft QBASIC, using a rudimentary GUI (graphic user interface), followed and was shipped with DOS 5 whilst Quick BASIC, the first fully compiled BASIC appeared around the same time, and Visual Basic (VB) for Windows shortly thereafter, this having compilation as an option.

VB4 was still somewhat clumsy to use, but VB5 is very user friendly. VB5 is quick, but not as quick as the original computer language, FORTRAN, or the later C++. There are still reminders of its predecessors, for example the QBColor( ) function.

VB6 and VB7 or VB.NET, however, are about as quick as C++ when compiled so that BASIC is finally competitive speedwise.

Appendix A

The original BASIC feature of having a command interpreter allows programs to run on an almost 'line by line basis without full compilation so you don't type the whole program in, compile and receive a long list of cryptic error messages which don't even tell you where the program stopped. Instead mistyped lines produce an immediate error as you type them.

When you do run the program, therefore, there will be only one error message at a time, telling you when the program stopped and you go to that line and correct the error, and thus work your way through what should be only a few errors.

QBASIC, the version of BASIC used in most of the coding given in this book, can be downloaded free from the internet, as can QuickBASIC, a later version which includes a compiler.

In versions of Windows such as Windows XP and Vista, QBASIC must be run in Command Prompt mode.

In later versions of Windows from Windows 7 to Windows 10, QB4.exe can be obtained in 32-bit and 64-bit versions from www.QB64.org by clicking DOWNLOAD under 'QB64 v1.3 out now!' and on the page that then appears, choosing to download either of the zip files: qb64_1.3_win_x64.7z (64 bit) or qb64_1.3_win_x86.7z (32 bit), and also help_1.3.zip.

The qb64 programs convert the QBASIC code to executable C++ with the output from PRINT commands displayed in a separate window.

[QBASIC programs can also be run via a free program which uses a 'DOS box', but this is confusing to use.]

A.2. Introduction to BASIC programming

BASIC commands

The most elementary BASIC commands are:

> RUN - to run a program
> SAVE - to store a program
> ENTER - to add lines
> REN - to renumber program lines (with default 'gaps' of 10)
> LIST - to list the program (on screen)
> BYE - to leave BASIC

Arithmetic operations

The following program determines the square toot of a number using Newton's method in which the root is given by iterating the recursion relation

$$x_{new} = (x_{old} + num/x_{old})/2$$

where num = number for which the square root is required

> x_{old} = initial estimate of the square root

APPENDIX A

Then, using a tolerance number TOL as a termination criterion the program is:

```
10 Rem SQRT using Newton's method
20 INPUT "Input, xold, num,tol", XOLD, NUM, TOL
30 XNEW = 0.5*(XOLD+NUM/XOLD)
40 DIFF = ABS(XNEW-XOLD)
50 IF DIFF<TOL THEN GOTO 80
60 XOLD = XNEW
70 GOTO 30
80 PRINT "SQRT =", NEW
```

and to test the program typical input is 1,4,0.001 to obtain Ö4 = 2.

Note that ABS( ) is a library function for the absolute value and that in some versions of BASIC a final line, 90 END is required (and in VB a first line Sub MYPROG( ) is needed to declare a subroutine).

In early versions of BASIC line numbers were necessary and in very early versions of BASIC variable names were restricted to two a single alphabetic character plus a single optional digit.

In QBASIC (and VB) line numbers are not necessary and variable names can be many characters but statements are upper case (converted thus if typed otherwise). Then when computation is redirected by a GOTO (or THEN GOTO, for which only half the statement is actually required) statement the target line must have a *label* (e.g. LAB1:) which is given in the GOTO statement. Thus the foregoing example can be written more briefly as

```
INPUT xold, num, tol
LAB1: xnew = (xold + num/xold)/2 : diff = ABS(xnew-xold)
IF diff<tol GOTO LAB2
xold = xnew: GOTO LAB1
LAB2:PRINT xnew
```

where a semicolon is used as a *statement separator*. Line numbers are used in most coding given in the present book, however, in part because they help describe how programs work (i.e. "lines 110 - 160 do - - - ').

Strings

Ease of string handling is one of the traditional advantages of BASIC. The following program reads three names (given in the DATA statements at the end) and prints them (on screen) with three spaces between. It then prints an integer and a real number using PRINT USING to *format* these.

```
10 READ a$, b$, c$
20 x$ = SPACES$(3)
30 PRINT A$;x$;b$;x$;c$
40 P$="#####" : Q$ = "#####.##"
50 n = 2 : c = 14/3
60 PRINT USING P$ ; n ; : PRINT USING Q$;c
70 DATA 'Bob", "Jim", "Ted"
```

Appendix A

Note that a ; follows the 'n' of the first PRINT USING statement to print both numbers on the same line, otherwise the second number will appear on a second line. Here in line 40 P$ is in *integer* format and Q$ is in *real number* format. Strictly variables should be *declared* at the start of the program as *integer, real, double precision* etc.

Arrays and Loops

The following *database* program dimensions (i.e., declares their size) *arrays* and then uses a *loop* (on i) to read some names and ages and print them out, right justifying the names using the LEN function.

```
DIM names$(10),num(10)
FOR i = 1 to 3
READ names$(i), num(i)
j = LEN(names(i)) : x$ = SPACE$( j )
PRINT x$;names$(i),num(i) : NEXT
DATA "Jane" , 25
DATA "June" , 35
DATA "Caroline" , 15
```

Functions

The following is a simple example of a user defined function to calculate the square of a number. Note the way the variable X is passed to the function as an *argument* and the function result is returned in the same way.

```
10 DECLARE FUNCTION SQ(Z)
20 Z=2
30 Y = SQ(Z)
40 PRINT Z
100 FUNCTION SQ(Z)
110 Z=Z*Z
END FUNCTION
```

Note that QBASIC automatically stores the function as a *subroutine* in a separate *workspace* accessed via the VIEW menu from the menu bar (at the top of the screen).

Standard functions

Standard arithmetic, mathematical and string functions used in BASIC include

INT( ) - gives the integer (truncated) value of a number
ABS( ) - gives absolute value of a number (unsigned)
RND(x) - gives a random number [x <0 gives same number, x> 0 (or x not given) gives the next number in the sequence, = 0 gives the last number]
SQR( ) - gives square root
SIN( ) - gives SIN( ) of an angle in radians
LEN(A$) - see example program in "Arrays and loops" earlier in this section
CHR$(n) - gives the ASCII character corresponding to integer n
   (e.g. n = 65 gives A)

Appendix A

Subroutines

The simplest way of forming subroutines is using the GOSUB command to move to program segments appended after the END statement

```
10 PRINT "main"
20 GOSUB 50
30 PRINT "main"
40 END
50 PRINT "sub"
60 RETURN
```

Alternatively subroutines are stored as separate programs and called by a main program. The following program is called MAIN. It has a subroutine 'datin' which is called and numbers passed to it, omitting one number so that it prints as zero when the number list is printed while in the subroutine.

```
DECLARE SUB datin (N, M)
REM MAIN
DIM X(10), Y(10)
COMMON SHARED Y()
X(1) = 5: Y(2) = 3: N = 10: M = 10
datin N, M
PRINT "main", X(1), Y(2), N, M
END

SUB datin (N, M)
DIM X(10)
PRINT "sub", X(1), Y(2), N, M
END SUB
```

Here the argument list passes N, M to the subroutine and the COMMON SHARED statement allows listed variables to be accessed by all other subroutines. As the array X() is not included in the shared statement, X(1) will print from the subroutine as zero.

Data files

Here we give a examples of a data files (as distinct from program files) using the following program.

```
OPEN "c:\basic\temdat" FOR OUTPUT AS #7
OPEN "c:\basic\gmdata" FOR RANDOM AS #8 LEN = 100
x = 2: y = 3
PUT #8, 1, x :PUT #8, 2, y
WRITE #7, x, y
CLOSE #7
OPEN "c:\basic\temdat" FOR INPUT AS #7
GET #8, 2, z : PRINT z
INPUT #7, z : PRINT z
```

Appendix A

Here two files are used for *sequential* access and *direct* or *random* access, in the second case overestimating the *record* length and reading back only the second number written to it.

As another example the following code accesses a .DBF file in which a list of names, account numbers, balances and dates is stored:

```
OPEN "\gmwork\accs.dbf" FOR INPUT AS #8
ON ERROR GOTO pend
PRINT "Start"
FOR i = 1 TO 4: INPUT #8, a$
PRINT a$: PRINT: NEXT
pend: PRINT "end"
END
```

The file had data for only three people and was set up using Lotus Approach but .DBF files are used by other programs such as Q&A and Sortit. The ERROR statement is to end the program without error message interruption when end of file (EOF) is encountered. As should be expected, the recovered data includes headings and is printed without formatting. In this instance the account number heading was 'a/c #' which did disturb reading of the headings slightly.

Searching and comparing data

The following code is a very simple example of comparing data, in this case string data. In conjunction with search, therefore, such comparisons can be used to locate specific data.

```
10 a$ = "jim" : b$ = "jim"
30 IF a$ = b$ THEN PRINT "OK"
40 b$="ted"
50 IF a$ = b$ THEN PRINT "OK" ELSE PRINT "NO"
```

In the previous example program such comparisons might be used to extract negative numbers (perhaps corresponding to negative account balances) and the associated personal details from a file.

A.3. Sorting routines

The simplest type of sort is a *bubble sort* in which we successively pass down through the numbers, interchanging pairs of numbers when the second exceeds the first. Eventually the numbers fall into descending order but it takes over 2000 calculations to sort 100 short integer numbers.

More efficient is *search sorting* which seeks out the maximum number of those remaining to be sorted and places this at the top of these. This takes over 400 calculations for the 100 number sort.

More efficient are *hybrid* sorting routines which combine the two approaches and sometimes use *recursion* (i.e., the subroutine calls itself) and take only about 250 calculations for the 100 number sort.

APPENDIX A

A program using the *Quick Sort* method is given below, this using recursion. It lives up to its name and takes about 180 calculations for the 100 number test.

```
DIM H, L, ii AS LONG
DECLARE SUB quicksort (a(), L, H)
DECLARE SUB partition (L, H, ii, a())
DIM a(101)
FOR i = 1 TO 100: VALUE = RND(.5) * 100: a(i) = INT(VALUE): NEXT
calcs = 0
CALL quicksort(a(), 1, 100)
FOR i = 1 TO 100: PRINT a(i); : NEXT
PRINT "Calcs = ", calcs

SUB partition (L, H, ii, a())
SHARED calcs: DIM i, j AS LONG
piv = a(L): i = L: j = H + 1
REM Choose pivot as first element in range
DO
  DO
   i = i + 1: REM From start look for larger # (if there is)
  LOOP UNTIL a(i) > piv OR i >= H
  DO
   j = j - 1: REM From end look for smaller # (if there is)
  LOOP UNTIL a(j) < piv OR j <= L
        REM If they haven't crossed swap them
  IF i < j THEN
    temp = a(i): a(i) = a(j): a(j) = temp: calcs = calcs + 1
  END IF
LOOP UNTIL j <= i: REM Swap pivot with the split in the array
a(L) = a(j): a(j) = piv: calcs = calcs + 1
ii = j: REM Return index of # in correct location for next 'split sort'
END SUB

SUB quicksort (a(), L, H)
REM If the range is valid then sort
IF L < H THEN
REM Split the array & return index of the item in the correct location
CALL partition(L, H, ii, a())
REM Sort the lower portion
CALL quicksort(a(), L, ii - 1)
REM Sort the upper portion
CALL quicksort(a(), ii + 1, H)
END IF
END SUB
```

Appendix A

Finally note that it is sometimes necessary, and generally a wise precaution, to declare variable types as *integer, real* (the default), or *double precision* using the DEFINT, DEFSNG, DEFDBL statements. Alternatively this can be done globally as the first line of a program using:

DefSng A-H, O-Z: DefInt I-N

to reserve I-N for integers, as is the default in FORTRAN, the original programming language.

A.4. Visual BASIC (VB)

Visual basic programs usually begin with a form, Form1, for which the coding:

Private Sub Form-Load( )

End Sub

is automatically added when VB starts the new program with Form1.

Then one can add BASIC coding, to obtain, for example:

Private Sub Form-Load( )
Show
x = 2
y = 3
z = x + y
Print "z =", z
End Sub

Here the command Show is necessary to print on the form.
Alternatively, one can have VB add a coding Module to contain the commands of one's program. This will take the form:

Sub main( )
y = 2
x = 3
z = x+ y
Form1.Print "z = ", z
End Sub

and to run this include the command line

Call main

in the coding for Form1.

Regrettably, perhaps, VB does not have DATA statements, so that data must be read from a separate file, though for just a few values of variables, of course, these can be 'declared' as above.

Appendix A

As a VB example, the following coding plots simple vibrations.

The coding for Form1, which has a Command button added to it that is pressed to start the program, is

```
Private Sub Command2_Click()
Call main
End Sub

Private Sub Form_Load()

End Sub
```

The coding in the program module for the vibration plotting is:

```
Public output As Object
Sub main()
Rem Time stepping vibration program
Set output = Form1
output.FontSize = 20
output.Print "            VIBRATION PLOT"
output.Line (0, 0)-(0, 0): output.DrawWidth = 5
A1 = 0: B1 = 0: A2 = 0: B2 = 0: XL = 0: SL = 0: F = 40
output.Line (0, 0)-(0, 8000): output.Line (0, 4000)-(8000, 4000)
For T = 0 To 2.5 Step 0.1
S = 0: If T <= 0.5 Then S = 1
A3 = 1.5 * A2 + B2 / 2 - A1: B3 = S + A2 / 2 + B2 - B1: X = 120 * T
Z = 100 - 20 * SL: Y = 100 - 20 * S: X = F * X: Z = F * Z: Y = F * Y
output.Line (XL, Z)-(X, Y)
Z = 100 - 20 * B2: Y = 100 - 20 * B3: Z = F * Z: Y = F * Y
output.Line (XL, Z)-(X, Y)
Z = 100 - 20 * A2: Y = 100 - 20 * A3: Z = F * Z: Y = F * Y
output.Line (XL, Z)-(X, Y)
A1 = A2: B1 = B2: A2 = A3: B2 = B3
XL = X: SL = S: Next
End Sub
```

After running the program the resulting plotting on Form 1 comes out as follows, showing the a small initial disturbance, along with the vibration of two parameters which, for example, might be the movement at two levels of a building subjected to an earthquake.

APPENDIX A

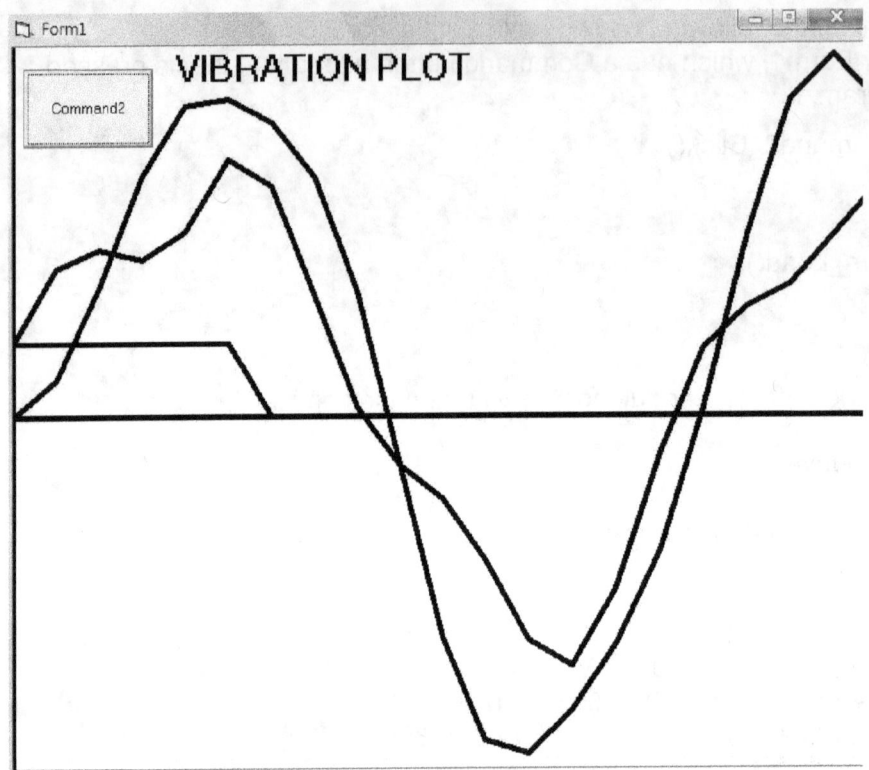

As a further VB example, the following is a VB5/6 listing for the steepest descent program given in Sec. 6.4. A quick search with the four step lengths noted there, and also at the start of this listing, will give a good solution.

The program has a form *Form1* to which is attached a command button. When this is clicked a program module *Module1* is called and an input box appears asking for the value of the penalty factor B. Input 1 and the box asks for search step S. Input trial values and when this search is complete use S = 0 to terminate the search, when a new B value (and then S) is requested.

To terminate execution use S = 0 followed by B = 0.

The coding for Form1 is:

```
Private Sub Command1_Click()
Call main
End Sub

Private Sub Form_Load()

End Sub
```

Appendix A

The coding for routine and subroutine of Module 1 is:

```
Attribute VB_Name = "Module1"
DefSng A-H, M, O-Z: DefInt I-L, N
Private op As Object: Public X1, X2, B, F
Sub main()
Rem searches: B=1, 0.082 & 0.14; B=100, 0.0047 & 0.00035
Set op = Form1: op.DrawWidth = 3: op.FontItalic = True
Dim C(10, 10): I = 0: M = 1.05: S = 0: op.FontSize = 14: op.FontBold = True
op.PSet (2400, 1400), RGB(255, 255, 255): op.Print "Optimum"
op.PSet (1100, 2100), RGB(255, 255, 255): op.Print ">= constraint"
op.PSet (700, 500), RGB(255, 255, 255): op.Print "= constraint"
op.PSet (3200, 1000), RGB(255, 255, 255): op.Print "Solution path"
X = 0: Y = 1000: op.Line (X, Y)-(X, Y)
For Z = 0 To 2 Step 0.01
X = Z: Y = 1 - X * X / 4: X = 2000 * X: Y = 3000 - 2000 * Y
op.Line -(X, Y): Next Z
op.Line (0, 2000)-(4000, 0): op.Line (0, 3000)-(6000, 3000): op.Line (0, 3000)-(0, 0)
X1 = 2: X2 = 2: C(1, 1) = X1: C(1, 2) = X2
X = 2000 * X1: Y = 3000 - 2000 * X2: op.Line (X, Y)-(X, Y)
NEWB: a$ = InputBox("B", , , 5000, 4000): B = CSng(a$)
I = I + 1: C(I, 1) = X1: C(I, 2) = X2: S1 = 0: If B = 0 Then GoTo PEND
Call Subb: Debug.Print "IF =", F
F1 = F: X1 = X1 * M: Call Subb: F2 = F: X1 = X1 / M
G1 = (F2 - F1) / (X1 * (M - 1))
X2 = X2 * M: Call Subb: F2 = F: X2 = X2 / M: G2 = (F2 - F1) / (X2 * (M - 1))
NEWS: a$ = InputBox("S", , , 5000, 4000): S = CSng(a$): If S = 0 Then GoTo NEWB
X1 = X1 + (S1 - S) * G1: X2 = X2 + (S1 - S) * G2
Call Subb: Debug.Print X1; " "; X2; "F= "; F
S1 = S
X = 2000 * X1: Y = 3000 - 2000 * X2: op.Line -(X, Y)
GoTo NEWS
PEND: End Sub

Sub Subb()
G = 1 - X1 * X1 / 4 - X2: E = X1 - 2 * X2 + 1: If G > 0 Then G = 0
FU = (X1 - 2) ^ 2 + (X2 - 1) ^ 2
F = FU + B * G * G + B * E * E
End Sub
```

Appendix A

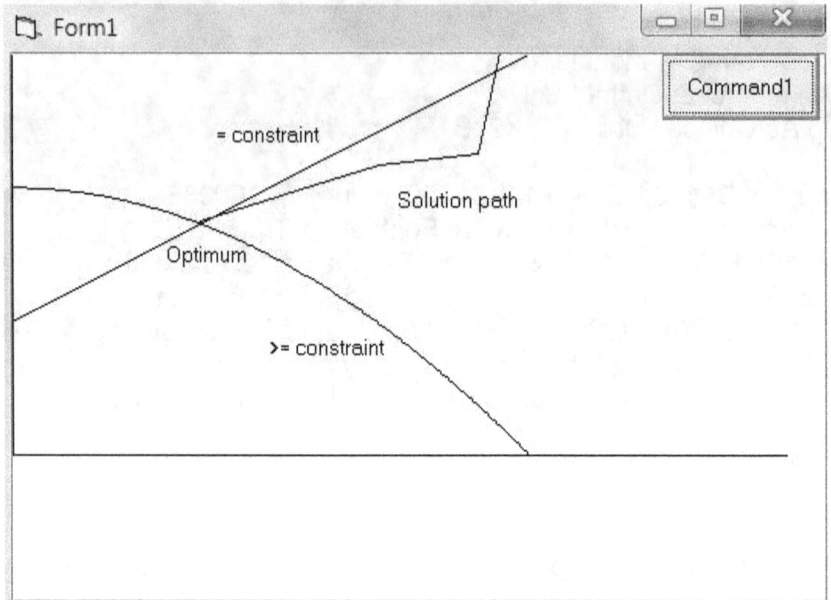

The solution progress plotted on Form 1 with the penalty factors and search lengths stated in the 5th Rem line of Module 1 is shown above.

The main VB differences are that progress results are printed in the immediate window using Debug.Print and plotted on Form1. Generally, however, numerical results would be printed on Form1 and data sets would be read from a file using
   Open "\newvb\dsndat.txt" For Input As #8
   15 Dim rf(20), cord(20, 2)
   20 Input #8, np, ne, ns, nq
Note that in this short example a program module need not be used and the code could have been attached to Form1, this without a command button (or any other control) but with the statement *Show* preceding any executable statements. Then the program is started by the F5 key as for QBASIC.

A.5. Using programs listed in this book

To use/run the programs listed in this book type them into a word processor and save them as MS-DOS ----.txt files. Then rename them as ----.BAS files which can then be read into and run in QBASIC in command prompt mode, or for later versions of windows in QB64, as noted at the end of Section A.1.

Appendix A

A.6. References

Brown S, *Visual Basic in Record Time,* Sybex, Alameda CA 1998.

Capron HL, Williams BK, *Computers and Data Processing*, Benjamin Cummings, Menlo Park CA, 1982.

Cochran C, *MegaBasic Users Manual*, American Planning Corp., Alexandria VA 1984.,

Fox D, *Pure Visual Basic*, Sams 1999.

Kreitzberg CB, Scheidman B, *The Elements of FORTRAN Style,* HBJ, New York, 1972.

Lien DA, *The BASIC Handbook,* 3rd edn, Microtech, Dubai, UAE, 1989.

Perry G, *Introduction to Computer Programming*, SAMS, New York, 2001.

Price WT, *Fundamentals of Computers and Data Processing with Basic*, Holt, Rinehardt and Winston, New York NY, 1983.

Time-Life (eds), *Computer Languages*, Time-Life Inc. 1986.

MS GW-BASIC User's Guide and User's Reference, MS Corp., 1987.

Appendix A

Appendix B

BLOCK EQUATION SOLUTION ROUTINE

The following is a listing for a solution routine which carries out the forward reduction on the equations in blocks and writes the results to a temporary file c:\store.txt opened in line 20 (note that this file must be created/available for the program to work). These blocks are recalled in reverse order during back substitution.

Forward reduction is carried out by, after deploying the first element matrix, cycling through the node numbers and 'picking up' elements as their association with the next node is detected, the number of elements impinging a node (the *nodal valency*) being limited to 8 in line 110.

Line 50 DIM allocates 80 x 41 for memory storage of equations and 'isiz' and LB are the actual storage sizes used, minimum test values of these being set in line 60.

Then in line 560, if the current pivot row + total band width (NTW) equals 'isiz' blocks of six 'ibuf' X LB are written to storage from the top of the equation block (lines 570 - 600), shifting up the remaining rows (lines 610 - 620), the clear buffer area at the bottom (cleared in line 625 - 626) now being filled as forward reduction continues. The process is reversed during back substitution in lines 810 - 875.

Like the program in Section 12.5, this program is set up to deal with IOA problems and banded symmetric or unsymmetric matrices are handled.

Line 52 reads the number of nodes (NP), the number of elements (NE) and the *inclusive* half band width (NBW), that is,

NBW = (max node # diff. in any element + 1) X NDF. (B.1)

Note that the program given in Section 12.5 uses the *exclusive* half band width as NBW, i.e. less by NDF = 1 here.

Line 51 sets the degrees of freedom per node (NDF), the number of nodes per element (NCN) and the length of the band to the left of the pivot (NM). To signal unsymmetric matrices put NM = 1 in line 51 and then the correct value for NM is calculated in line 55, that is NM = NBW -1, where NBW is given by Equation B.1.

Appendix B

Then for unsymmetric matrices the total band width is 2*NBW - 1 set after line 55.

Line 53 reads the nodal loads and the remaining data lines are the node numbers for each element followed by its element matrix.

```
DEFSNG A-H, O-Z: DEFINT I-N
10 REM BAND SOLUTION ROUTINE FOR I-O ANALYSIS
20 OPEN "c:\store.txt" FOR RANDOM AS #2 LEN = 4
50 DIM ESM(6, 6), SK(80, 41), SKP(41), Q(100), NOP(10, 6), DIS(2, 50)
51 NDF = 1: NCN = 4: nm = 1: REM RESTORE 1000
52 READ NP, NE, NBW: NLOAD = NP * NDF
53 FOR i = 1 TO NLOAD: READ Q(i): NEXT
55 lb = NBW + NDF: IF nm <> 0 THEN nm = NBW - 1
if nm<>0 then lb = 2 * NBW - 1
57 REM ISIZ=80:LB=40
60 isiz = lb + 1: ibuf = isiz - lb: nblock = 0
65 NRW = 0: NTW = NBW + NDF
70 L = 0: N = 1: REM isiz,LB ARE BLOCK DEPTH & WIDTH
75 FOR j = 1 TO NCN: READ NOP(N, j): NEXT
77 IDF = NDF * NCN
80 FOR i = 1 TO IDF: FOR j = 1 TO IDF
90 READ ESM(i, j): NEXT: NEXT: REM READ FIRST k (ELEMENT MATRIX)
100 L = L + 1: REM COMMENCE FORWARD REDUCTION ###########
110 FOR M = 1 TO 8
130 FOR i = 1 TO NCN
140 IF NOP(N, i) = L THEN GOTO 170: REM CHECK IF NEXT k NEEDED YET
150 NEXT
160 GOTO 280
170 REM
180 FOR i = 1 TO NCN: FOR j = 1 TO NCN
190 FOR IL = 1 TO NDF: IE = (i - 1) * NDF + IL: NR = (NOP(N, i) - 1) * NDF + IL
200 NRE = NR - NRW: REM NRW = NO. ROWS OF K FILED
210 FOR JL = 1 TO NDF
 JE = (j - 1) * NDF + JL: NC = (NOP(N, j) - 1) * NDF + JL
220 NCB = NC - NR + 1: NCB = NCB + nm: IF NR > NC AND nm = 0 THEN GOTO 240
230 SK(NRE, NCB) = SK(NRE, NCB) + ESM(IE, JE)
REM FORM SYSTEM MATRIX
240 NEXT: NEXT: NEXT: NEXT
245 IF N = NE THEN GOTO 265
248 FOR j = 1 TO NCN: READ NOP(N + 1, j): NEXT
250 FOR i = 1 TO IDF: FOR j = 1 TO IDF
260 READ ESM(i, j): NEXT: NEXT: REM READ NEXT k
265 N = N + 1
270 NEXT M
```

APPENDIX B

```
280 REM
290 NDIF = (NP - L + 1) * NDF: IF NDIF > NBW THEN LIM = NBW + NDF
320 FOR ID = 1 TO NDF
330 LIM = LIM - 1: IP = ID + NDF * (L - 1): IPE = IP - NRW: R = Q(IP): NOB = 0
385 REM ! L,ID
390 XK = 1 / SK(IPE, nm + 1): Q(IP) = Q(IP) * XK
440 FOR j = 1 TO LIM: IA = IPE + j: JA = nm + 1 - j: IF nm = 0 THEN IA = IPE
IF nm = 0 THEN JA = j + 1
442 IF JA < 1 THEN GOTO 446
445 SKP(j) = SK(IA, JA)
446 NEXT
450 NC = LIM + 1
460 FOR j = 2 TO NC: SK(IPE, j + nm) = SK(IPE, j + nm) * XK: NEXT
REM R/PIVOT
480 IF (L + ID - NP - NDF) = 0 THEN GOTO 660: REM END TEST
490 FOR i = 1 TO LIM: NR = IP + i: NRE = IPE + i
500 IF SKP(i) = 0 THEN GOTO 550
505 LC = nm - i + 2: IF nm = 0 THEN LC = 1
507 NC = LC + LIM
510 FOR j = LC TO NC: JP = j + i
520 SK(NRE, j) = SK(NRE, j) - SK(IPE, JP) * SKP(i): NEXT: REM  REDUCTION
540 Q(NR) = Q(NR) - SKP(i) * Q(IP)
550 NEXT i
560 IF (IPE + NTW) < isiz THEN GOTO 630
REM TEST IF STIFFNESS BLOCK FULL
570 IF (NLOAD - NRW) <= isiz THEN GOTO 630
575 nblock = nblock + 1
580 FOR i = 1 TO ibuf: FOR j = 1 TO lb
585 nrec = (nblock - 1) * ibuf * lb + (i - 1) * lb + j
590 PUT #2, nrec, SK(i, j): NEXT: NEXT
REM FILE PART OF STIFFNESS BLOCK
595 flag = nblock
600 NRW = NRW + ibuf: REM NRW = NO. ROWS OF K FILED
610 FOR i = 1 TO lb: FOR j = 1 TO lb: IA = i + ibuf
615 REM If SK(IA, 1) = 0 Then op.Print L; ID; I
620 SK(i, j) = SK(IA, j): NEXT: NEXT: REM SHIFT REMAINING ROWS UP
625 FOR i = 1 TO ibuf: FOR j = 1 TO lb
626 SK(lb + i, j) = 0: NEXT: NEXT
630 REM
640 NEXT ID
650 GOTO 100: REM END FORWARD REDUCTION LOOP #############
660 REM
670 NR = NDF * NP: NRE = NR - NRW: DIS(NDF, NP) = Q(NR)
REM LAST VALUE
```

Appendix B

```
680 Q(NR) = 0: i = NDF: L = NP
690 GOTO 810
700 L = L - 1: REM LOOP ON NODES FOR BACK SUBSTITUTION
710 i = i - 1: REM LOOP ON D.F./NODE FOR BACK SUBSTITUTION
720 NR = NDF * (L - 1) + i: NRE = NR - NRW
730 DIS(i, L) = Q(NR): Q(NR) = 0
740 IF LIM < (NBW + NDF - 1) THEN LIM = LIM + 1
750 FOR j = 1 TO LIM: JA = j + 1 + nm
760 LJ = L + INT((j + i - 1) / NDF): K = i + j - (LJ - L) * NDF
770 DIS(i, L) = DIS(i, L) - SK(NRE, JA) * DIS(K, LJ): NEXT: REM BACK SUBST.
810 IF (NRE - NTW) > 0 OR NRW = 0 THEN GOTO 890
820 FOR ii = 1 TO lb: FOR j = 1 TO lb
830 IA = isiz - ii + 1: IB = lb - ii + 1
840 SK(IA, j) = SK(IB, j): NEXT: NEXT
850 NRW = NRW - ibuf
860 FOR ii = 1 TO ibuf: FOR j = 1 TO lb
REM READ BACK FILED PARTS OF MATRIX
865 nrec = (nblock - 1) * ibuf * lb + (ii - 1) * lb + j
870 GET #2, nrec, SK(ii, j): NEXT: NEXT: REM REDUCED K AS NEEDED
875 nblock = nblock - 1
890 IF (i + L - 2) = 0 THEN GOTO 930: REM END TEST
900 IF i <> 1 THEN GOTO 710: REM END LOOP ON FREEDOMS/NODE
910 i = NDF + 1
920 GOTO 700: REM END BACKSUB LOOP ON NODES
930 REM
935 PRINT "SOLUTIONS"
940 FOR N = 1 TO NP
950 PRINT N, DIS(1, N), DIS(2, N)
960 NEXT
970 PRINT "# blocks = "; flag: CLOSE : KILL "c:\store.txt"

DATA 8,2,4
DATA 1,7,12,17,1,7,12,17
DATA 1,2,3,4
DATA 1,-.2,-.1,-.05
DATA -.3,1,-.2,-.1
DATA -.4,-.3,1,-.2
DATA -.5,-.3,-.4,1
DATA 5,6,7,8
DATA 1,-.2,-.1,-.05
DATA -.2,1,-.2,-.1
DATA -.1,-.2,1,-.2
DATA -.05,-.1,-.2,1
```

APPENDIX B

```
1000 DATA 6,2,4
1005 DATA 1,7,13,24,12,17
1010 DATA 1,2,3,4
1020 DATA 1,-.2,-.1,-.05
1030 DATA -.3,1,-.2,-.1
1040 DATA -.4,-.3,1,-.2
1050 DATA -.5,-.3,-.4,1
1060 DATA 3,4,5,6
1115 DATA 1,-.2,-.1,-.05
1120 DATA -.2,1,-.2,-.1
1130 DATA -.1,-.2,1,-.2
1140 DATA -.05,-.1,-.2,1
```

The first data set appended is for case (a) in Table 12.3, that is with two unconnected elements with NM =1 set in line 51 for unsymmetric matrices. Note that in the first data line of this data the third entry for NBW is increased (from 3 to 4) from the value used in Section 12.5 as the above program uses *inclusive* half band width.

Though the block size (isiz) is set as small as possible in line 60 equation storage will not be needed for this small problem as here isiz = lb + 1 = 8, where lb = 2*NBW - 1 = 7, and the buffer size = ibuf = 1. Thus isiz + ibuf exceeds the problem size NP X NDF = 8 To test storage set NM = 0 in line 51, giving case (b) in Table 12.3. Now lb = NBW + NDF = 5, so that isiz + ibuf (block size + buffer size) = 6, two less than the problem size so that two blocks (of one row) are stored and this will be reported by program.

Lines 1000 - 1140 give the data for case (c) in Table 12.3c. Remove REM before the RESTORE statement in line 51 to use this data.

References

Mohr GA, *Finite Elements for Solids, Fluids, and Optimization*, Oxford University Press, Oxford, 1992.

Mohr GA, Numerical procedures for input-output analysis, *Applied Mathematics & Computation* 101 (1999) 89-98.

Mohr GA, *The Scientific MBA*, 5th ed., *Balboa Press,* Bloomington IN (2017).

Appendix B

Finite Elements & Optimization for Modern Management

Key chapters of this important book include:
> Mathematics and Optimization.
> Numerical Methods.
> Finite Element Network Models.
> Linear Programming.
> Nonlinear Programming.
> Finite Element Distribution Models.
> Finite Element Traffic Flow Models.
> Mohr's Flow Ratio Design Method.
> The Critical Path Method.
> Production and Operations Management.
> Numerical Method for Econometrics.
> Two Dimensional Finite Elements.
> A useful introduction to BASIC programming.

G. A. Mohr did his PhD at Churchill College, Cambridge.
He published circa 60 journal papers and 40+ books, including:

A Microcomputer Introduction to the Finite Element Method
Finite Elements for Solids, Fluids, and Optimization
The Pretentious Persuaders, A Brief History & Science of Mass Persuasion
Curing Cancer & Heart Disease;   The Variant Virus
The Doomsday Calculation, The End Of The Human Race
Heart Disease, Cancer, & Ageing: Proven Neutraceutical & Lifestyle Solutions
2045: A Remote Town Survives Global Holocaust
The History & Psychology of Human Conflict;   The War of the Sexes
Elementary Thinking for the 21st Century
The 8-Week+ Program to Reverse Cardiovascular Disease
The Scientific MBA;   Mohr's Law of Hierarchies
The DIY Cardiovascular Cure;   Combating Cancer
New Ideas for the 21st Century;   Economics: A Basic Introduction

Also with R.S. Mohr/Richard Sinclair & P.E. Mohr/Edwin Fear:
The Evolving Universe: Relativity, Redshift and Life from Space
World Religions: The History, Psychology, Issues & Truth
World War 3, When & How Will It End?
The Brainwashed, From Consumer Zombies to Islamic Jihad
Human Intelligence, Learning & Behaviour
New Theories of The Universe, Evolution, and Relativity
The Psychology of Hope;   The Population Explosion
Brainwashed Zombies: Religious, Political & Consumer Persuasion
Human Conflict: An Attitudinal Psychology Model

www.ingramcontent.com/pod-product-compliance
Lightning Source LLC
Chambersburg PA
CBHW081424220526
45466CB00008B/2265